The Submariners

The Submariners

LIFE IN BRITISH SUBMARINES 1901–1999

AN ANTHOLOGY OF PERSONAL EXPERIENCE

❖

CHOSEN AND EDITED BY

John Winton

CONSTABLE · LONDON

Constable Publishers
3 The Lanchesters
162 Fulham Palace Road
London W6 9ER
www.constablerobinson.com

First published in UK 1999
by Constable and Company Limited

This paperback edition, published by Constable,
an imprint of Constable & Robinson Ltd. 2001

A copy of the British Library Cataloguing in
Publication data is available from the British Library

ISBN 0-09-480220-3

Printed and bound in the EU

Contents

Part One:
EARLY DAYS

Part Two:
THE FIRST WORLD WAR

Part Three:
BETWEEN THE WARS

Part Four:
THE SECOND WORLD WAR

Part Five:
POSTWAR

Acknowledgements

Acknowledgements and thanks are due to Macmillan & Co. for THE TRADE, by Rudyard Kipling; Mrs Michael Riviere, Captain Guy D'Oyly Hughes' daughter, and Mr Duncan Dunbar-Nasmith, Admiral Dunbar-Nasmith VC's grandson, for LETTER HOME FROM E.11; Admiral of the Fleet Sir Edward Ashmore GCB DSC for E.18 IN THE BALTIC 1915 by his father, Vice Admiral Leslie Ashmore CB DSO; the Executors of the late Captain H. K. Oram and Wendy Harris for ESCAPE FROM THETIS; Mrs Malcolm Burr, for MY WORST PATROL by her father, Rear Admiral Ben Bryant CB DSO** DSC; Cdr. Edward Young DSO DSC RNVR and Wordsworth Editions for TWELVE LITTLE S-BOATS, 'YOU BLOODY BASTARD, YOU'VE SUNK A BRITISH SUBMARINE!', and SURFACE AND GUN ATTACK; the Rev. Lt.-Cdr. Rupert Lonsdale for THE SURRENDER OF SEAL; Petty Officer Telegraphist Joe Lewis DSM for TIMOSHENKO; Gatwick Submarine Old Comrades' Archives for SOLE SURVIVOR by Chief Stoker Petty Officer John Capes BEM, THE 'SCARLET PIMPERNEL' BOAT by Leading Stoker Bill Britton, and SHAKESPEARE – THE UNSINKABLE SUBMARINE by Leading Telegraphist Ken Wade DSM; Mrs Kathleen Fitt and family for RUM, TOBACCO AND SATISFACTION by her father, Chief Torpedo Gunner's Mate Joe Brighton DSM*; Captain M. R. G. Wingfield DSO DSC* RN for TAURUS VERSUS BULGARS ON HORSEBACK; Pamela Mellor, for SUBMARINE SKETCHES by her brother, Lt. Henty Henty-Creer RNVR; Lt.-Cdr. George Honour DSC VRD NVR for D-DAY JUNE 1944 – OPERATION 'GAMBIT'; Chief Petty Officer George Luck DSM for YOUNG MURRAY; Lt.-Cdr Ian Fraser VC DSC RNR for THE XE.3 MIDGET SUBMARINE

ATTACK ON *TAKAO*; Mrs Sylvia Coote for THE 'PERISHER'; Cdr. Tim Hale RN for HMS DREADNOUGHT; Captain D. G. Littlejohns RN for DIVING DEBACLE and CRABOLOGY; Captain R. G. Sharpe RN for ON LOCATION; Lady Maureen Mackenzie and the Royal Navy Submarine Museum for CHIEF POLARIS EXECUTIVE; Vice Admiral Sir Louis Le Bailly KBE CB DL for THE FIRST POLARIS TEST FIRING; Cdr. David Lund RN for SUBMARINE LIBRARY; Captain Christopher Wreford-Brown DSO RN for *CONQUEROR'S* WAR PATROL; Lt.-Cdr. Andrew Johnson MBE RN for THE 116-DAY WAR PATROL; Mrs Sybil Stevens for SUBMARINE OLD COMRADES.

Part One:

EARLY DAYS

The Weapon of the Weaker Nation

Britain's first steps towards acquiring submarines were very cautious. In April 1900, the Parliamentary Secretary to Viscount Goschen, the First Lord of the Admiralty, told the House of Commons: 'The Admiralty are not prepared to take any steps in regard to the submarines because this vessel is only the weapon of the weaker nation. If, however, this vessel can be rendered practical, the nation which possesses it will cease to be weak and may become really powerful. More than any other nation we should have to fear the attacks of submarines.'

This seemed to be a conclusive dismissal of submarines, an echo of Lord St Vincent's remarks nearly a hundred years before. But in December 1900 the Admiralty were concerned to note that the French had provided for more submarines in their Naval Estimates. The French were our traditional enemies. If the French were building submarines, then submarines had to be taken seriously. Britain had no submarine designers. The first submarines would have to come from abroad. The design chosen was that by John P. Holland, of New Jersey, to be built by Vickers Son & Maxim, at Barrow-in-Furness.

In April 1901, the First Lord of the Admiralty, by now Lord Selborne, stated in the Naval Estimates in the Commons: 'five submarine vessels of the type invented by Mr Holland have been

3

ordered, the first of which should be delivered next Autumn. What the future value of these boats may be in Naval warfare can only be a matter of conjecture, but experiments with these boats will assist the Admiralty in assessing their true value.'

The first submarine appointments were made almost casually, at a time when the general opinion of submarines and submariners in the Navy was succinctly expressed by Rear-Admiral Arthur Wilson VC, when he was Controller of the Navy in 1902, who is alleged to have said: 'Underwater weapons, they call 'em. I call them underhand, unfair, and damned un-English. They'll never be any use in war and I'll tell you why: I'm going to get the First Lord to announce that we intend to treat all submarines as pirate vessels in wartime and that we'll hang all the crews.'

The First Inspecting Captain of Submarines

While I was at Greenwich a statement was made in Parliament to the effect that the Admiralty had decided to build five submarine boats for trial.

It struck me that the naval officer who ought to be selected to command these should be an ex-torpedo lieutenant, for their equipment would largely consist of electrical appliances and torpedoes.

I therefore applied to be given the command, and this was approved.

On taking up my appointment (as Inspecting Captain of Submarine Boats), I called on Sir William White, the Director of Naval Construction, and Sir John Dunston, the Engineer-in-Chief. Both washed their hands entirely of submarines and refused to have anything to do with them.

Sir William advised me never to go below water, as he had once made a descent in a submarine in London dock in 1887 and had been stuck in the mud on the bottom for an hour or so.

... I knew nothing about submarines; nor did anyone else, so the first thing to do was to sit down and think out what were the difficulties that we were likely to come across, and arrive at methods by which they could be forestalled. The result was rather peculiar; for all the problems that I originally considered to be likely to be difficult turned out to be simple, and several of those that appeared to be simple gave, in the end, an infinity of trouble.

As soon as the first 'Holland' boat neared completion, I asked for a gunboat to be stationed at Barrow as a mother ship, and for the crews for the boats to be selected. The 'Hazard' was commissioned and volunteers for the first crew called for.

The following were the first officers and men appointed to the Submarine Service, September 1901:

Lieutenant F. D. Arnold-Forster	
Lieutenant S. Bowle Evans	
Lieutenant J. B. Morton	
Engineer Robert Spence	
William R. Waller	Petty Officer First Class
F. C. Knight	,,
Joseph B. Rees	,,
Ernest E. Neville	,,
William J. Robinson	Engine-Room Artificer, 3rd Class
William Muirhead	,,

ADMIRAL SIR REGINALD BACON KCB KCVO DSO

The Royal Navy's first submarine was launched at Barrow on 2 November 1901. Her first captain describes in some detail those first days in

Holland One

The boat then completing at Barrow-in-Furness under the supervision of Captain now Admiral, Sir Reginald Bacon, was one of the American 'Holland' type. As I was to be her first captain, I was anxious to see the boat directly I got there, but found that nobody in the yard seemed to have heard of any submarine at all.

Eventually I discovered her in a shed labelled 'Yacht Shed' in large white letters, where she was being built in the utmost secrecy. Only selected, trustworthy men were allowed inside. All frames and other parts made in the yard were marked 'For Pontoon No. One' so she had aroused no special interest in the busy workshops.

What surprised me most when I did find the boat was her small size. She was only sixty-three feet long and was shaped like a very fat and stumpy cigar. She had fins and a tail, with a single propeller and two rudders, one for steering and the other for diving. There was a small conning tower on top, just big enough to put one's head and shoulders in. Her speed turned out afterwards to be seven knots on the surface and never more than about four or five knots under water.

The ingenious designer in New York evidently did not realise that the average naval officer has only two eyes and two hands; the little conning tower was simply plastered with wheels, levers, valves and gauges, with which some superman was to fire torpedoes, dive and steer, and do everything else at the same time, and the inside of the boat was stuffed with wonderful automatic boxes.

Alterations were made, and whilst the boat was being made ship-shape and less like a box of conjuring tricks, those with artistic ideas tried their hands at painting periscopes in various ways to make them invisible. The early periscopes were long and bulky, not like the neater little fittings on modern submarines, and there was plenty of surface for paint. A barber's pole gave one enthusiast an idea. He painted a dummy periscope in spiral stripes of all the primary colours. When whizzed round by a small electric motor it ought to have been invisible – but it wasn't, and the periscope painting craze gradually died out.

Another queer diversion whilst awaiting the completion of the boat was what we called 'fug trials'. Awful things had been prophesied about the danger of breathing the same air for several hours inside a submerged submarine. To see what would happen, half a dozen of us used to shut ourselves up with the doctor in the hermetically sealed bread-room of the small gunboat *Hazard*, then lying in the basin at Barrow. We had cards and music, and every hour the doctor took everyone's pulse and temperature, including his own. Though apparently something serious should have happened, nobody felt any the worse. The seances in the bread-room led later on to breathing trials on more scientific lines in the submarine itself.

When the boat was ready, we tried trimming her down and blowing her up again in the basin, with big chains passed underneath her to pull us up if we got stuck at the bottom. The first real dive and underwater run was made in Morecambe Bay, and an American crew that had done some trial runs in the United States were sent over by the Holland Boat Company to go out with us for our first effort.

After the boat was carefully trimmed down everyone except the American working the diving rudder wheel, the 'boss diver', as he called himself, was seated about the boat on canvas stools opposite their work, and warned that if they moved they might upset the balance, and perhaps cause a nose-dive into the mud.

7

Then the motor went ahead, the diving rudder was put down and green water was seen through the conning tower windows. Gradually the depth gauge showed we were running under water for the first time, and those who could see it watched anxiously whilst listening to the hum of the motor and the queer-sounding American orders given by our temporary captain.

The boat ran, as these boats always did, with her nose well down and to those who could not see the depth gauge it seemed as though we were bound for the bottom. When a bucket got loose and clattered down the engine-room floorplates it sent hearts into mouths.

The working of the diving rudder wheel was rather a cunning business in those early boats, and when the American crew left after the first underwater run, care had to be taken to select suitable petty officers to train as 'diving coxswain', the English version of 'Boss Diver'.

After a little practice the boat was found to be very handy underwater, but on the surface she was a brute. They are proud of the great expanse of their basin at Barrow, but it was not nearly big enough for little *Number One Holland* to manoeuvre in comfortably.

Being short and stumpy, she was awkward to steer on the surface, and one day she alarmed the inmates of the sick-bay in the *Hazard*, her parent ship, by poking her big nose through the ship's side into their berths. Her plates were so stout that it did not hurt her at all, but the ship had to go into dock.

When it was at all rough, the boat, when running on the surface, was all awash, and nothing could be seen from the little conning tower. Everything had to be battened down; those below had to stop there; and those on deck, the captain and the coxswain, had to hang on as best they could. They could stop inside, of course, the captain using the periscope for looking out, but its lenses had an annoying habit of clouding over at critical moments; then he was done, and had to trust entirely to Providence and the compass.

It was in these Holland boats that the famous white mice were kept in cages. The idea came originally from the coal mines. If certain defects occurred in the petrol engine, small quantities of carbon monoxide, a highly poisonous gas, found its way into the boat. White mice are far more sensitive than man to the ill-effects of this gas, and their behaviour in the submarine gave warning to the crew of its presence. If a mouse actually died, it was high time to come to the surface, open up everything, and blow the boat through with the fans. The presence of petrol vapour or battery gases, which were also dangerous could be detected in good time by smell.

REAR-ADMIRAL D. ARNOLD-FORSTER CMG

*

One of the first, if not the very first, man in the Royal Navy to realise the enormous potential of submarines as weapons of war was Admiral Sir John Fisher, who became First Sea Lord in October 1904. He noted on January 5 that year: 'Satan disguised as an Angel of Light wouldn't succeed in persuading the Admiralty or the Navy that in the course of some few years Submarines will prevent any Fleet remaining at sea continuously either in the Mediterranean or the English Channel.' *He also wrote a letter* 'to a High Official in 1904, and which I had forgotten, until I came across it recently [while compiling his book *Records*, published in 1919]. It's somewhat violent, but so true that I insert it. I went as First Sea Lord of the Admiralty shortly after – very unexpectedly – and so was able to give effect (though surreptitiously) to my convictions. Not only Admirals afloat, but even Politicians ashore, dubbed submarines as "playthings", so the money had to be got by subterfuge.'

That letter of April 1904 did indeed read like

The Trumpet of a Prophecy

ADMIRALTY HOUSE
PORTSMOUTH
April 20th 1904

My Dear Friend

I will begin with the last thing in your letter, which is far the most important, and that is our paucity of submarines. I consider it the most serious thing at present affecting the British Empire! – That sounds *big*, but it's true. Had either the Russians or the Japanese had submarines the whole face of their war would have been changed for both sides. It really makes me laugh to read of 'Admiral Togo's *eighth* attack on Port Arthur!' Why! had he possessed submarines it would have been *one* attack and one attack only! It would have been all over with the whole Russian Fleet, caught like rats in a trap! Similarly, the Japanese Admiral Togo outside would never have dared to let his transports full of troops pursue the even tenor of their way to Chemulpo and elsewhere!

It's astounding to me, *perfectly astounding*, how the very best amongst us absolutely fail to realise the vast impending revolution in naval warfare and naval strategy that the submarine will accomplish! (I have written a paper on this, but it's so violent I'm keeping it!) Here, just to take a simple instance, is the battleship 'Empress of India', engaged in manoeuvres and knowing of the proximity of Submarines, the Flagship of the Second Admiral of the Home Fleet nine miles beyond the Nab Light (out in the open sea), so self-confident of safety and so oblivious of the possibilities of modern warfare that the Admiral is smoking his cigarette, the captain is calmly seeing defaulters down on the half-deck, no one caring an iota for what is going on, and suddenly they see a Whitehead torpedo

10

miss their stern by a few feet! And how fired? From a submarine of the 'pre-Adamite' period, small, slow, badly fitted; *with no periscope at all* – it had been carried away by a destroyer lying over her, fishing for her! – and yet this submarine followed that battleship for a solid two hours under water, coming up gingerly about a mile off, every now and then (like a beaver!), just to take a fresh compass bearing of her prey, and then down again!

Remember, that this is done (and I want specially to emphasise the point), with the Lieutenant in command of the boat out in her for the first time in his life on his own account, and half the crew never out before either! why, it's wonderful! And so what results may we expect with bigger and faster boats and periscopes more powerful than the naked eye (such as the latest pattern one I saw the other day), and with experienced officers and crews, and with nests of these submarines acting together?

I have not disguised my opinion in season and out of season as to the essential, imperative, immediate, vital, pressing, urgent (I can't think of any more adjectives!) necessity for more submarines at once, at the very least 25 in addition to those now ordered and building, and a hundred more as soon as practicable, or we shall be caught with our breeches down just as the Russians have been!

And then, my dear Friend, you have the astounding audacity to say to me, 'I presume you only think they (the submarines) can act on the *defensive*!' ... Why, my dear fellow! not take the offensive? Good Lord! if our Admiral is worth his salt, he will tow his submarines at 18 knots speed and put them into the hostile Port (like ferrets after the rabbits!) before war is officially declared, just as the Japanese acted before the Russian Naval Officers knew that war was declared!

In all seriousness I don't think it is even *faintly* realised – *The immense impending revolution which the submarines will effect as offensive weapons of war.*

When you calmly sit down and work out what will happen in the narrow waters of the Channel and the Mediterranean – how totally the submarines will alter the effect of Gibraltar, Port Said, Lemnos, and Malta, it makes one's hair stand on end!

I hope you do not think this letter too personal!

Ever Yours
J. A. Fisher

*

The first British-designed submarines were the 'A' Class; 165 tons on the surface, 180 tons dived; 100 feet long with a hull diameter of 11 feet 6 inches; armed with two 18-inch bow torpedo tubes; propelled by a 500 hp petrol engine, making 11 knots on the surface, and 150 hp main motor, giving 7 knots dived. The complement was two officers and eleven men. A.1 was laid down at Vickers, Barrow, on 19 February 1902 and launched on 9 July.

A.1 took part with Holland boats in the Naval Manoeuvres of 1904. On the final day, 18 March, A.1 was carrying out a submerged attack on the cruiser Juno *off the Nab Tower when she was run down and sunk by the liner* Berwick Castle. *Her captain, Lieut. L. C. D. Mansergh and his whole crew were lost in this the Royal Navy's first submarine accident.*

In spite of this setback, the Submarine Service was expanding rapidly, with new officers and ratings joining all the time, and life in submarines was already developing a distinctive flavour of its own.

Early Days in 'A' Boats

In October 1904, Max Horton and I met at the 'Keppel's Head' at Portsmouth before catching the seven o'clock boat to join HMS *Thames*, the first parent ship for submarines, moored high up Fareham Creek. Having both done our 'Gunnery' and 'Torpedo' courses at Plymouth, we were strangers to 'The Nut' [bar], but soon saw familiar faces and followed them to the inner bar. Answering a greeting, Horton there announced in his loud forthright fashion – 'Yes, six bob a day and ashore by the 7-bell boat for us'. We had butted unknowingly into the *Thames* private corner and the remark was icily received.

The score of lieutenants manning the only British submarines in commission were in their early twenties, volunteers attracted either by the pay or the challenge of the new weapon – the cash tangible and much talked about, the challenge harder to measure and not mentioned. The loss in March of *A.1* with all hands, at a time of rapid growth and transition had interrupted training. It had also brought a reaction from overconfidence into a small band, not yet a community with a tradition, and Horton's jibe jarred.

The eight sub-lieutenants of the new training class had been told to join with their sea chests, and the small and ancient steamboat gave added warning that the *Thames* might lack amenities, and that we were not quite clear of the gunroom. As three or four of us were trying to find room for ourselves and perhaps a suitcase, the veterans of the 'Nut' arrived at the jetty, and the next moment I was back at Dartmouth, joining the *Britannia* in 1898. 'Subs out of the stern sheets' was shouted down at us in a familiar raucous voice that had often from the *Britannia*'s gangway hustled us as 'News'. It came from a former fourth term chief cadet captain, now a submariner of twelve months standing. Reaching the ship after a long damp trip we got no warmer welcome. The *Thames*, an ageing cruiser, bereft of the guns meant in 1880 to outmatch those of a Russian class, had been given the title and some requirements of a submarine depot ship. Submarines being dangerous and discreditable, she had been banished to the furthermost corner of Portsmouth Harbour, in company with the powder and quarantine hulks.

The only executive officer on board with more than two stripes was her red whiskered 'hungry hundred' first lieutenant, a character to whom we were merely eight more bodies to fit into an already crowded chest flat. The scanty senior officers of the Trade were either on the seagoing tender *Hazard* or scurrying between Vickers and the Admiralty planning the future.

In the *Thames* next morning, persistence revealed a reluctant Engineer Commander 'in charge of training', a bearded bewildered old gentleman left over from her last spell in reserve. He knew nothing of the younger engineers appointed 'for submarines', at least one or two of whom might have been able and willing to impart something useful to us.

The chaos and crowding in the *Thames* was due to personnel temporarily outrunning construction. New *A*'s were being rapidly completed at Vickers, but the loss of *A.1* had brought an order to fit a water-tight hatch under the *A* boats' conning towers – a dockyard job.

Hitherto recruits had been attached as they arrived to one or other of the submarines in running order, to pick up knowledge from their shipmates. There were two crews for every submarine and hardly an *A* boat running. A *Holland* boat's crew was eight strong and two the maximum number of passengers she could comfortably take. Submarines lying alongside the *Thames* were overcrowded during working hours and enquiring students unwelcome. One's first dive was everybody's ambition, but had to be fought for.

Skinner of our term was a veteran of a few months and 'No. 2' of *Holland 3*, and through him Horton and I soon got ours. Her spare captain was Little and her crew that day a blend of the No. 1 and the 'Spare' crew. Torpedo and dummy attacks were not then the routine exercises they were to become, boats more often went out merely to practise trimming (then always done statically), diving and depth keeping. The recognised area was Sandown Bay, and diving only permitted in the vicinity of a tender flying a large red flag.

The overall length of a *Holland* boat was a yard short of a cricket pitch and the No. 2 standing beside the captain at the periscope, could reach in one stride any member of the crew at his station. Horton and I, squatting on the deck formed of the boards over the battery, were primarily concerned in keeping out of the way. After the deafening rattle of the 4-cylinder engines on the way out, the interior, at diving stations seemed unnaturally quiet and we could hear each low voiced order, and watch it carried out. 'Trimming' seemed to take a long time. Even the gentle swell off Sandown kept the indicator bubble wandering between 3 degrees up and 3 degrees down by the bow. Once the two main ballast tanks were full, little buoyancy remained, and flooding whether of a fore or an after tank was only for a few seconds at a time.

Little, large and calm, stood central abaft the periscope beneath the two foot high conning tower, the only place where he could stand upright. Skinner, dodging round him, eyes everywhere, alone was mobile. At last orders to the tanks were succeeded by 'Go ahead' and the coxswain started the strenuous yet delicate juggling with the diving wheel which governed the fore and aft angle of a submarine. Watching the bubble, he revolved the wheel gently against its movement. The silence and immobility of everybody else as *H.3* still almost horizontal, gathered way, began to suggest that diving was simpler than we had expected.

Suddenly calm was shattered as she plunged steeply by the nose. We passengers, the only people not holding on to a wheel or a valve, slid forward along the boards to the rear of the torpedo tube, a few feet away. I saw Skinner leap to the cause of the error, the brass pointer on the indicator arm of the diving helm. It had disconnected – stuck at 5 degrees 'Rise', though the coxswain had turned the wheel against the bubble towards 'Dive'. Instantaneously the motors speeded up, the coxswain hastily put his helm up hard and *H.3* gave us an exhibition of her lively diving qualities. Her change to rise was equally rapid as Horton and I, trying to look nonchalant, scrambled back to our places. I don't remember what depth we reached, gauges then only read to 100 feet and we might have hit the bottom before that. But for the lightning movement of Skinner's, the stolid coxswain would have kept his wheel down and, with two or three seconds longer under dive helm, the angle of the boat could have been disastrous, spilling the acid from the battery – a more serious danger than hitting the bottom.

'SEA GEE' (REAR-ADMIRAL C. G. BRODIE)

Skinner was one of the first two of Brodie's term to go into submarines; Hart, also one of Brodie's best friends, was the other. Skinner was killed in an explosion in A.5 *alongside* Hazard *in February, 1905, Hart in a similar internal explosion accident in* C.8 *in 1907. 'Tiny' Little rose to become Admiral Sir Charles Little GCB GBE and died in 1973.*

*

Events in 1905 showed how dangerous those early submarines were. In June, A.8 foundered with the loss of sixteen lives whilst changing crews in Plymouth Sound. In October, in Stokes Bay, Portsmouth,

A.4 *carried out communications trials with an insulated megaphone strapped to her hull while* Torpedo Boat 26 *steamed round in circles, ringing a large brass bell.* A.4 *was submerged with a narrow ventilating tube protruding above the surface when a steamer unknowingly passed close enough to send water pouring down the tube.* A.4 *plunged to a depth of 90 feet with a bow down angle of 40 degrees. Sea water reached the battery which gave off chlorine gas and all the lights went out. In the darkness and choking gas, Lieutenant Godfrey Herbert, the first lieutenant, felt his way to the controls and blew the ballast tanks.* A.4 *hesitantly but thankfully surfaced.*

A.4*'s CO, Lieutenant Martin Nasmith, was court-martialled, charged with 'negligently or by default hazarding'* A.4. *He was convicted of default but acquitted of negligence, the Court ruling that 'taking into consideration the prisoner's coolness and presence of mind under difficult circumstances after the boat had submerged, the Court sentences him to be reprimanded'. However, the Commander-in-Chief, Portsmouth, Admiral Sir Archibald Douglas, later made a general signal:*

The Commander-in-Chief having read the minutes of a court martial held on the officer in command of Submarine A.4, wishes to make known to all the officers and men of the Fleet that he is deeply impressed with the behaviour of the officers and crew on the occasion which led to that court martial. Their pluck and devotion to duty under the most trying circumstances was most commendable, and aptly described by the President of the Court in his report forwarded to the Admiralty as worthy of the best traditions of the service.

*

Fred Parsons joined the old wooden three-decker training ship HMS Impregnable *as a boy seaman, aged fifteen, at Devonport in 1893.*

In 1903, when he was serving as a Petty Officer First Class in the destroyer Gypsy, *he volunteered for submarines because, as a married man with children, he needed the extra money. Submarine pay was two shillings a day, a considerable sum in those days. But Gypsy's Captain thought Parsons had done it to get away from him. From that moment, Parsons could do nothing right. Eventually, he was unjustly disrated to Leading Seaman. He did manage, by appealing to the Commodore, to regain the rate of Petty Officer Second Class in six month's time. When he was told he was going to Portsmouth for the submarine service*

... I was delighted. I hadn't expected to hear any more of *that*, after I was disrated.

When I got to the Sick Bay to pass the Doctor I found another man, the same rating as myself, waiting there – two Leading Seamen, both Leading Torpedomen. When we saw the Doctor, the first thing he said was: 'Hello, two more for the suicide squad'. He could have been right. As submarines were still very new, there had been several accidents; and little did we know that one of us was doomed to die in one within a month or so.

We were drafted to Portsmouth to join HMS *Thames*, a light cruiser doing submarine depot ship duties. Fort Blockhouse, the present submarine headquarters at Gosport, was at that time being overhauled ready for its future role. I was sent there in a working party to help get things ready, and then, about April 1905, HMS *Forth* was fitted out as the submarine depot ship, and my pal who had joined with me and I, were sent to Plymouth with her.

We were both in the same training class. I had already done several trips in the 'Holland' boats – the first ones in service. We did several runs around Spithead before going down to Plymouth. When *Forth* arrived there, she was moored near the old *Impregnable*, and it reminded me of the days when we used to land with the band, and march away to the tune of 'A Life On The Ocean Wave'.

I was detailed to train in *A.7*, which, along with *A.8*, had been in Plymouth awaiting *Forth*'s arrival. Then we moved to the *Defiance*, the torpedo training school. We often did duty aboard the submarine, and one evening while I was sitting by the fore-hatch keeping an eye on the battery, which was on charge (this was about a month after our arrival), Lieut. Little went below in his boat, *A.7*. He saw me sitting there, and he knew me, as I was training in his boat.

'Hello, Parsons', he said. 'My Chief Petty Officer is leaving. Would you like to take his place?'

I was delighted. 'If you like, sir', I said.

'Not if I like – if *you* like', he told me, giving me an old-fashioned look.

I knew I'd put my foot in it, and years later when I met him as a retired Admiral, I said something and he gave me the same old look. Then I reminded him of this episode.

I was detailed for *A.7* but my pal was detailed for *A.8*. And there our ways parted for ever. One day we were out together doing exercises, and after surfacing and going ahead some way, *A.8* suddenly dived with her hatch open. This disaster occurred just off Plymouth Breakwater. The boat went straight to the bottom, and all on board were lost. My pal among them. I thought then of the Doctor's words '. . . the suicide squad'.

This happening caused several of the training class to change their minds and request to be returned to General Service. I lived to have one or two near things, but I always reckon my lucky star must have been shining about then. There were only two of us of the same rating in training, and no objection was made to anyone who wanted to leave. So, by a fifty-fifty chance, it could have been me. My wife was very frightened by this, but as I pointed out to her, you won't go before your number is up, so it was just as well for me to carry on.

FRED PARSONS

Fred Parsons later went with Captain Scott to the Antarctic in Terra Nova.

*

After the 'B' and 'C' Classes of 1905 and 1906, each bigger than its predecessors, D.1, the first of a new 550-ton, 16-knot Class was launched in 1908. The D Class were the first British submarines to have diesel engines instead of petrol, twin screws, saddle tanks instead of internal ballast tanks, and a W/T system incorporated in their design. D.4 was the first British submarine to mount a gun. The 'D' Class were the first to have a proper patrol capability, as was discovered in the Naval Manoeuvres of 1910 by the new Inspecting Captain of Submarines, Roger Keyes, whose brother Adrian was one of the first submariners, CO of A.2.

Inspecting Captain of Submarines

At that time our submarine service, with the exception of *D.1*, consisted of small craft, really only fit for local defence. *D.1*, however, the only submarine we possessed capable of operating at any distance from our coast, proceeded under her own power from Portsmouth to the west coast of Scotland, and in spite of having one engine disabled, cruised off the Blue base for two or three days and torpedoed two of the Colonsay cruisers. *D.1*'s enterprising exploit opened the eyes of the First Sea Lord, Admiral Sir Arthur

Wilson, to the offensive possibilities of submarines, which he had hitherto regarded as defensive vessels.

A couple of months after the manoeuvres, I was summoned to the Admiralty and offered the appointment of Inspecting Captain of Submarines. I protested that I knew nothing about submarines except second-hand from my brother, who was one of the pioneer submarine officers; that the existing Inspecting Captain and his two predecessors were torpedo specialists; that it was a highly technical service, and I was a mere 'Salt Horse' without any specialist attainments. The Naval Secretary, Rear-Admiral Troubridge, replied that that was just what Sir Arthur wanted, a sea-going officer who had every prospect of being a young Admiral, who could be relied upon to bring the submarine service into close touch and co-operation with the fleet. I felt highly honoured and accepted the appointment, and that was the beginning of my long association with a splendid body of officers and men whose deeds of enterprise, endurance and valour fill one with admiration and pride.

*

The post of Inspecting Captain of Submarines was unlike anything else in the Navy.

I had an office at the Admiralty, my headquarters were in HMS *Dolphin*, an old hulk secured alongside the submarine depot at Fort Blockhouse, and I was nominally in command of HMS *Mercury*, a hulk moored head and stern off Haslar Creek. There were seven submarine sections, as they were called in those days, and these were maintained by:

Fort Blockhouse, which had very primitive living quarters for officers and men, and none of the amenities of the naval barracks and other shore establishments; plant for charging submarine batteries, workshops, torpedo store, etc., and a floating dock. All officers and Portsmouth ratings were trained there.

HMS *Forth*, a sea-going depot ship and the *Onyx*, a small hulk at Devonport. West-country ratings were trained by this section.

HMS *Bonaventure* and *Antelope*, a sea-going depot ship and tender based on Portsmouth.

HMS *Mercury* (hulk) depot ship, and *Hazard*, sea-going tender based on Portsmouth.

HMS *Thames* and *Sharpshooter*, sea-going depot ship and tender based on Harwich. East-country ratings were trained in this section.

HMS *Vulcan* and *Hebe*, sea-going depot ship and tender, based on Dundee.

The depot ships, which were old cruisers, provided living quarters for officers and men; they were fitted with charging plant, workshops and store-rooms for spare torpedoes and submarine stores.

The tenders were old torpedo gunboats.

The crews of the submarines only lived in their vessels on passage.

That was the situation when I assumed command. My first step was to find a technical assistant, and I had no difficulty in selecting Commander Percy Addison, after inspecting his other sea-going sections.

I then visited the outlying units, embarked in the depot ships and tenders for cruises, watched submarine attacks from the surface, and took part in many, submerged.

As I have already said, the military value of a submarine lies in the skill of her captain and, I would add, his powers of leadership. It is given to some to excel at ball games, to others to be first-class shots with gun or rifle; if you can add the 'hunter's' instinct to a first-class eye and steady nerves, you will probably have a first-class submarine captain. But skill in attack is not enough. Unless the captain has the absolute confidence of his crew, unless the crew is trained to the highest pitch, and the machinery and weapons are maintained in a state of efficiency, you will not have a first-class submarine.

It was so interesting to stand beside a captain when he was delivering an attack and to watch his crew, they knew in whose hands their fate lay, and one could soon assess the military value of an individual submarine. In the very rare event of its being clear that the atmosphere was not a happy one, I had no hesitation in taking immediate steps to correct it.

They were the salt of the earth those pioneer submariners and I felt very proud when I found myself in command of a personnel knitted by the nature of their service into such a band of good comrades.

ADMIRAL OF THE FLEET SIR ROGER KEYES KCB KCVO CMG DSO

*

Any lingering doubts that submarines were no more than local coastal defence vessels were dispelled by the decision, in 1910, to send three 'C' Class from Portsmouth to Hong Kong, where the depot ship would be the converted sloop Rosario.

The Pioneer Voyage of HM Submarines C-36, C-37 and C-38, From Portsmouth to Hong Kong, During February–April 1911

These three boats, before sailing, had been put into dry dock at Portsmouth, but nothing important was done to them except the scraping of their bottoms and annealing their air-bottles. Such smaller items as larger stanchions and awnings had been added, and on the night of February 7, 1911, they were out of dockyard hands ready for sea. Apart from the Engine-room Artificers, the crews were mostly volunteers selected out of the Submarine Service. The officers consisted of a Lieutenant as captain, with another as First Lieutenant – for each boat – in addition to a couple of junior Lieutenants as 'spares'.

Thus: in *C-36* were Lieutenant G. Herbert, Lieutenant E. R. Lewes and Lieutenant G. M. Welman; in *C-37* were Lieutenant A. A. L. Fenner, Lieutenant K. Michell, whilst Lieutenant A. E. Whitehouse took passage as far as Malta; in *C-38* were Lieutenant J. R. A. Codrington, Lieutenant F. H. Taylor and Lieutenant R. N. Stopford.

Commanding the flotilla from the mother-ship was Lieutenant N. E. Archdale, who was also to be in charge of the depot ship at Hong Kong.

All hands turned out at 4.45 a.m. on February 8, a dark and very raw morning. After a cold breakfast the three little ships, led by Herbert, went out from Portsmouth in their numerical order, and outside picked up their escort, the cruiser *Bonaventure* (4360 tons), at 6 a.m. In fine weather, single-line ahead, the four reached Plymouth that afternoon, having averaged 11½ knots most of the way. Here the boats waited after the next day till a SW blow ended, and they could complete with petrol.

After calls at Vigo, Gibraltar, Port Farina in the Gulf of Tunis, and Malta, they arrived at Port Said on 10 March.

Early the next day pilots came aboard and took the boats separately down the Suez Canal at full speed, all traffic being ordered to give way. From Suez came the alteration of escorts, HMS *Pelorus* taking *C-36*, HMS *Highflyer* towing *C-37* and HMS *Edgar* having *C-38*. Departure was at 5.30 a.m. on March 13, in a calm, but during the evening it piped up, and after night-fall a nasty sea got up on the port quarter, which made steering so difficult that 'an hour at the wheel was all a man could stand'. About 1 a.m. all three boats parted their tow-ropes, and the fun began.

On account of the waves none of the boats for the present could connect up again, so no other choice than using their own engines

and a limited amount of fuel could be made. As for C-37, thanks
to sand having got into her petrol tanks, and this sediment being
shaken up by the boat's motion, she had endless trouble, which
meant frequent shifting of plugs and strainers. Those below in the
engine-room were enduring the buffeting and annoyance with the
thermometer at 105! Their patience in the heat and not too pure air
was remarkable.

At 9 a.m. on 15th, *Highflyer*'s Captain, the senior officer present,
signalled to the *Pelorus* that he was convinced the submarines could
never be towed out to China. *Pelorus* was to make for Port Sudan
and telegraph this conclusion to the Admiralty.

However, *Pelorus* semaphored to C-36, asking Herbert if he could
attach the towing hawser again. Herbert replied that he could. Strip-
ping off his uniform, he crawled forward along the casing, while
the submarine bucked up and down, frequently ducking him several
feet under water, and it looked as though he would be swept off at
any time. At last, he caught up the cable and resecured it.

About 5 p.m., C-37 made a gallant attempt to pick up the tow,
but failed owing to the heavy sea. Night came, and at 10 p.m. a
second attempt failed, but in the morning *Highflyer* was asked to
give this submarine 'a lee' and the rope was at last secured, largely
due to the pluck of Lieutenant Michell, who went for'ard along the
deck and was dipped completely under water every time the lively
submarine pitched her bows. Two stout hawsers were now in place,
joined together, making such a very long line that she towed and
steered much more easily.

Fortunate it was that they could now shut off engines, for they
had not petrol enough to carry to Perim, and Red Sea harbours are
few. By the 17th the weather improved, so that the *Highflyer* was
able to lower a boat, bringing provisions and ice. The latter seemed
a godsend, for with a light wind astern no air could get down into
the submarine, where the heat had become oppressive. And any

cooking made life unbearable. After passing the Straits of Bab-el-Mandeb, and spending a wretched night shipping green seas most of the while, they made Aden.

Two days later and they were again smashing through such waves that a good deal of water got down below and did not lessen the discomforts; yet March 24th began a week of glorious weather, with a light NE monsoon, calm sea, cloudless days and beautiful sunsets. Occasionally escort would stop to lower ice and provisions, and opportunity was thus made for exchanging some of the submarine's crew so that tired men could be rested by a spell on board the surface ship. It was March 29 when the dawn revealed Ceylon, and the sun rose magnificently over Adam's Peak. The cruiser *Monmouth* was waiting to escort them all the way to Hong Kong, in lieu of *Edgar*.

The seven days, April 3–9, were spent on passage from Colombo to Singapore, with a south-west swell that seemed to affect the *Monmouth* more than the submarines; just as in the Bay of Biscay, the three boats liked the long ocean swell better than did *Diana* and *Bonaventure*. This phenomenon is worthy of note. Any inconvenience on the way to the Malacca Straits was caused by the numerous rain-storms, which at times were so bad that a submarine could not see her cruiser. 'I counted as many as fifteen rain-storms going on at the same time', observed C-37's captain. It was while lying alongside the *Monmouth* at Singapore that a French steamer was trying to turn in a narrow area athwart the stream. The latter's engines, through some mistake, went astern instead of ahead, and she got out of control. Fenner saw what was about to happen, cleared his men out of the submarine, and then followed the crash of steel against steel. Fortunately the incident might have been much more serious, the steamer struck with her rudder, damaging several of the submarine's plates, but no water came in.

The last stage of this long voyage began with HMS *Flora* taking the place of *Highflyer*, and so they departed in company, passing a couple of Japanese ships on the way to England for the King's coronation. The final two days of the submarines' journey resembled those exciting hours in the Red Sea. A strong NE wind turned the swell into a wicked waste of angry waters. The *Monmouth*, in spite of her 9,800 tons, was having a bad time, but her officers with anxiety watched the three little C's battened down and once more taking it green. Indeed the cruiser's people marvelled that such craft could stand so much. Frequently the boats would disappear under the waves, and the watchers never expected to see them again.

Through forty-eight miserable hours this continued, with salt water leaking down, wetting everybody's clothes and bedding. The boats rolled and wallowed a great deal, spilling more acid from their batteries, and at the worst moment one of C-37's men cut a vein whilst trying to open a sardine tin. Blood spurted all over the place and intensified the general adversity, until tourniquets were applied and the man could be given attention. It was a very battered and rusty trio of boats which arrived in Hong Kong harbour on the morning of April 20; but they had proved to the world the ancient truth that small vessels will usually go through more weather than any human being has the heart to drive them.

During this memorable voyage everyone felt most trying the cramped space, lack of exercise, and being battened down for hour after hour with little air and excessive heat. On a number of occasions it became necessary to stop all cooking, and in fine weather an electric boiler was rigged up abaft the conning-tower. For most of the journey C-37 carried only two officers, which meant watch-and-watch, four hours on and four hours off by day, but at night three hours on and off. The seamen were in four watches likewise. In a surface ship, during almost any weather, you can at least walk about, but here in these boats no space was available, so that the personnel used to suffer a good deal from cramp.

In order to admit all possible air, the conning-tower hatch remained open till the last second; but some one had to stand by, all the time, ready to close it when a sea came romping along. Two or three hours of that duty meant heavy work, and even the men below off watch might be summoned on deck hurriedly to slip the tow-rope. Bathing in tropical shark-infested waters presented a problem, but a canvas bag was rigged up on the upper deck and filled with fresh water.

As to provisions, the men were each given 9½d. a day, and before quitting each port purchased what was required for the passage. Every three or four days the parent-ship would stop and send along those articles previously asked for by signal; it was a novel method of deep-sea shopping. For the officers each boat began with six boxes containing everything to mess three persons during a week, apart from eggs, vegetables and fruit. Very few incidents of sickness occurred during those weeks of varied temperatures, and notwithstanding all the dampness. Each evening the submarine's captain mustered his men, serving out pills, castor oil or quinine as required.

In short, the record voyage had been achieved not less by means of discipline and good organisation than by patient endurance with pluck.

FROM THE DIARY KEPT BY LT. A. A. L. FENNER, CO OF *C-37*

*

The Submarine Service had already acquired a rich assortment of characters, one such described by the CO of C-15, one of the flotilla attached to HMS Bonaventure, the sea-going submarine depot ship at Portsmouth in 1911.

The 'Bonaventure''s captain, Commander Frank Brandt, was one of the outstanding personalities in the Submarine Service in those days.

In moments of exasperation his gift of invective was unsurpassed by anyone that I have ever met in the Service or out of it. Should he, perchance standing on the quarterdeck of his ship, happen to witness some particularly unseamanlike behaviour on the part of a submarine skipper bringing his boat alongside, Brandt would call for a megaphone, and an admiring audience would be treated to a torrent of language, which for its novelty and picturesqueness was without rival. A masterpiece of its kind, it was the envy of all who heard it. None of us took the least offence; we knew that he really did not mean a word of what he was saying, for he was the kindest of souls, and all his officers had the greatest admiration and affection for him.

His clothes were as unorthodox as his language. The climax came, so far as his carelessness in dress was concerned, when the C-in-C of the Port arrived unexpectedly on board his ship. Brandt, hastily summoned from below, met his admiral at the top of the gangway in carpet slippers, his trousers turned up, and his unbuttoned monkey jacket, displaying to the scandalised eyes of the flag officer a vast expanse of pink flannel shirt.

'Frankie' Brandt, a loveable man and a gallant gentleman, perished on the bridge of his ship, HMS 'Monmouth', as she sank in flames at the battle of Coronel.

COMMANDER C. L. KERR

*

On the eve of the First World War, Admiral Sir Percy Scott, justifiably called 'the father of modern naval gunnery' realised that the Admiralty were failing to appreciate the potential of the submarine or the deadliness of the torpedo, believing that the submarine was an untried weapon and the torpedo was not accurate. Letters from Sir Percy began to appear in the press, in the Daily Mail *on 2 June 1914.*

In wartime the scouting aeroplanes will always be high above, on the look-out, and the submarines in constant readiness, as are the engines at a fire station. If an enemy is sighted, the gong sounds, and the leash of a flotilla of submarines will be slipped. Whether it is night or day, fine or rough, they must go out to search for their quarry; if they find her, she is doomed. Will any battleship expose herself to such a dead Certainty of destruction? I say 'No'. Not only is the open sea unsafe; a battleship is not immune from attack even in a closed harbour; for the so-called protecting-boom at the entrance can easily be blown up. With a flotilla of submarines commanded by dashing young officers, of whom we (the British Navy) have plenty, I would undertake to get through any boom into the harbour and sink or materially damage all the ships in that harbour. If the battleship is not safe either on the high seas or in a harbour, what is the use of a battleship? What we (England) require is an enormous fleet of submarines, airships and aeroplanes, and a few fast cruisers, provided we can find a place to keep them in safety during wartime. I do not think that the importance of submarines has been fully recognised, neither do I think that it has been realised how completely their advent has revolutionised naval warfare. In my opinion, as the motor has driven the horse from the road, so has the submarine driven the battleship from the sea.

And a long letter in The Times *on 4 June, which Scott himself summarised*

'That as we had sufficient battleships, but not sufficient submarines and aircraft, we should stop building battleships, and spend the money for their construction on the submarines and the aircraft that we urgently needed.

'That submarines and aircraft had entirely revolutionised naval warfare.

'That if we are at war with a country within striking distance of submarines, battleships on the high seas would be in great danger; that even in harbour they would not be immune from attack unless the harbour was quite a safe one.

'That probably if we went to war, we should at once lock our battleships up in a safe harbour, and that the enemy would do the same.

'That all naval strategy was upset, as no fleet could hide from the eye of the aeroplane.

'That submarines could deliver a deadly attack in broad daylight.

'That battleships could not bombard an enemy if his ports were adequately protected by submarines.

'That the enemy's submarines would come to our coasts and destroy everything they could see.'

For Admiral Sir Percy Scott, the master gunner, architect of so many gunnery innovations, the great apostle of the big gun, to write in this vein caused the veil of the ark of the tabernacle at HMS Excellent, *the gunnery school at Whale Island, to be rent from top to bottom. After a moment's pause for stupefaction, Scott's naval readers reacted with a torrent of violently hostile criticism. Admiral Sir Edmund Fremantle said it was 'a mischievous scare'. Lord Sydenham said it was 'a fantastic dream'. The* Pall Mall Gazette *said Scott's ideas 'approached the boundaries of mid-summer madness'. 'As a romance, or even a prophecy' wrote the* Manchester Courier *'the forecast is fantastic, but as practical tactics it is so premature as to be almost certainly fatal'. 'The imaginative, fancy-picture-making spirit of the thing is out of place over Sir Percy Scott's name' said the* Manchester Guardian. *The* Spectator *called the letter 'a most approved example of the mare's-nest'. Mr Hannon, Secretary of the Navy League, said in the* Globe *that Sir Percy's letter contained statements that were 'premature, ill-advised and calculated to do serious harm to the cause of the maintenance of British supremacy at sea'. Occasionally, there were some who thought Sir Percy might have a point. 'Is Sir Percy Scott a dreamer of dreams like Admiral Aube? Or is he a precursor of practical achievements?'* said the Daily Graphic. *'Let us not forget that the dreams of today are often the realities of tomorrow.'*

In July, Sir Percy replied to his critics and in so doing repeated an argument first vehemently put forward by Fisher, 'All war is, of course, barbarous, but in war the purpose of the enemy is to crush his foe; to arrive at this he will attack where his foe is most vulnerable. Our most vulnerable point is our food and oil supply. The submarine has introduced a new method of attacking these supplies. Will feelings of humanity restrain our enemy from using it?'

Part Two:

THE FIRST WORLD WAR

❖

Sir Percy and all his critics were to have their answer very soon. On 5 September 1914, the small light cruiser Pathfinder, *2,940 tons, leader of the 8th Destroyer Flotilla, was patrolling the line St Abb's Head–May Island–Bass Rock off the entrance to the Firth of Forth when she was torpedoed by U.21. The explosion counter-mined the ammunition in* Pathfinder's *forward magazine and the ship virtually disintegrated. Some men were picked up, but 259 of her crew were lost. This was the first warship ever sunk in the open sea by a genuine submarine.*

The next was only just over a week later:

Patrol Report of HM Submarine *E.9*, September 1914

12th September

Midnight   Arrived position; rested on bottom 120 feet

13th September

5.11 a.m.   Rose and proceeded as per chart
6.30 a.m.   Surface. Weather thick and raining hard, slight swell
6.32 a.m.   Dived 70 feet

7.15 a.m.   20 feet: sighted Heligoland, distant 5 miles on port bow, also cruiser [the *Hela*] approximately 1½ to 2 miles off, and wisps of smoke in various directions; attacked cruiser; weather cleared

7.28 a.m.   Position 600 yards abeam of cruiser (two funnels). Submarine very lively diving. Fired both bow torpedoes at her starboard side at intervals of about 15 seconds

7.29 a.m.   Heard single loud explosion. Submarine at 70 feet, course parallel to cruiser

7.32 a.m.   Rose to 32 feet, observed cruiser between waves; appeared to have stopped and to have list to starboard. Splashes from shot on our port side and ahead of cruiser. Turned periscope to see where shots were coming from, but submarine was very deep, and only observed wisps of smoke and mast very close. Dived to 70 feet and picked up trim

8.35 a.m.   20 feet; sighted trawlers where cruiser had been, 4 or 5 in number in a cluster. Horizon slightly misty, one trawler, one cable on beam. Dived 70 feet

9.07 a.m.   20 feet; destroyer on beam 100 yards; 70 feet

9.23 a.m.   Rested on bottom 90 feet

12.30 p.m.   Heard several destroyers pass over us from southward apparently from Weser River

3.50 p.m.   Rose to 20 feet; destroyers in sight, patrolling

4.55 p.m.   20 feet; destroyers

5.05 p.m.   Rested on bottom 100 feet; destroyers passing over us at intervals

9.26 p.m.   Rose and charged. Horizon clear, loppy swell

11.10 p.m.   Rested on bottom 110 feet

14th September

4.45 a.m.   Rose 20 feet. Course as per chart, but observed nothing but trawlers patrolling in the Bight

6.09 a.m.   Heligoland well in sight, also outer anchorages all clear of ships except trawlers

7.18 a.m.   Turned to westward and moved out to endeavour to catch enemy's submarines patrolling. Continued search submerged till dusk, charging on the surface from 11.40 a.m. to 1.25 p.m. Visibility from clear to 1 mile. Occasional heavy rain

6.45 p.m.   Proceeded on surface to westward; sea increasing

Midnight   Very heavy seas. Bent stanchions and splash plate. Endeavoured to rest on bottom, but disturbance continued to such a depth, i.e. 120 feet, that the submarine, despite 8 tons negative buoyancy, bumped. Rose from bottom and dived at 70 feet during the night

15th September

5.00 a.m.   Surface. Very heavy seas; unable to remain on bridge, proceeded on gas engine with conning tower closed and ventilator in conning tower open, conning through the periscopes

1.53 p.m.   Sea abating. Proceeded on surface to port

(Signed) M. K. HORTON
Lt-Commander
16th September 1914

The German cruiser Hela *was the first enemy warship to be sunk by a British submarine. Horton was mentioned in despatches.*

*

At about this time, the Submarine Service acquired the title of 'The Trade', but as Rudyard Kipling explained

No one knows how the title of 'The Trade' came to be applied to the Submarine Service. Some say that the cruisers invented it because they pretend that submarine officers look like unwashed chauffeurs. Others think it sprang forth by itself, which means that it was coined by the Lower Deck, where they always have the proper names for things. Whatever the truth, the Submarine Service is now 'the Trade'; and if you ask them why, they will answer: 'What else could you call it? The Trade's "the trade" of course.'

THE TRADE

They bear, in place of classic names,
Letters and numbers on their skin.
They play their grisly blindfold games
In little boxes made of tin.
Sometimes they stalk the Zeppelin,
Sometimes they learn where mines are laid
Or where the Baltic ice is thin.
That is the custom of 'The Trade'.

Few prize-courts sit upon their claims.
They seldom tow their targets in.
They follow certain secret aims
Down under, far from strife or din.
When they are ready to begin
No flag is flown, no fuss is made
More than the shearing of a pin.
That is the custom of 'The Trade'.

The Scout's quadruple funnel flames
A mark from Sweden to the Swin,
The Cruiser's thunderous screw proclaims
Her comings out and goings in;
But only whiffs of paraffin
Or creamy rings that fizz and fade
Show where the one-eyed Death has been.
That is the custom of 'The Trade'.

Their feats, their fortunes and their fames
Are hidden from their nearest kin;
No eager public backs or blames,
No journal prints the yarns they spin
(The Censor would not let it in!)
When they return from run or raid.
Unheard they work, unseen they win.
That is the custom of 'The Trade'.

*

Brothers serving in the Submarine Service were unusual. Twin brothers were almost unique. C. G. Brodie, describing his twin brother T.S., gives a vivid picture of the kind of man who was a submarine CO early in the First World War.

Twin Brothers

Round-shouldered, with a head too big for his body, and a shy, deprecating manner, he had a habit of avoiding attention. It is not easy to see a twin, one's other half, always in perspective, but after joining schools and the Navy hand-in-hand, no twin can have any illusions about his appearance. One boy with a big head and very fair hair is conspicuous enough, two exactly alike are everyone's joke and need labels. Cadet's wit is seldom subtle, and a youthful and hateful pimple of mine started us as Spot and Non-Spot. T.S. breathed to me: 'Thank heaven they haven't thought of Spot and Plain'. But news of the Whitehead torpedo reached the *Britannia* about then and War Head and Dummy Head it became. That T.S. became known as Dummy Head and C.G. as War Head suggests that he was the more patient under rather monotonous humours, but he could be roused, as a few of the more tiresome prodders found.

T.S. did not join submarines until I had been some time in command. He had done a couple of years in destroyers, achieving a measure of fame as the only executive officer to survive his full period under the fiery Walter Cowan, then a very young and exacting Commander. This proved he was still patient, but that he also had other qualities. My own enthusiasm for 'The Trade' led him to enter submarines, at the unusual seniority of four years as lieutenant. Though without many years' experience in command, his record in practise attacks soon led him to *D.8* and his war work in her in the Heligoland Bight, though like most others devoid of targets, rewarded him with *E.15*, the latest in her class.

The Navy before the First World War hardly ever used Christian names, but we knew everyone's initials, and it was natural to call brothers T.S. and C.G. He was T.S. to me, and everyone else. T.S.'s lined face, bent shoulders, and weary air cast him for the role of aged mess cynic and misanthrope. A silent target provoking the quips of the wardroom wags, he would at last stir and loose a pointed shaft of wit to everyone's satisfaction. No misogynist but fastidious where women were concerned, the full day's work and play the bachelor life of a wardroom then provided, wholly sufficed for him. A supremely good dancer, when waltzing was the sole test, his violin playing gave greater pleasure than that of many professionals, and he was a first-class bridge player in any company. Called 'The Old Man' when he was 22, at 30 he was often affectionately referred to as 'The Old Wreck'. But his physique was deceptive. Early in 1915 he wrote, to cheer me at Christmas, an account of an episode in the *Maidstone* that showed he was not too old at 30.

At that time there must have been at Harwich nearly sixty officers of an age between 20 and 30, getting all the exercise they could between patrols. Lying alongside Parkstone Quay facilities for games were good if not varied. T.S. put a challenge on the wardroom notice board backing 'Young Hopeful' against the chosen champions of the mess, for a stake of two pounds, at the four games available for single combat, golf, badminton, billiards and cards. He returned from his patrol to find it accepted and his identity unguessed. He won the badminton easily, halved the golf, won the best of five at whisky poker (I suppose it is now known by its American name of draw poker) and was leading at billiards when interrupted by a Zeppelin scare. It was lucky for him Stoker was not there, but the feat shows he was fairly fit, and the only strenuous game, badminton, gave him his easiest victory. Though not rivalling Nasmith's fine physique or experience, T.S., like Boyle and Stoker, was a not unworthy representative as a man, or as an officer, of the 'Trade' and the navy of 1915.

'SEA GEE' (REAR ADMIRAL C. G. BRODIE)

*

After the final failure of the Navy's attempt to force the Straits on 18 March 1915, thoughts turned to a military landing on the Gallipoli peninsula, and to the possibility that submarines might penetrate the Straits and operate where surface ships could not, in the Sea of Marmara. The problem was to get through the Dardanelles Straits.

With their shoals and shallows, their narrows, reducing to only just over a mile wide at one point, minefields, batteries of Turkish guns, howitzers and even torpedo tubes ashore, patrols by day and search-lights by night, and a westerly current of between two and five knots running into the Mediterranean, the Straits were a formidable proposition for a submarine. At a conference with Commodore Keyes and his staff, everyone present said it was not possible – except T.S. who said he could do it.

E.15 began the attempt to penetrate the Straits before dawn on 17 April. C.G. wrote 'At daylight T.S.'s serenity passed to me. Suddenly, as surely as if he had spoken aloud, I was aware that all was supremely well with him'. But all was not well. T.S. had dived to run under the minefield when the current swept E.15 ashore at Kephez Point, twelve miles into the Straits and directly under Turkish guns, which opened fire. T.S. blew all main ballast tanks and went full astern to try and free E.15, but the boat was hard aground. As T.S. opened the conning-tower hatch, a shell exploded against the hull and killed him. After another shell hit, the crew made their way up on to the casing and surrendered. E.15 was finally destroyed in situ by our own forces.

*

The next attempts to penetrate the Straits were made by the Australian E Class submarine AE.2 (Lt.-Cdr. Hew Stoker), who set off on 25 April, and E.14 (Lt.-Cdr. Edward Boyle), on 27th. Both reached the Sea of Marmara, and they met each other on 28th, but while Boyle went on to make the first prolonged and highly successful patrol in the Marmara, which thoroughly disrupted Turkish ship-ping and induced a near-panic in the area, and for which he was awarded the Victoria Cross, Stoker was not so fortunate, and describes

The Loss of *AE.2*

Close to E.14 we went, and exchanged cheery greetings through megaphones. Her commanding officer was senior to me, and therefore with him lay the future direction of our operations. He asked what our plans for the morrow had been, and I replied that we had proposed going to Constantinople. He, however, considered it would be advisable to wait until he had received the Admiral's orders by wireless that night, and therefore directed us to meet him at the same rendezvous at 10 a.m. on the morrow. And so we parted for the night.

Next morning, as we were making for the rendezvous, we sighted what we believed to be E.14, some five miles ahead of us. Half an hour later we were at the position ourselves, but nothing could then be seen of E.14, who had, we imagined, dived to investigate some smoke farther along to the westward.

This smoke, which was approaching, soon singled out to indicate only one ship, and such dense volumes of it were arising that one assumed she must be fairly big. When, however, her mast and funnels hove in sight one could see she was only a torpedo craft moving at high speed, and as her course lay direct for us it would be necessary to dive out of the way until she went past.

After an adjustment of the ballast tanks, we dived to 50 feet, and shaped a southerly course to investigate another ship we had sighted in that direction. The submarine was diving easily and comfortably; not a suspicion of impending disaster lay in our minds.

Suddenly, and for no accountable reason, the boat took a large inclination up by the bows and started rising rapidly in the water. All efforts at regaining control proved futile. The diving rudders had not the slightest effect towards bringing her back to the horizontal position or stopping her rising in the water. We increased to full speed in order to give the rudders their maximum power, and shifted water ballast forward as quickly as possible, but still she continued to rise, and at last broke surface. Through the periscope I saw a torpedo-boat a bare hundred yards off, firing hard. At all costs we must get under again at once. I ordered one of the forward tanks to be flooded, and a few minutes later the submarine took an inclination down by the bows and slipped under water. Closing off the forward tank, and stopping the movement of water ballast from aft to forward, we endeavoured to catch her at 50 feet, but now again the diving rudders seemed powerless to right her, and with an ever-increasing inclination down by the bows she went to 60 then 70 feet, and was obviously quite out of control. Water ballast was expelled as quickly as possible, yet down and down she went – 80, 90 and 100 feet. Here was the limit of our gauges; when that depth was passed she was still sinking rapidly. We could not tell to what depths she was reaching. I ordered full speed astern on the motors . . . In a few moments – moments in which death seemed close to every man – there came a cry from the coxswain: 'She's coming up, sir!' and the needle seemed to jerk itself reluctantly away from the 100-feet mark, and then rise rapidly.

The amount of water expelled from the ballast tanks had now made the boat light; so with increasing speed she jumped to the surface, and remained there an appreciable time. While I attended to the reflooding of the tanks, another officer looked through the periscope. He reported the torpedo-boat circling around us, and a gunboat approaching fast from the southward. It afterwards transpired that the torpedo-boat then fired two torpedoes at us; yet they missed this practically standing target at such short range.

Under we must get again – and away we went with the same terrible inclination down by the bows, this time expelling water ballast immediately she began to dive in desperate attempts to regain control. But down and down and down she went, faster even than before, 60, 80, and 100 feet. The inclination down by the bows became more and more pronounced – she seemed to be trying to stand on her nose. Eggs, bread, food of all sorts, knives, forks, plates, came tumbling forward from the petty officers' mess. Everything that could fall over fell; men slipping and struggling, grasped hold of valves, gauges, rods, anything to hold them up in position to their posts.

Full speed astern again . . . A thousand years passed – well, this time we were gone for ever.

In Heaven's name, what depth are we at? . . . Why did not the sides of the boat cave in under the pressure and finish it? . . .

And then, once again that fateful needle jumped back from its limit mark, and AE.2 rushed stern first to the surface.

BANG! . . . A cloud of smoke in the engine-room. We were hit and holed! And again in quick succession two more holes.

Finished! We were caught! We could no longer dive and our defence was gone. It but remained to avoid useless sacrifice of life. All hands were ordered on deck and overboard.

The holes in the hull were all above water, and therefore not in themselves sufficient to sink the boat, though preventing all possibility of diving. While the crew scrambled up on deck, an officer remained with me below to take the necessary steps for sinking. The third officer, on the bridge, watched the rising water to give warning in time for our escape. A shout from him and we clambered up; but through the conning tower windows I saw there was still a minute to spare. I jumped down again and had a last look round – for, you see, I was fond of AE.2.

What a sight! Pandemonium – I cannot attempt to describe it – food, clothing, flotsam and jetsam of the weirdest sorts floating up on the fast entering water in the place we had been so proud to keep neat and clean . . .

An anxious shout from above: 'Hurry, sir, she's going down!'

In the wardroom my eye was caught by my private dispatch-case, which contained, I remembered, some money. That was bound to be useful – I ran and picked it up, and darted up the conning tower.

As I reached the bridge the water was about two feet from the top of the conning tower; besides this only a small portion of the stern was out of water. On it were clustered the last half-dozen of the crew, the remainder were overboard.

Curious incidents impress one at such times. As those last six men took to the water the neat dive of one of the engine-room ratings will remain pictured in my mind for ever.

Perhaps a minute passed, and then slowly and gracefully, like the lady she was, without sound or sigh, without causing an eddy or a ripple on the water, AE.2 just slid away on her last and longest dive.

CDR. H. G. STOKER DSO RN

Stoker and his ship's company became prisoners-of-war of the Turks. Stoker was awarded the DSO in 1919, after he returned home.

*

The next to penetrate the Straits was Lt. Martin Nasmith in E.11. He had been ordered by Commodore Keyes to 'Go and run amuck in the Marmara' and he needed no second urging. But Nasmith was a curious blend of caution and aggression. He flew over the Dardanelles and the Marmara beforehand in a Farman biplane 'to look at the jumps' and he prudently waited to confer with Boyle, who returned on 18 May, before setting off the next day on a patrol which was the stuff of legend, described in a letter to his family by E.11's First Lieutenant, Guy D'Oyly-Hughes:

H.M. Submarine E.11
June 12th, 1915

My dear Father and Mother

We have indeed had a month full of crowded life. We got out of the Dardanelles on June 7th at 4 p.m. – with a real live mine hanging on our port hydroplane. We had carried the little fellow with us for over two hours and he wasn't a very comfortable travelling companion as every now and then his mooring chains would rattle and clank on our side and we would look at each other and wonder if the bump was coming now or later on. However I seem to have started at the wrong end of this yarn, so I'll begin again.

At 2 a.m. on April 19th [*sic: actually May 19th*] we were escorted by a destroyer well inside the entrance to the Dardanelles. She left us shortly after 2.30 a.m. and after wishing us luck through a megaphone, she turned round and went out.

We dived at the first streak of daylight and at once went deep to go under the Kephev mine field – we bumped on Chanak corner as we rounded it at 80 feet but we wriggled off again alright. By 9 a.m. with the battery finished we were crawling past Gallipoli and had to sit on the bottom all day till darkness fell and we could come to the surface to try and charge. We were interrupted by their patrols rushing at us four times but we were too quick for them (having been well grounded in the art of rapid diving off Heligoland). And by 7 a.m. next morning we were well into Marmora with the battery right up.

We went right out into the Middle of Marmora and slept. We hadn't had any for nearly 40 hours and by jove we wanted it.

After that the fun began – our first bag was a 22 knot gunboat off Constantinople – (the most beautiful town in the world, I should say). At 8 a.m. on a glorious Sunday morning the population of Constantinople must have been roused by a terrific report and the rather depressing sight of a gaily painted vessel in flames and rapidly sinking. She sank very quickly – but not before one man (who must

47

have been coolness personified) rushed to a six-pounder and fired one round at our periscope (just as I was having a look) hitting it square about 18 inches from the top and of course utterly ruining it and leaving us with only one periscope between us and utter blindness! 'Some shot' as the Yanks would say.

Well – I can't possibly relate all our adventures here as I would take a whole day to write them down. I will get hold of a copy of our report to the Admiralty and send it along when we get to Malta. We had a magnificent time – the only thing being that the strenuous life and long hours with no exercise and considerable anxiety laid up first of all Nasmith and then myself for the best part of a week. We both had the same complaint – fever, headaches, and an awful lassitude. Simply couldn't move a limb for love nor money.

Then to add to our difficulties our starboard main shaft cracked and our port main motor developed a full brilliance earth so we reckoned it was madness to go on – so having sunk eight ships we decided to come out. We bagged a big transport as we came out and then picked up a mine on our hydroplane. However, we got out and found a destroyer waiting for us with the Admiralty photographer on board. We got a tremendous reception from the whole fleet as we got into Lemnos Harbour at sunset. All the ship's companies of every ship were on deck cheering frantically – signals of congratulation pouring in – 'Well done E.11' from the Admiral – General Hamilton thanked us in the name of all the soldiers ashore for what we had done for them. The French ships simply went off their heads – they didn't stop shouting till long after we had got alongside our parent ship and were tucked up in bed snoring.

Well – it was great fun but at times (especially when we went right into Constantinople) rather too exciting for my peace loving tastes. The good God brought E.11 out of Constantinople – because none of *us* knew where we were going.

We stopped one night at Lemnos and then set sail for Malta for a short and quick refit before returning. We are 40 miles off Malta now and should be in by sunset. I shall of course be frightfully busy refitting the boat but we ought to have a pretty decent time for three weeks before returning to the fray. We don't seem to get any great 'push' into the fighting ashore. I suppose it's fearful country the wretched soldiers have to tackle but they are just the same today as they were on the first night after landing, two months ago now. I'm afraid it's our old British policy of nibbling at the job – losing thousands of good lives and then waking up to the fact and sending out adequate men and supplies and doing the job thoroughly.

We come back to civilisation to find that the whole Cabinet seems to have turned upside down and done a shift. Winny has got the push apparently. This sort of thing doesn't exactly fill one with confidence. What's the matter with 'em all anyhow?

Lord – how I'd love to have a drop of leave to have a good yarn with you about everything –

Well – heaps of love and kisses – will write again soon.

Yours ever,
Guy

In cold figures, E.11 sank eleven ships – a large gunboat, two transports, three store ships, an ammunition ship and four other vessels. But the patrol's effect on the enemy was as much psychological as physical. E.11 twice penetrated Constantinople harbour (like a Turkish submarine appearing in the Pool of London) to sink a troop-carrying barge and throw the population into a panic. Nasmith was awarded the Victoria Cross, D'Oyly Hughes and E.11's other officer, Lieutenant Robert Brown RNR, were both awarded DSCs and all thirty members of the ship's company were awarded DSMs.

In October 1914, E.1 (Lt.-Cdr. N. F. Lawrence) and E.9 (Lt.-Cdr. M. Horton) were sent to operate in the Baltic. They were followed in August 1915 by E.8 (Lt.-Cdr. F. H. J. Goodhart) and E.13 (Lt.-Cdr. G. Layton, and in September by E.18 (Lt.-Cdr. R. C. Halahan) and E.19 (Lt.-Cdr. F N. A. Cromie). Entry into the Baltic involved another difficult passage for submarines – through The Sound, the narrow strait between Denmark and Sweden. E.18's Navigating Officer was Sub Lt. (later Vice-Admiral) Leslie H. Ashmore.

E.18 in the Baltic

The Drogden Light Vessel marks the end of the Flint Channel (leading into the Baltic) and I knew that until we reached a certain bearing from it we could not safely dive. The bearing of its two dimmed lights drew aft with agonising slowness. At intervals Halahan's voice, tense with impatience, would stab at me. 'Can we dive yet Sub?'

'No, sir, not yet. Not until the bearing is right!'

I knew and shared his anxiety. Unable to dive, discovery at that stage would be our end. And suddenly, there indeed was a destroyer, a bare 200 yards to starboard overtaking us. It seemed unbelievable that we had not been discovered. Any moment now she must turn to ram us. Halahan called down to the petty officer steering in the control room below.

'I've got the wheel, coxswain. Steering from the bridge.' To me he muttered furiously, 'I'll ram the bastard if he comes towards us.'

Then in silence we watched the black shadow draw slowly ahead and melt into the darkness, and a sigh of relief broke from us. Every minute now was taking us into deeper water. But there was still too little to cover us completely when, to our horror, another destroyer loomed up ahead.

'How's that bearing, Sub?' Halahan grunted.

'Another few degrees yet, sir, before deep water,' I replied.

'To hell with it. We've got to get down', decided Halahan, and sounded the diving klaxon. I dropped quietly into the conning tower, followed by Halahan, and, as the hatch slammed behind him, the first lieutenant took the boat down.

Hardly had we reached the control room when the submarine hit the bottom with a tremendous crash with only ten feet showing on the gauge. And now I was treated to an exquisite little lesson in leadership by my captain. As looks of dismay and alarm spread over the faces of the control room crew, he turned to his sailor servant standing behind him. In a voice utterly confident, calm, he said, 'Get me a cup of cocoa, will you Welsh?'

At once all traces of anxiety left the faces of the men around him and they turned quietly to carry on with their various duties.

For the next two and a half hours we progressed in a fashion to make any submariner's hair stand on end. With both motors at half speed we bounded along the rocky bottom at some four knots, rising nearly to the surface at one moment and plunging to the bottom at the next. At last, at 4 a.m. on 9th September, we ran thankfully into deep water and Halahan took us to the sea bed for a rest.

VICE-ADMIRAL LESLIE H. ASHMORE CB DSO

*

As part of their unrestricted submarine warfare campaign in 1915, the U-boats began sinking East Coast fishing trawlers. To counter this, decoy trawlers were used, to act the part of a 'tethered goat' while towing a submarine, the two vessels being connected by a telephone cable. When a U-boat was sighted, the trawler would inform the submarine by telephone and, at the appropriate moment, slip the tow.

*On the morning of 23 June 1915, in the North Sea off Aberdeen,
the armed Trawler* Taraniki *(Lt.-Cdr. H. D. Edwards) was towing*
C.24 *(Lt. F. H. Taylor) when a U-boat (actually* U.40*) was sighted,
and* Taraniki *duly played her part as*

The Tethered Goat

When going on these trawler towing patrols the submarine and
trawler used to leave Aberdeen separately, well before dawn. Also
the trawler used to be berthed in the harbour well away from the
submarines so as to try to prevent any unauthorised person from
finding out that we were working together.

We used to pick up the fishing fleet separately, and then get in
tow of the trawler and start diving before it was light. The towing
wire was secured to the towing slip in the bows of the submarine,
and the end of the telephone cable was spliced to a short length of
cable which was led through a watertight connection in one of the
ventilating shaft caps. When slipping the tow it was hoped that this
splice would carry away – it being the weakest part of the cable.

When towed we used to dive at about forty feet. As soon as we
were in good trim we used to set a watch of one Officer and two
men at the diving planes. We rang up the trawler at regular intervals
to make certain that the telephone was working all right.

We had been diving for about two hours on our first patrol when
the trawler rang up to say a German submarine had appeared on
the surface and was firing at her to force the crew to abandon ship.

We went straight into action stations. As soon as Taylor had got
rough position from the trawler he gave the order to slip the tow.
We then found that the wheel working the horse-shoe securing the
hinged pin could not be moved at all. We put all the pressure on it

we dared, but it refused to budge. When Taylor realised it was hopeless to do anything from our end, he told the trawler to slip the tow from their end. As soon as they had done this, we of course began to sink heavily by the bow. However, Taylor caught the trim and got to periscope depth. In the meantime the bow tubes were got ready. We had an absolutely sitting shot at the German as she was stopped beam on to us. When she sank we blew and came to the surface to pick up survivors. Immediately afterwards I found that we couldn't move our propeller as the telephone cable had floated aft and had got properly wrapped round it and the shaft. The trawler had to take us in tow and return to Aberdeen.

We were rather pleased with ourselves as the torpedo which sank *UC.40* [sic] was, I believe, one of the oldest in use at the time – Mk. V. No. 10. The C.O. of the German submarine who was one of the survivors, told me that it made such a small explosion that he thought he had been sunk by an internal explosion, and that when he came to the surface he thought we had just come to the surface by coincidence. His No. 1, who was a survivor, was most indignant with him for not having kept on the move when on the surface, a point with which I was in entire agreement.

LT.-CDR. G. J. MACKNESS (THEN *C.24*'S FIRST LIEUTENANT)

U.40's three survivors were the CO, Kapitänleutnant Gerhard Furbringer, and two of his officers. The other twenty-nine men in U.40 were all lost. When Furbringer was brought on board Taranaki *he complained bitterly that he had been sunk by a 'dirty trick'.*

*

In the majority of submarine attack exercises, the target was a surface ship. But submarines had shots at U-boats often enough to make it worthwhile having exercises with submarines as targets. On

53

15 August 1916, E.4, E.31, E.41 and E.16 sailed from Harwich for just such an exercise.

The plan was for E.4 (Lt.-Cdr. J. Tenison) and E.31 (Lt.-Cdr. F. E. B. Feilman) to attack E.41 (Lt. A. Winser) and then E.16. The roles would then be reversed and the attackers become the targets for E.41 and E.16. The destroyer Firedrake *was in attendance to supervise the exercises and recover expended torpedoes.*

In one run, when E.4 was the target on the surface, being attacked by the dived E.4, E.4 collided with E.41. Both submarines sank. E.4 was lost with all hands. Some twenty men from E.41 were picked up by Firedrake. *That was assumed to be all the survivors, but a full hour-and-a-half later, another man came bobbing like a cork to the surface. So, a disastrous day was to some extent redeemed by this.*

Miraculous Escape

Something was heard to come in contact with the bottom of the boat for'ard. It hit twice in quick succession. Then the engine-room telegraph rang: 'Out clutches.' I took out the port clutch and closed the muffler valve, then I heard the report that the boat was making water. I proceeded for'ard to ascertain the position of the leak, and came to the conclusion she was holed low down. My first impulse was to close the lower conning-tower hatch. At this point the chief engine-room artificer asked me if all hands were out of the engine room. I replied that I would go and find out. On going aft I met one man coming for'ard. I ordered him to put his life belt on, keep his head and go to the conning-tower hatch and wait his turn. Finding there was nobody else aft, I came for'ard and put on a life belt and closed the valve on the air trunk through the engine-room bulkhead. Then I noticed the water begin to come down the conning-tower hatch, and the boat took a dip by the bows.

I then went aft and shouted to the hands for'ard to come to the engine room. There was no response. The midships compartment was in darkness and partly flooded. Chlorine gas began to come through. I closed the engine-room door and began to unscrew the clips of the torpedo hatch above me. At this juncture the engine room was in complete darkness, with the exception of the port pilot lamp which was evidently burning through 'earth'. The water was slowly rising in the engine room through the voice pipes which I had left open to relieve the pressure on the bulkhead door.

I proceeded to disconnect the torpedo hatch from its gearing, which meant the removal of two split pins and two pins from the links. Before the foremost one could be moved I had to unship the strong-back and wait for sufficient pressure in the boat to ease the hatch off the strong-back.

The heat at this time was excessive, therefore I rested awhile and considered the best way of flooding the engine room. I eventually decided that the best way would be to flood it through the stern tube or the weed trap of the circulating system, or by dropping the exhaust and induction valves and opening the muffler valve. I tried the stern tube first, but I could open neither the stern cap nor the rear door. Then I came for'ard again. While passing the switchboards I received several shocks. I tried to open the weed trap of the circulating inlet but it was in an awkward position, and as the water was coming over the top of me I could not ease back the butterfly nuts. So I proceeded for'ard again and opened the muffler valve, also the test cocks on the group-exhaust valves. I tried them and found the water coming in. I then climbed on top of the engines underneath the torpedo hatch and unshipped the strong-back, drawing the pin out of the link with a spanner I had with me. In order to flood the boat completely, I opened the scuttle in the engine-room bulkhead.

Chlorine gas came in as well as water. I tried three times to lift the hatch but each time could open it only half way, and each time air rushed out through it and the hatch fell down. I clipped the hatch again and had to dive down to fetch the clip bolts; then as the pressure increased again I knocked off the clip bolts. The hatch flew open, but not enough to let me out. I managed to lift it sufficiently to clear my hand and let it down again. I then decided to flood the boat rapidly through the dead-light, till the water came up level with the hatch coaming. I was then able to raise the hatch and come to the surface.

STOKER PETTY OFFICER WILLIAM BROWN

In spite of his badly-crushed hand and his terrible ordeal, as soon as he was pulled out of the water, the resourceful William Brown was able to give detailed information about where he thought the damage was, which valves were open and which shut, which bulkhead doors were shut, and much other information of great value to the salvage operation. E.41 and E.4 were both located, raised and put back into service, E.41 as the Navy's first submarine minelayer.

*

Early in 1915, it was reported that the Germans were building submarines with much higher surface speeds than ours. In time, this was shown to be untrue, but meanwhile it encouraged the idea, which had already been discussed, of building submarines fast enough to be able to operate with the fleet.

This notion went against all previous experience, which had clearly demonstrated that the submarine was like the cat that walked by itself. The first impulse of any warship on sighting a submarine was to sink it first and ask questions afterwards. Furthermore, as experience was to show, submarines operating at high speed in close formation with surface ships were very vulnerable to collisions.

Nevertheless, the project went ahead, and as the fleet speed of 24 knots could not be achieved by diesel engines, the only solution was steam. In spite of the utter failure of Swordfish, the Navy's first steam-driven submarine, completed in 1916, the construction of the steam-driven 'K' Class was put in hand. Over 300 feet long, 2,600 tons dived, sluggish in diving, and requiring numerous large hull openings to admit air to the boilers and allow boiler smoke out, the 'K' Class were somewhat accident-prone, as was shown by the fate, on 29 January 1917, of

K.13

I was appointed to H.M. Submarine E.50, in command, which was nearing completion at John Brown's Yard on the Clyde. The acceptance trials for E.50 took place on the Gare Loch, Scotland, on the same day and in the same place as the ill-fated submarine K.13 was also carrying out her trials. The complete details of this tragedy have never, as far as I am aware, been published and I will try now to give all the facts as I saw them from start to finish.

After a strenuous forenoon with the Manager of John Brown and several of the workpeople who helped to build my boat, my trials were complete by mid-day, having submerged to about 100ft. without a drip anywhere. I came to the surface, the contractor's men were landed and we settled down to a clean-up and picnic lunch on board.

K.13 carried out her trials at the same time near me and at lunchtime the majority of the officers and crew were entertained to lunch in the contractor's tug. Now K.13 was commanded by Bertie

[Godfrey] Herbert, Commander, a very old friend of mine. I knew him as a man of wonderful courage, who had come through dreadful disasters in a most imperturbable and convivial manner. He had a round fat face, always cheerful, a king of stunts and good company.

After lunch he hailed me and asked me to keep well clear as he was making a further experimental dive, having had a slight leak in his boiler-room during the forenoon. Now K.13 was one of the new steam-driven submarines and apparently the boiler-room was too hot during their trials to get at the leak.

I lay off at a good distance from his ship so as to keep well clear. He dived just off the Gare Loch Hydro Hotel about three p.m. I was standing on my conning-tower just awash, all ready to dive when he came up. His dive appeared to be quite normal, except at the end he went down rather fast, but I did not take much notice of this until I noticed a great disturbance of water coming up from where he dived.

I did not know until long afterwards that one of the maids in the Gare Loch Hotel saw two heads appear in the wash as she disappeared. It was subsequently found when K.13 was eventually raised that two of the engine-room staff were missing and evidently, as the engine-room filled on diving, they opened the engine-room hatch and came out with the rush of air. Nearly all the rest of the engine-room staff were trapped as the watertight door between the engine-room and the control-room had to be closed, and this accounts for the two heads seen by the maid at the Hydro. I did not observe this as I was lying too far off or else I would have tried to save them.

Knowing how fond Herbert was of stunting, I did not move over for about half an hour as I did not want to risk K.13 surfacing under me, especially as Herbert had asked me to keep well clear. It was mid-winter, very cold, and by four o'clock I realised the K.13 for some reason was on the bottom and could not come up.

I then sent my First Lieutenant ashore to telephone to the Senior Naval Officer, the contractors and others, asking for salvage gear to be sent immediately. I then anchored close to the spot where air disturbance was still appearing in the water. It was now dark and I placed my dinghy on patrol over this spot so as to be handy if anybody or anything came to the surface.

I was mystified by the fact that the underwater signalling apparatus was silent. However, at dawn, with my signalman and with lead and line, we obtained contact with the hull. Now it is rather difficult to read Morse by tapping with a hammer, but my signalman read quite distinctly: 'All well before the engine-room bulkhead'. That gave me a clue as to what had happened and that some of them were still alive.

In the meantime Captain Barthelot, the Senior Naval Officer of the Clyde, some of the contractors' directors, some divers, and Captain [Lt. RNR] Kay in an old gunboat [*Thrush*] used as a salvage ship and a trawler, had arrived. I asked the divers to put down several buoys on the hull of the submarine and arranged with Kay to try and sweep a wire under the bows as apparently the stern was full of water.

Captain Barthelot then asked me to attend a conference he was holding on board one of the ships, as I was the Senior Submarine Officer present. At the conference the contractors said they would build a steel tube to go from the surface and fit round the torpedo hatch with a watertight joint. This they said would take from fifty to sixty hours to complete. I pointed out that this was too long and asked Captain Barthelot for permission to try to raise the bows above water, so as to rescue those still alive, either through the torpedo tubes or the fore hatch, allowing the stern to rest on the bed of the Gare Loch about 80ft. down. This mean raising the boat about thirty degrees from the bottom. Much to my amazement the contractors said that they believed the boat under these conditions would break in half. However, I felt quite confident that this was the only way to make an attempt to get the survivors out.

Captain Barthelot then ordered me to take charge of the salvage operations and go ahead and try to get up the bows. Now I don't want anyone to think that I was the only person to bring our efforts to the successful end that did eventually transpire. Kay and his engineer and crew were magnificent in the way they went about the rescue.

I will now try to put down the chain of events that ended so successfully. A heavy flexible wire was swept under the bows of the K.13, one end secured in the gunboat and the other end to a luff-upon-luff tackle on the trawler's winch. About mid-day we had just got the first strain on this wire – I was looking over the side of the trawler, hoping, of course to see the hull of K.13, when an enormous bubble appeared in the water and in the centre of this who should appear but Herbert, the Captain of the boat.

He bobbed up under the sea gangway of the gunboat and I jumped over to try and help him out. We got him on deck and rubbed him down. He was cold and rather exhausted and at first all he could say was: 'Where is Goodhart?' Apparently, we learnt afterwards, Commander Goodhart was training with Herbert to take over command of another K. submarine [K.14] and Herbert had endeavoured to blow him out of the conning-tower with details of the best way he considered help could be given. Unfortunately, Goodhart was caught in the conning-tower casing and failed to surface, where he was found later in proceedings, drowned.

I always feel that, having just got the first lift on the submarine, it probably saved Herbert's life by enabling him to get through the conning-tower casing hatch. Herbert's scheme to send Goodhart to give us information was a very brave effort and the bubble of air that was supposed to bring Goodhart up undoubtedly sucked Herbert out in his place. After he had told us as much as he knew as to the cause of the accident and the lack of air now in the forepart, together with a certain amount of chlorine from the batteries, we warmed him up and sent him ashore to the Hydro.

We then hastened the divers, who had become very cold and fatigued, to fix air leads on to the charging nozzle on the hull of K.13 and my submarine started a full power trial on our new compressors. They ran splendidly and my engineers did all they could to push the air in, but it was of no avail. We signalled with lead lines and a submarine lamp secured to the periscope prism, to press them to open the valve inside, which eventually we understood had been done.

This was a great disappointment and I was reluctant to send the divers down again to disconnect. We then discovered that the air pipes were blocked with ice and frozen snow, caused by the intensely cold water through which they had to pass. We obtained new air hoses but all this took time and it was not until about three o'clock the next morning that the air suddenly started to pass through into the boat. This apparently revived them considerably and, after frantic appeals, I suddenly saw the periscope rise out of the water. I roused Kay and his ship's company and we took in the slack of the wire. We kept the compressors going full bore all the time.

We then received from the shore a flexible armoured hose, fitted with an adapter to screw on to the ammunition supply pipe on deck. Again the divers were called upon to make this joint. After a considerable delay this was done. We could not get much response from inside the boat and for two or three hours I was slung in a bo'sun's chair under the fo'c'sle of the trawler, signalling with a lead on the hull, over and over again: 'Open ammunition valve'.

They eventually did this but inside they were alarmed because the water in the hose came through, as they did not understand the idea. Eventually they tried again. They drained it and I was sitting in my bo'sun's chair with the end secured close to me, all ready to speak to them, but at first the rush of foul air almost asphyxiated me. I then realised more what the conditions were like inside the boat.

We then passed another air hose down inside the armoured hose and with this gave them some more fresh air, which seemed to bring them to life. Bottles of hot tea and cocoa were prepared and passed down, also through the large armoured hose. This unfortunately came to a full stop as a soda water bottle got jammed inside and took some time to clear. All this time Kay was heaving in inch by inch on the wire and early in the morning reported that she was tending to slip back and he could not heave any more.

The Commodore of the Liverpool Salvage Company, Commodore Young, then arrived with two empty mud-hoppers. I said I wished to hand over to him but he would not have it. The sterns of the empty hoppers were then trimmed down aft, the wires under the bows taken in and slowly pumped out to help to take the strain off the other wires. By the afternoon the forepart of K.13 was well above the water and we had every hope of getting the crew out through the torpedo tubes. In fact I prepared the crew to make ready for their escape this way but the tide was rising and we could not raise the bows any more.

The dockyard then sent off a boat with oxy-acetylene gas cylinders. The boat unfortunately caught fire. A race then started to get more equipment to cut through the upper casing into the torpedo compartment before the tide came too high. It took a long time for the submarine crew, who were quite strange to the boat, to find and open the casing drains. However, this was done, and a hole was cut through the hull. Out came the 31(?) survivors, mostly in very bad shape. They were taken straight ashore and not long afterwards the tide flooded through the holes and the boat sank back to the bottom.

My job was done! I had had no sleep for about fifty hours and was glad to get to bed.

COMMANDER KENNETH MICHELL DSO MVO DSC* RN

K.13 sank because the engine-room ventilators had been left open. The red light of an indicator was seen to be flickering in the control room, but this was taken to be due to faulty wiring, causing a bad contact. There were eighty men on board when K.13 dived – her normal complement of fifty-three plus civilian employees of Fairfields the builders, and some naval personnel. Of these thirty-two were drowned when the after section flooded. K.13 was later raised, recommissioned as K.22 and was involved in a series of collisions in the Firth of Forth on 31 January 1918 when two more of this class, K.4 and K.17 were lost.

*

A submarine's entire crew could be lost through the most trivial of causes, as was demonstrated on 16 April 1917, three-quarters of a mile north of the Rough Wreck Light Vessel, some seven miles east of Harwich.

The Loss of C.16

Fate prevented me from joining C.16. Some weeks after I should have joined her she was lost with all hands. I was told the circumstances of her loss some time later.

She was carrying out a dummy attack in the exercise area off Harwich when, owing to a misjudgement, she was struck on the top of her conning tower by the target vessel [the destroyer *Melampus*]. A hole of about six inches was knocked off the edge of her brass conning tower, and the copper pipe to her whistle which was attached to her conning tower was broken. Water came in through the hole, and some signal gear jammed the lower conning tower hatch which was only partly closed. The stop cock to the whistle inside the hull had inadvertently not been closed on diving, so that the air in the reservoirs for surfacing vented out of the broken pipe above. She went to the bottom in 60 feet. As she lay on the bottom with water pouring in, circuits must have shorted, and chlorine fumes must have spread from the salt water in the batteries.

Eventually, the captain, Lieut. Boase, decided to flood up the boat and try to effect an escape through the fore hatch. In the meantime they tried to fire the First Lieutenant, Lieut. Anderson, out of one of the tubes. This failed and he was drowned therein. The escape effort through the hatch failed. When the boat was raised not long afterwards, it was found that a fender had jammed in the hatch. Before the end, before the flooding up in fact, Lieut. Boase had made out a brief report on what had happened and put it in a bottle, which was found when the boat was raised. The death of this crew was not in vain, for when the circumstances came to light, steps were taken to tighten up diving drill, and a start was made towards the development of escape drill and apparatus.

CAPTAIN A. L. BESANT CBE RN

When the fore hatch was opened, a fender above it jammed against the superstructure casing, preventing the hatch from rising more than about ten inches. When the hatch was dropped, a pig of lead attached to the fender swung in under the hatch joint, and held the hatch open by about two inches. With the hatch unable to be properly shut, the compartment below flooded and everyone drowned.

*

Good Advice

... He talked on for about twenty minutes with practical, helpful advice, and after a pause he said, 'after the last war I swore that if there was ever to be another I would be the officer who said, "And you might switch off that light."'

'What do you mean sir?'

'Well, I suppose it applies to you too, for very shortly you will find yourself in command of a flotilla and so I beg you to take some trouble in giving your commanding officers that encouragement and sympathetic understanding that will give them confidence in you and in your interest in their affairs when they are out on patrol. I am sure you will as you are a submarine officer – but that brings me to "You might switch off the light"; – a phrase that has stuck in my mind since the bitter winters of 1915, 1916 and 1917. For much of that time I was based at Blyth and we normally sailed after midnight so that no U-boat would see us leave. By dawn we would be far beyond the swept channel and in a suitable depth for diving. It was Commander S's orders that we were to report to him before sailing. I remember those interviews so well, in fact I wish I could forget them, but I can't.

'They went like this. I would go up to "Shanks" Willis cabin in "Titania" and knock on the door, and knock at intervals of five seconds until there was a grunt of,

"Come in, who's that?"

"Coltart, sir."

"What do you want?"

"I'm sailing for patrol in ten minutes."

"Oh – where to?"

"Well, sir, you have told me to spend the next three weeks forty miles NNW of Heligoland."

"Oh yes, an excellent patrol position – by the way what's the weather like?"

"NE gale blowing, sir. It's snowing rather hard and the visibility is 200 yards."

"Oh, yes, well plug into it. I say, you might switch off that light!" '

I understood his message very clearly.

REAR-ADMIRAL G. W. G. SIMPSON CB CBE

*

In January 1918, Lt. Geoffrey White, commanding Boyle's old submarine, E.14, made a very daring attempt to penetrate the Dardanelles and torpedo the German battlecruiser Goeben, *which had run aground in the Straits. But the enterprise went wrong and* E.14 *was sunk by shore batteries on 28 January. A Turkish communiqué announced that they had sunk a submarine. The first definite news of her fate came in a letter from a Turkish PoW camp in May 1918.*

Dear Sir,

No doubt the officers and men on HMS 'Adamant' [*the submarine depot ship*] would like to know what became of the Captain and two officers. I am very sorry to say that Mr White was almost blown to pieces by a large shell which wounded three other men, and I believe it killed Mr Drew [*the navigating officer*], as I was with both of them. I saw the Captain's body, but nothing of Mr Drew, so I think he must have been killed and fell into the sea. Mr Blissett [*the First Lieutenant*] was last seen in the engine-room, so went down with the boat. It was a credit to us all to think we had such a brave Captain, and sir, if only I could mention a few things about him; but owing to his coolness he saved the boat half a dozen times. It is a great pity that no officer was saved to tell the tale. I also mention AB Mitchell and Signalman Trimbell for gallantry in diving overboard and saving the life of Prichard Ord. Tel., who was badly wounded, and would have lost his life had it not been for both these men keeping him afloat until assistance arrived. I am glad to say that all men who were wounded were sent to hospital ten minutes after being captured, and were treated very well. The remaining five men, except Stoker Reed, have had a bad attack of fever since being captured, and we are all very sorry that so few men were saved, and, as I have said, our gallant Captain. This is all I have to report.

PETTY OFFICER ROBERT PERKINS, E.14'S COXSWAIN
AND SENIOR SURVIVOR

Perkins was one of only nine survivors. His letter makes no mention of his own plight, put to forced labour in a cement works, and suffering great privation. When he and the others were repatriated early in 1919 and told the story of E.14's last fight, Perkins was awarded the DSM, White a posthumous Victoria Cross.

*

Then, on 11 November 1918, it was

Armistice Day

On Armistice Day I was on patrol in the new submarine R.*12*. We were proceeding to a position off the north-west coast of Ireland to waylay a German submarine flotilla reported homeward bound from the Mediterranean. On the morning of November 11 we were proceeding as requisite on the surface. Lieutenant Barry [R.12's CO] and I leaning with our arms over the periscope standard and facing in opposite directions. Suddenly the first lieutenant [Lieutenant

67

Lowther RNR] struggled through the hatch and handed Barry a signal. I glanced at Barry's face and seeing the expression on it threw caution to the winds while I read the signal he handed to me:

ARMISTICE WILL BE SIGNED 11 A.M. CEASE HOSTILITIES
UNLESS ATTACKED.

It would be foolish to try to explain my feelings. I can tell, however, what we did. The first thing was to send a signal asking if we might return from patrol. The reply we got was very curt and plain.

REMAIN ON PATROL UNTIL ORDERED TO RETURN.

That was that. The war was over but there was still a Navy – a disciplined Navy. Of that Navy, the submarine service was credited with sinking during the period of hostilities 54 enemy warships and 274 transports and supply ships, or ships engaged in contraband trade. These numbers do not include those ships of the enemy forces which were torpedoed by our boats and succeeded in reaching port. They do include, however, the nineteen enemy U-Boats which fell prey to the marksmanship of our submarine commanders.

LIEUTENANT WILLIAM GUY CARR, RN, *R.12*'S NAVIGATING OFFICER

However, fifty-nine British submarines were lost through various causes during the war.

Part Three
BETWEEN THE WARS

———— ❖ ————

After the war, Rear-Admiral Submarines called for reports from submarine COs and staff medical officers on

The Health of Submarine Crews on Patrol

'Very few submarine officers knew how to apply an antiseptic dressing properly and it was common practice for the crew to help themselves to articles in the chest indiscriminately, thereby soiling rolls of cotton wool, cyanide gauze and bandages. Scissors were frequently used for purposes for which they were not designed and in one boat the crew habitually consumed soda-mint tablets as sweetmeats.'

SURGEON COMMANDER A. D. COWBURN RNVR, DEPOT SHIP
HMS *AMBROSE*

'I do not think that five submarine sailors in 100 clean their teeth at sea. Their teeth are usually in an unsanitary condition and, due partly to this and partly to constipation, their breath is normally bad at sea. I think the constipation of ratings is due to their own carelessness and ignorance, and it is difficult for officers to deal with this as the men do not willingly report their condition.'

COMMANDER J. G. BROWN DSO RN, COMMANDING OFFICER *K.12*

'The chief handicap to the efficiency of the submarine seaman is his tendency to constipation induced by over-eating, lack of exercise and inadequacy of conveniences. Some boats had no W.C. at all. Relief was generally discouraged until the boat came to the surface at night and I have heard of cases where men went without relief for four or five days. Personally I made a man take a pill every two days unless I was assured he had no need of it.'

LIEUTENANT-COMMANDER G. P. THOMPSON OBE,
COMMANDING OFFICER *E.35*

'Excluding the various forms of gas poisoning, I have seen no condition peculiar to the submarine service.'

SURGEON-COMMANDER C. R. RICKARD, DEPOT SHIP HMS *MAIDSTONE*

'The practice of using the right eye only at the periscope is very common. I cannot see how it can be done away with entirely but efforts should be made individually to use both eyes equally.'

COMMANDER C. S. BENNING DSO, HMS *ADAMANT*

'I myself suffered from a form of this disease (Pyorrhoea) known as 'French mouth' and a dental specialist blamed it on tinned food.

This view was sufficiently well looked on by the Admiralty to make them refund me a very large bill for dental treatment.'

LIEUTENANT-COMMANDER G. P. THOMPSON OBE,
COMMANDING OFFICER _E.35_

*

After the war, some COs came back to command submarines after a considerable period away, and were not at all sure of their welcome. However, they need not have worried, as in

The Giant _M.1_

I had not handled a submarine since C.9 in 1912, so I felt my future as well as that of the 'M' Class was in the scales. 'M.1' was nearly 3,000 tons, a 'K' Class hull with a 12-inch gun on top and by good design and fortune, the handiest submarine I ever knew, a contrast to the clumsy, dangerous 'K's. Her crew of 60 included several old friends of early Holland days, sifted by years of searching tests in peace and war and now in key positions. Nearly all the rest were experienced selected men. Having seen the pioneers in 1904 from the point of view of a novice, it was odd to be among them again, conscious once more of my technical inadequacy, and wondering if I'd lost my good eye at the periscope – my sole justification for command. After years of command of parent ships, among brass hats or bowlers, it was rejuvenating to live in a submarine again, and I soon began to enjoy handling 'M.1' in our working up period. Reporting at Blockhouse before going north to join the flotilla. I was hugely delighted by a fortuitous eavesdrop. At the Fort the 'convenience' nearest to the jetties had a partition and the officer users on one side could see the mens' boots under it, and hear their voices over the top. My own name from the other side caught my ear, and then, 'Brodie?' – 'Oh, he's alright. He don't know nothing about it, but we'll see him through.' The phrase was not wholly flattering but I've never heard praise that pleased me more. I knew I'd been accepted by that fine team. We had an interesting commission and they did see me through, and got me my fourth stripe.

'SEA GEE' (REAR-ADMIRAL C. G. BRODIE)

*

L.8 *made the passage to Hong Kong in 1919. Like every submarine, she had her share of submarine characters.*

There was the Chief Engine-Room Artificer, Murdoch, a gigantic, sad-faced, silent Scot. I never knew him to volunteer any information, even to his messmates, on any subject other than his job. He only came up on to the bridge twice between Portsmouth and Hong Kong, and on each occasion it was to give a quick glance at the exhaust smoke to see if he had improved it by a recent adjustment of his beloved Diesel engines.

If the engines were running well, he would parade up and down the narrow space between them like one of his native pipers, rubbing his huge hands together and glancing here and there at a pressure gauge with that slight relaxing of the features which, for him, did duty for a smile.

If adjustment or repair were required, his great body would insinuate itself between the revolving camshaft and the dancing exhaust springs with an agility gained by much practice, though marvellous in a man of his bulk. There was one small adjustment which he could not manage himself because his hands were too big. Another

ERA would be sent for, and Murdoch would nod sadly at the valve, and then stand behind his mate breathing heavily.

What little slumber he allowed himself was spent on the ERA's mess table. He had once tried a bunk, but it had buckled under his weight, and he didn't risk it again. His sleep never interfered with the working of his sub-conscious mind. If the engine developed the slightest knock – and it frequently did – or the vibration altered due to a change of speed, he would roll off his table and bolt into the engine-room.

One night I found him asleep. Clad in threadbare overalls and a pair of shoes, he was lying flat on the table, his arms folded crusader-wise across a doormat of a chest. Just above his head a 50 candle-power light glared on to his face. On one huge forearm was tattooed a nude, well-nourished dancing girl. On the other arm, dimly visible through the oily fur, was a tombstone bearing one word, 'Mother'. Yes, he had his human side, but it was manifested by art rather than speech.

Murdoch went ashore once during the commission. I was astonished to meet him stalking sorrowfully along towards the dockyard gates in Hong Kong about six o'clock one evening. Then I remembered that it was 30th November. At about two o'clock next morning I was woken by a frightful hullabaloo in *L.8* secured alongside *Titania*. Looking out of my scuttle I saw two sleepy ERAs making a hurried 'get-away' along the gang-plank into the ship. I didn't discover the cause of the row; there are occasions when inquiries are superfluous, but I'm sure St. Andrew had a good deal to do with it. Next day, Murdoch, assisted by a nervous stoker, put in a solid twelve hours of hard work behind the port engine without even coming out for meals – what a man!

LT.-CDR. T. A. POWELL RN

*

Even in peacetime exercises the 'K' boats were as unhandy and as accident-prone as ever. They were slow to dive, but once they began to dive, the forces of inertia made it difficult for them to stop. This very probably contributed to the accident to K.5, south-west of the Isles of Scilly on 20 January 1921, in the opinion of the First Lieutenant of K.9 in

Hic Jacet!

'Down you get, signalman! Press the hooters as you go!'

The signalman showed alacrity. Laden with paraphernalia – Aldis lamp and lead, telescope, hand-flags, bunting, signal halyards, and lord knows what besides – he vanished through the manhole into the wheelhouse.

'Midships! Meet her! . . . Steady! Close the voice-pipe!'

As I was speaking I heard the signalman obey my last injunction. There may be those who will sleep on when the last trump sounds, but I doubt if anyone has ever ignored the summons of a submarine's hooters.

We had been steaming, I think, at sixteen knots. Almost on the instant I felt the thrust of the turbines cease. A series of explosive sighs, from near and far, betokened the opening of the external vents. These boats had about 500 tons of surface buoyancy, maintained only by the vents which sealed the tank tops in the space between the two hulls, now that the seals were broken, ballast water was flooding in at about 125 tons a minute.

Glancing for'a'd, I saw the foreplanes coming out like a pair of ears that had lain retracted within the animal's head. When I looked aft, the funnels had disappeared, but wisps of smoke and steam still hung about their wells. By this time she was settling fast, and the thump of a heavy sea against the wall of the conning-tower, the lift of its frustrated tongue, hastened my going.

I, too, had armfuls of gear to salve. I negotiated the manhole above the wheelhouse, but stuck in the conning-tower hatch, like Father Christmas in a chimney too narrow for his bulk.

'Below there . . .'

Some kind soul climbed the ladder and stretched up rescuing hands. Mine were thus freed to pull the lid down on top of me and put my weight on the clips.

At the foot of the ladder I paused to take stock. A strange lot of pirates they looked, but they were all there, gravely intent. The red light was burning, and the gauge showed that 8 or 10 feet of conning-tower was still above the surface. I nipped through the bulkhead door into the wardroom and shed my superfluities.

Back in the control-room, I began to feel worried. The gauges still flickered round 14 feet as the seas tumbled over her. But it was time she started to move down.

The captain spoke, with one eye glued to the after periscope.

'There goes *K.5* – a beautiful dive!'

I looked at the telemotor panel. All sixteen levers, in parallel rows, proclaimed that the vents should be open. I thought of something Cuddeford [*K.5*'s First Lieutenant] and I had agreed upon – that submarine vents should be hand-worked, just like bathroom taps (as indeed they were in all other submarines of our acquaintance). Here was a vast cobweb of pipes radiating to all parts of the boat – a system of liquid pressure, in which anything might fail. Supposing one couldn't shut them? How, then, could one blow? Answer, one couldn't! Irrelevant train of thought, interrupted by a chant –

'One and two full, sir!' 'Three and four full, sir!' 'Five and six full, sir!' 'All externals full, sir!'

Thank heaven for that!

'Close external vents!'

Still she was reluctant to leave the surface. With flippers and tail depressed, she bumped and thrashed her way through the sea-way at about 15 feet. Meanwhile, doubtless, submarine look-outs in all the oncoming ships were reporting a conning-tower awash: The captain's patience showed signs of strain.

'What the hell's the matter, Number One?'

Rhetorical question! Or I hoped so!

The bubble on the coxswain's spirit-level was forward. The externals being full, that meant she was light forward – very considerably so. It struck me as unaccountable that the trim should be so much at fault, but the captain could only act on plain evidence.

'Flood "B",' he said. 'B' was an empty internal tank of 18 tons capacity, under the wardroom.

In moments of tension, most people prefer doing something with their hands to looking on. I went through the bulkhead and spun the big wheel of the kingston valve (or sea connection) myself. From under came the noise as though I had lifted the sluice of a dam. In the control-room the hiss of escaping air was followed by a choking gurgle – and then a splash, as the inboard vent of 'B' vomited water.

'"B" full, sir!'

The gauges move a foot or so – no more. The captain was still preoccupied in watching the enemy. I thought it well to make sure that he was aware of what had been done. Making the report as casual and conversational as I could said –

'We should be 18 tons heavy for'a'd, sir!'

Silence – as mordant as any form of words.

At that point memory yielded a photographic flash – uncertain and out of focus. What had I seen, watching the fore-planes come out? Or hadn't I? I signed to a man to raise the fore periscope. As the eye-piece came out of the well, I checked him and squinted forward. The foredeck, of course, was under water, but the raised bow uncovered intermittently. Its beautiful shining surface was unbroken – instead of which there should have been two round black cavities, proclaiming open vents.

'Bow vents!' I said, pointing an accusatory finger at the man on the telemotor panel, scarcely three feet away.

The operating lever was to 'open', but on either side of all these levers were unobtrusive little stop-valves, designed to isolate each pair of vents should a leak develop in the pressure system. They should of course, have been open when we put to sea, but one (out of thirty-two) had somehow been overlooked, with the result that there was this great air-filled blister, right up in the eyes of her.

Smith (as I will call him, asking a great family to forgive me) shot out a hand to open it, but I seized him by the wrist.

'Open "B" kingston! Blow "B"!'

When 'B' was empty we opened the bow vents. A few seconds later she slid down to periscope depth in perfect trim.

Who was to blame? Smith and I! I was guilty on two counts – (a) for not making sure that Smith had done his job, and (b) for being a fool. My eyes had seen, but my brain had failed to register.

There were no recriminations. But the question in my mind was this: If Smith had spotted his oversight *after* we had flooded 'B', and quietly rectified it, could we have caught her? Eighteen tons too much on the front end of the sea-saw? The answer would depend, I dare say, on how quickly we had tumbled to it. But ifs and ands are academic things, and were never more so than in 'K' boats.

We surfaced an hour or two later – if memory is playing fair – in an almost calm sea, with a tumbling swell. The horizon was bare.

Having reported our position, by dead reckoning, to *Inconstant* we were asked if *K.5* was in sight. The reply of course, was negative and was the prelude, I think, to some hours' delay, so far as we were concerned.

Doubtless, signals were being exchanged with all ships of the fleet, on wave-lengths that were not our business. The short winter's day was drawing in when we were ordered to go back to the position where the two boats had dived.

Navigation was not my problem. The captain shared it with the third hand. In their place I should have wondered whether it was possible to obey this injunction with as much accuracy as circumstances might require. A submarine's D.R., during a submerged exercise of the kind we had been engaged in, is apt to be an afterthought. And ocean currents do not register themselves.

However that may be, all too certainly we found the spot. A familiar reek was in our nostrils and foreboding in our hearts for some minutes before we ran into an iridescent lake of oil fuel. I should think there was a square mile of its unholy calm.

In the midst of it were two objects in indeterminate shape floating close to one another. Carrying our way, with engines stopped, we plashed through the viscous fluid towards them, until the gentle ripple radiating from our stem warded them off, and in so doing caused them to roll over. Inanimate things can seldom have conveyed a message more dramatic. They were two short baulks of timber, splintered at either end. One would not suppose, perhaps, that objects so nearly nondescript could talk at all. But it is always the simple things that make themselves most familiar. Their sides were painted red, with consecutive numbers picked out in white thereon, at intervals of about eighteen inches. They were, in fact, fragments of the cross-beams that form part of the structure of a submarine's battery tanks. The numbers provided a means of identifying cells. When Cuddeford and I dined together, the carpet under our feet covered movable floor-boards which rested on such beams as these.

Evidently the interior of the boat – or at least the compartment which had disgorged these fragments – had been watertight until the pressure of the sea had crushed it. Had there been an inrush of water from some cause or other, the pressure within and without would have equalised, and this violent disruption could not have occurred. Beyond that I do not care to speculate.

We made our position 120 miles west-south-west of Scilly. I have no chart by me, but I remember glancing at one at the time and wondering if she lay in six hundred feet or twelve thousand. For there or thereabouts is the sill on the ocean bottom which may be said to mark the limits of the Western Approaches. Westward of it, soundings are colossal.

Almost in silence – our mood as overcast as the night that was upon us – we turned from the grave of our fellow-farers, in that ancient and ample cemetery wherein there are no monuments, and set course for Spain.

COMMANDER JOHN MURRAY RN

*

Nevertheless, submariners were still regarded as reasonable insurance risks.

Life Insurance

I spent seventeen years in submarines, between 1919 and 1936. As I was a young married man I decided to insure my life with an insurance company, which undertook, in the event of my death from any cause – including the result of an accident in a submarine – to pay a lump sum. To my surprise I found that the annual premium was no more than if I had been, say, a clerk, working in an office.

This was not because the insurance company was being kind-hearted to a submariner; it was because experts called actuaries, who examine and calculate the risks of every profession, reckoned that I was no more likely to meet my end in peace-time service in submarines than in the daily hurly-burly of civilian life, where people have to travel in all sorts of fast-moving vehicles, as well as cross the busy roads in our traffic-infested island. In my case the insurance people turned out to be right, for in the years during which I served in submarines, from the Baltic to the China Seas, I recollect only one really dangerous moment . . .

COMMANDER GILBERT HACKFORTH-JONES RN

*

By the 1920s, submarine training had already established itself in the format it was to retain for many years; lectures on submarine systems, equipment and techniques backed up by practical experience at sea in running boats, where, even on training trips, the real world of submarines impinged, as in

Training Class 1924

After the trials and tribulations attendant upon these [sub-lieutenants'] courses, some of us, having volunteered for the Submarine Service, proceeded to Fort Blockhouse, the submarine base at Gosport, to be initiated into the workings of these strange craft.

When one went down into one of these mechanical underwater beetles for the first time, one felt that one would never get the hang of such a complicated mass of machinery. The instruction given at the base was excellent, interspersed as it was with trips to sea in submarines, to gain practical experience of their working.

Even in peace-time the risks attendant upon life in them was higher than in surface-craft. The submarines were, at that time, manned entirely by volunteers, though at a later date this practice had to be discontinued, as there were many for whom the life held little appeal. Personally I think it is the grandest life, for it produces a camaraderie which it would be hard to equal elsewhere either ashore or afloat.

As trainees we were split up into twos and threes and distributed around various submarines. The object was to carry out an attack upon the Home Fleet as they steamed south to rendezvous for exercises with the Mediterranean Fleet off Gibraltar.

Three of us dived together in order to attack the leading battleships. On rare occasions we were allowed out-of-date torpedoes which we could fire to hit. The more usual practice was to surface immediately after firing water-shots from the empty torpedo tubes to represent torpedoes, and to signal your exact time of firing and also your estimation of the target's course and speed.

It was this practice we were carrying out on this occasion. We watched our Captain raising the periscope until the eye-piece was only just clear of the deck. He was crouching down, and before it seemed possible for him to have done so in the time, he was passing the angle on the 'enemy's' bow and his estimation of her speed to the third hand, who was working the 'Is-was'. This was a simple disc which was fitted to the gyro repeater and really gave you the amount of 'throw-off' that you had to have on the periscope at the moment that the target steamed into the cross-wires upon the glass of it. The torpedo leaving the tube at that moment would travel through the water, and must then arrive at a certain spot at the same time as the target, provided your estimations had been accurate.

The final stages of an attack, even in peace-time, were tense with suppressed excitement. The men on the planes were anxious to keep the boat down at her correct depth, to prevent the tops of the periscopes being sighted. In the fore-end of the vessel the torpedo party eagerly awaited the order 'Fire' in order to admit the air which would send the torpedo rushing out of the tube.

In the smaller submarines, such as the 'H' Class, it was no easy matter to prevent the boat from breaking surface if you were firing a salvo of four torpedoes. At the forward end of this tube-like vessel you would automatically lighten yourself by six tons on their discharge until the sea had had time to rush in and fill the spaces recently occupied by them.

On this occasion we waited for the Captain to raise the periscope once more. He gripped the handles of it and swung it round until the red-line met the figure which the operator of the 'Is-was' had called out to him. Glancing through the eye-piece, he ordered 'Stand by' in calm, firm tones. It was reported to the fore-end. 'Stand by, sir', came the reply.

'Fire,' came the order, and was quickly followed by four water-shots.

The Captain had lowered the periscope into the well, and was watching the second hand of his watch for the interval to elapse before a torpedo would have reached its mark.

'Surface,' he ordered, and, opening the lower conning-tower lid, he gripped the clips which held the upper lid in place. The signalman, snatching his Aldis lamp, stood on the ladder below him. The Engine-Room Artificer, known as the outside E.R.A. because of his work in the boat outside the engine-room, had been busy with his wheel-spanner, and the valves that he had opened were allowing high-pressure air to rush into the tanks and expel the water in them through the kingston valves. The planes were put to 'Hard a'rise'. The First Lieutenant was watching the needle of the depth-gauge flickering back towards the zero mark.

'Twenty feet', he called out, 'seventeen, fifteen.'

The Captain pulled the clips free and the lid flew open. We swallowed to clear the painful feeling in our ears.

The blue sky was visible above us now. The needle had receded to the seven-foot marking, and a sailor with a bucket was busily engaged in draining the water from the voice-pipe which led up on to the bridge.

'Stop both motors – keep her on course,' the Captain shouted down.

The First Lieutenant had raised one periscope and was looking at the target.

'He's done it again,' he said quietly – 'beautiful position. Could not have missed.'

Everybody in the control-room beamed.

The Captain summoned him to the voice-pipe.

'Number One,' he was saying, 'tell them that it was an unseen attack on H.M.S. "Resolution" – range seven hundred yards – and we've been given it right away with congratulations. I can see the other "H" boat, but no sign of "L 24" yet. She's taking a hell of a long time to surface.'

We waited for 'L 24' to come to the surface, and it was not until some considerable time had elapsed that a feeling of uneasiness was noticeable.

Once more the Captain was speaking to the First Lieutenant.

'We've just got a signal ordering us to dive in this vicinity and call "L 24" on our Fessenden [underwater communication equipment]. We are to continue calling for half-an-hour if no reply is received before then. Stand by to take her down right away.'

The plaintive notes of this particular apparatus were sent out time and time again to attract the attention of 'L 24'. We called in vain, and finally the pair of us surfaced and returned to Portsmouth. Even as we did so we heard the sickening broadcast: 'The Admiralty much regret to announce . . . with all hands'.

Our training class had lost two of its number . . .

CDR. MARTYN SHERWOOD RN

L.24 was sunk with all hands in collision with the battleship HMS Resolution off Portland on 10 January 1924.

*

The sanitary arrangements in some submarines required what can best be described as

Toilet Training

The sanitary arrangements in 'R.4' were limited and it was customary to make the minor concessions to nature over the side of the bridge.

The wireless aerial ran round outside the bridge and, liquid not being too bad a conductor of high voltage electricity, it was possible to receive a paralysing shock if one was forgetful. Wireless communication was accorded second priority for this purpose and the order to 'Stop Transmitting' was frequently to be heard being passed to the long-suffering Telegraphists.

REAR-ADMIRAL BEN BRYANT CB DSO** DSC

*

Rule of the Road

Those familiar with Portsmouth will know that there is – or rather was – a floating bridge connecting Portsmouth with Gosport which passed fairly near the mouth of the Blockhouse Creek.

One day somebody thought to ask the Master whether he was

ever troubled by submarines emerging from the creek, to which the reply was:

'No, sir. No. When I see a submarine coming out of the creek I just stops. But when I sees that there Mr. "X" in "R-4" coming out, I goes back.'

CDR. PHIPPS-HORNBY

*

About some new designs of submarine, there was still room for

Two Opinions

In February 1932 I joined the submarine 'Thames', the first of the new 'Thames' class, building at Vickers-Armstrong, Barrow. Commander Claud Barry was captain and so I had the unusual experience of going back once more to the duties of first lieutenant, but was assured that my appointment was a good one. It proved both an invaluable and happy experience. Barry, the winner of a DSO in command of submarines in war, was very senior for the post, but had been appointed because of its special features. He had recently served in the Admiralty on the material side and was in part responsible for the 'Thames' design and was its keen protagonist. I found him delightful to serve, being clear in what he wanted and trusting his subordinates to get on with the job . . .

After a few days and a thorough study of the submarine I said to Commander Barry, 'What is this submarine designed for? She offers a huge target to the enemy, she cannot be quick and handy when turning submerged, she costs double an ordinary submarine and she cannot accompany the fleet, since battleship speed is now

25 knots'. Barry looked rather upset and changed the subject. Next day he said to me, 'To answer your question about "Thames". Whilst I am in command she is the fastest, cleanest and most efficient and most beautiful submarine afloat! I will have no criticism of her, Number One.'

I remark upon this incident because it is a good example of what could and occasionally did happen in submarine construction, the enthusiasms of individual submarine officers at that time carrying too much weight, opinions changing, leading to inconsistency and finally a showdown.

REAR-ADMIRAL G. W. G. SIMPSON

*

On 1 June 1939, the new submarine Thetis *(Lt.-Cdr. G. H. Bolus) sailed from her builders Cammell Lairds in Birkenhead for diving trials in Liverpool Bay. She had on board her normal complement of fifty-three officers and men and fifty passengers – officers of other submarines building at Cammell Lairds, Admiralty Overseeing Officers, employees of Cammell Lairds and Vickers Armstrongs, two employees of City Caterers, who supplied the food on board that day, and a Mersey pilot. When, soon after lunch, it was time for* Thetis *to dive, all these passengers opted to stay on board. At first* Thetis *seemed reluctant to dive. But when she did she went down with a rush. Those on board her felt a sharp rise in air pressure and knew something was badly wrong. The Torpedo Officer had been ordered to test whether the bow torpedo tubes were full of water. By an unfortunate combination of circumstances, the rear door of No. 5 Tube was opened while the bow cap was open, thus admitting the submarine to the full force of the sea. It was impossible to shut the rear door against the pressure of incoming water and by a further unfortunate circumstance the bulkhead door between the forward*

*tube space and the much larger torpedo stowage compartment next
to it could not be properly shut. The upshot was that both compartments were flooded with 150 tons of water. Thetis sank to the seabed
and lay there at a depth of 150 feet.*

*With two compartments flooded, and many more men on board
than usual, the quality of the air began to deteriorate rapidly. It was
even more unfortunate for* Thetis *that her predicament was not
realised by the Navy in general for some time and rescue was slow
in coming. When, by next morning there were still no signs of rescue
it was decided to blow the submarine's stern nearer to the surface
so as to allow men to escape in pairs from the two-man escape
chamber aft. Captain H. P. K. 'Joe' Oram, a submariner of great
experience and the Captain of the Flotilla which* Thetis *was due to
join, who was on board as an observer to familiarise himself with
the submarine and her ship's company, and Lieutenant Woods, the
Torpedo Officer, who knew the submarine and all her fittings inti-
mately (and was the officer who had actually opened the fatal tube
rear door) were chosen as the first pair. At about 8.45 a.m. on 2
June they attempted to*

Escape from *Thetis*

Carbon dioxide poisoning acts on the mind in a strange way. Picture
a wheel with spokes radiating out from the central hub and imagine
the spaces between the spokes each contain a separate thought.
Under normal circumstances you can rotate this wheel at will and
engage whichever 'thought space' you need. You might want the
one which is playing a game of golf, say, or you might want the
one for doing the monthly accounts. Once you have finished with one
thought you can disengage the wheel and move it round to the next

one. You can slip it in and out of gear to engage the right thought automatically. You don't even realise you are doing it. Occasionally, very occasionally, it slips out of gear without you noticing and then you feel as though you've been day-dreaming. But even then you still have control over the thoughts and you can get back into gear, rotate the wheel and see where you are.

With CO_2 poisoning you lose control of the wheel altogether. You become disengaged from the thought that you want and the wheel more or less spins at random. You may think about a number of different things before you finally drift back to the original thought. What is more you don't realise you have been for a little spin and you have no idea how long it has taken.

It took me three-quarters of an hour to climb aft through the submarine to the escape chamber. I didn't know that at the time. It just seemed a bit of a sweat. It wasn't far from the control room through the engine room to the chamber but the submarine was at a 35 degree angle and I was panting uphill. I remember passing men who sat with their heads in their hands and others who lay back sprawled against the bulkheads. No one broke down. No one was out of control. There were hands outstretched to pull Chapman,* Woods and I through, and even words of encouragement for the escape party as it made its laborious way aft. I cannot speak too highly of those on board. Their cheerfulness and dignity in the face of great adversity and discomfort were remarkable. Conditions had become so bad now that men's eyes watered almost continuously and they yawned and retched from lack of air. Soon it would be over. All we needed was to get that HP airline on from the surface.

Our party needed to rest for some moments before the escape itself could be undertaken. Once we felt able to proceed, Woods and I broke the lead seals on the DSEA boxes and put on our escape

* *Thetis'* First Lieutenant

apparatus. By today's standards, when men can escape in totally sealed suits which will ensure their survival on the surface for up to twelve hours even in Arctic conditions, the Davis kit was pretty primitive. But it was all we had and, one must remember, the science of escape had not then been very thoroughly investigated. We didn't know that it was possible to escape from a depth of 100 feet without any apparatus at all, for example. Most submariners were completely unfamiliar with the way their bodies would react in water of any depth and were therefore unable to help themselves. Today, training in the 'escape tank' is all part and parcel of the business of being a submariner. Men are taught not to be afraid of the water. They are taught to feel at ease in it and how to use it to their best advantage, even when they may be tens of feet below the surface.

The Davis Submarine Escape Apparatus was a rubber bag attached to a harness with an oxygen flask which we carried on our chests. It was connected to a mouthpiece with a small cock which we could open and shut. We also had a nose clip and a pair of red rubber goggles. The nose clip helped to equalise the pressure in the eustacian tubes behind the ear drums and prevent damage under pressure. Rather like 'popping' the ears to clear them when you are on board an aircraft. There were two valves on the bag, one which allowed oxygen to flow into it from the flask and another which acted as an exhaust and allowed for the expansion of gas under pressure. When we had sufficient oxygen to inflate the bag partially, we could shut the intake valve and breathe from the bag which doubled as a buoyancy aid. There was also an apron which acted as a drogue to slow descent.

As one ascends, of course, the volume of gas both in one's lungs and in the bag expands. Hence the need for an exhaust valve. Our escape was only being made from an effective depth of something less than thirty feet, including the height of the escape chamber, but the greatest pressure change actually occurs between this depth and surface. In round figures air pressure is 15 lbs per square inch at sea level. For every 10 metres of depth you add on another 15 lbs or 'bar' as it is called. (Think of the weather forecasts you hear broadcast on radio and television. They often give you the air pressure at the centre of a very low depression in millibars or thousandths of a bar.) It is easy to see that at ten metres the pressure doubles, is half as much as that again at twenty metres and so on, therefore the rate of expansion of air in the lungs changes accordingly on the way back up.

When we wanted to replenish the oxygen supply we just opened the valve on the bottom right-hand side of the bag which was a very simple artificial lung. Woods refreshed my memory on the use of the apparatus and Chapman ran through the escape chamber routine. He checked that the upper hatch was shut, then opened the small lower door and Woods and I stepped inside. With a final 'All right, sir? 'All right, Lieutenant,' the door was shut and clipped tight. We prepared ourselves for Chapman to flood up.

We stood face to face, almost touching each other, inside a seven-foot-tall cylinder which ran from the deck up to the pressure hull above our heads. A grim sort of intimacy. The interior was coated in white paint and the floor was tiled. At the top there was a hatch about thirty inches in diameter with an outboard vent in it which we would open manually. The hatch would hinge up vertically when the clip was released after we had equalised the pressure from within. The spring would give it a bit of help. The hatch could be opened and shut remotely from inside the submarine. After our escape Chapman would then check the state of the hatch visually, open the bottom door and the next two escapees would be loaded inside.

We signalled to Chapman to start flooding up and in swirled the water, cold, dark, and foul-smelling. It was not a pleasant experience standing there waiting until the level rose high enough for us to climb the ladder on the wall of the chamber and equalise the pressure. When it got to about chest height I thought I'd better try breathing through the escape apparatus so I opened the valve on my bag to clear it of air and get oxygen in from the bottle. I put the mouth piece in and started to breathe. Nothing happened. No air came through. The water was still rising and Chapman was keeping an eye on things through the glass scuttles. I banged on the inside of the escape chamber to signal that I was in trouble and Chapman immediately stopped flooding and started draining down. Meanwhile Woods helped me to check my apparatus and discovered that I had not opened the cock on the mouth piece so, although there was oxygen in the bag, it could get no further. Had I drifted off into a day-dream? Had the wheel of consciousness ceased to turn for a few vital seconds? It was impossible to judge at the time but, with hindsight, perhaps that is what happened. I adjusted the cock and took a few experimental breaths. Everything was all right. I was very thankful to both Chapman and Woods for recognising my difficulty and rescuing me from it. We signalled to Chapman and he flooded us up a second time.

As icy water hissed and gurgled in and as the tank filled I grasped the rungs of the ladder and more or less floated up to the top. I was still not too sure whether in fact I was going to be able to do what I had outlined to Bolus. It would be a question of swimming for a bit to reach the tail or the buoy and then getting a purchase. If I failed, at least the DSEA would give me some buoyancy so, if the worst came to the worst, there was a fair chance of my body being found in time and the message being recovered. As the pressure increased I had the sensation of two thumbs pressing hard into the bones on each side of my nose. It was intensely cold. Just as we were about to knock the clip off the hatch and pop out we heard the loud bangs of explosive charges close at hand. We had been found. It was too late to abort the escape.

Suddenly we were out, into the blackness. It felt like being fired through Chaos. I practically hit the boat that was waiting for us as I surfaced.

CAPTAIN 'JOE' ORAM RN

The explosive charges had been dropped by the destroyer HMS Brazen *which had just arrived on the scene and took Oram and Woods on board. An hour later, two more men, Leading Stoker W. Arnold and Mr F. Shaw, an employee of Cammell Lairds, appeared on the surface. More ships arrived and a frantic rescue attempt began, in which hopes were raised and dashed, while the whole country waited in an agony of suspense. But there were no more escapes. The ninety-nine men still in* Thetis *all drowned or died of carbon dioxide poisoning.* Thetis *was eventually salvaged and recommissioned as HMS* Thunderbolt.

Part Four:

THE SECOND WORLD WAR

The war began badly for the Submarine Service. On 10 September 1939, off the Norwegian coast, Oxley *was torpedoed and sunk in error by* Triton. *Early in 1940,* Undine *and* Seahorse *were both sunk in the same waters off Heligoland and on the same day, 7 January. Two days later, also off Heligoland, there was*

The Loss of *Starfish*

Nothing worthy of note took place during the first days of the patrol. At 0100 on the 9th *Starfish* entered the southernmost part of the patrol area. Course 190 degrees. Speed 6 knots. *Starfish* dived at 0540 and at 0800 course was altered to approximately 140 degrees. This course should have taken us to a position some five miles south-west of Heligoland, which, as far as I could recall, it was hoped would be sighted at dusk on the 9th. Weather was overcast with moderate to good visibility. Wind south-east, force 3 to 4.

At about 0930 Lieutenant Wardle (Torpedo Officer), who was on watch, reported an enemy destroyer in sight fine on the starboard bow. I proceeded to the control room and confirmed this report. The enemy craft appeared to be a destroyer – although, from the silhouette, carried her crows-nest slightly higher than most German destroyers. On sighting, *Starfish* was ½ degree on the enemy's port bow, her course being 330 degrees. I cannot now remember the sighting range, but I consider it to have been between four and five miles. I decided to attack. The order for diving stations was given, while all tubes were ordered to be brought to the ready. Course and speed were altered as necessary to carry out an advancing attack on the enemy's port bow, the initial alteration of course being a large one to starboard to increase the distance off track.

Some moments after the beginning of the attack, Electrical Artificer Yates, whose duty it was to transmit orders from the control room to the tubes, asked whether he should pass the orders by order-instrument or by word of mouth. Being intent on the attack I paid little attention to this request, but told him to carry on passing the orders by word of mouth, imagining that the reliability of the order-instrument was in doubt, when in point of fact the latter was in perfect order and his query both unnecessary and misleading. I then carried on with the attack, altering course as necessary to port to get on a broad firing track. On Electrical Artificer Yates' reporting that all the tubes were 'blown up' I told him that he was to fire numbers one, two, three and four tubes only (torpedoes were staggered at 8 and 12 feet), and in that order, at three-second intervals on the order 'Fire'. I also told him to report as soon as the tubes were ready. I was now reaching the final stages of the attack and, as the distance off track was still rather small, I fired up the track-angle and steadied on a course of 190 degrees. Electrical Artificer Yates reported: 'One, two, three, and four tubes ready'. At 1951, having grouped-up and the sights being on, I gave the order 'Fire'.

It was not possible to make use of the Asdic set during the attack as it had developed a minor fault, which was in the process of being repaired, shortly before the attack started. However, the hydrophones were employed and from the enemy's revolutions the speed was estimated at 19 knots and the range of firing at 500 yards.

Immediately after I had given the order to fire, I ordered 60 feet and started altering course through 180 degrees to 270 degrees. I was somewhat surprised that the trim of the boat was so little upset on firing. A few moments later Petty Officer Clark, the TGM [Torpedo Gunner's Mate], reported that no torpedoes had been fired. He had received no orders after the one to 'blow up' all tubes, and had never made any report to the control room that they were in the 'ready' position. I do not consider that this petty officer was in any way to blame for the misfiring of the torpedoes.

After this report I decided to make further observations of the enemy's movements in the hope of making an attack later. After listening on the hydrophones I ordered periscope depth. At 0956, having steadied on course 270 degrees and reduced speed to group down one, slow, I raised the periscope on a bearing on which I hoped to sight the enemy; it was not till I trained the periscope right aft that I did this. The enemy was lying stopped and beam on at a range of something less than one cable. This was the first sighting I had had of the enemy on a broad bearing and I now identified her as a minesweeper, and not a destroyer.

Considering it was possible that the periscope had been sighted, I ordered 60 feet and increased speed. As the submarine was levelling off at 60 feet two depth-charges were dropped in the vicinity, the time then being 0945. No damage was sustained, but both hydroplanes were reported inoperative in power. At this moment the angle on the boat was 4 degrees bow-up, with 15 degrees rise helm on the fore-planes. The boat started to come up and, in view of the shallowness, it was considered best to bottom. Both motors were stopped. The boat settled on an even keel, showing 85 feet on the forward gauge and 90 feet on the after one. All motors were stopped and complete silence kept.

I decided to remain bottomed for a short time only. I knew,

particularly after the experience of *Spearfish*, that it was best to remain underway if successful evasion was to be carried out. Accordingly, when at 1050 Electrical Artificer Yates asked permission to restart one of the Sperry motors to prevent gyro wandering, I granted it. No sooner had he done this than four depth-charges were dropped fairly close to the submarine. A large number of lights were broken and a large number of air leaks were started on the high pressure air-line, but these defects were soon remedied. It was impossible even at the time to determine whether or not the dropping of these four depth-charges came as a result of the starting of the Sperry motor or was purely coincidental; but it was difficult, particularly after the enemy's inactivity up to that moment, to feel that it was not a case of cause and effect. I therefore decided to remain stopped until the dark (sunset was 1630) when the chances of successful evasion and further offensive action seemed greater. *Starfish* had been fitted with a special unit (A/S4, for listening to German A/S impulses) prior to this patrol. This proved most efficient, although an alternative power supply had to be arranged. It was possible to listen throughout to the enemy's procedure, etc., and to form rough estimations of the range at which they were working.

One depth-charge was dropped at noon, causing no damage. At 1440 the enemy obtained contact. Two heavy attacks were made in close succession and some twenty depth-charges were dropped very close to the submarine, the enemy passing right overhead on both occasions. In the pressure hull the rivets had sheered and the shell-plating had sprung at the first frame abaft 'A' bulkhead, starboard side, causing a very heavy leak. The after bulkhead of 'A' had also been badly buckled and water was pouring through both the starboard side and the bottom. The compartment was shut off immediately. The after bulkhead remained watertight except for the starboard trench door, which owing to distortion leaked slightly. Both the conning-tower and the gun tower had been severely damaged and water started to weep through the lower hatches. Numbers of rivets throughout the boat had been rendered partially defective and there were numerous air leaks on the HP airline. Serious damage had been caused to the pressure hull beneath or near the drain oil tanks in the engine room, although it was impossible to assess the extent of this. Such repairs were made as was possible under the conditions.

At 1600 tea and soup were issued, and in view of the uncertainty of the situation all patrol orders were destroyed by tearing them up and placing them in oil fuel. All confidential books and signal publications were collected and locked in the CB chest.

At 1645 a small high-speed engine, which had been stopped for some minutes, was heard very distinctly overhead, while between 1700 and 1715 the enemy passed overhead on two occasions. No depth-charges were dropped. It had now become apparent from the enemy's A/S impulses that the minesweeper had been joined by an additional unit.

By 1800 the situation in the submarine was serious. Both the torpedo trenches and all the bilges were nearly full. The engine room crankcases and starboard main motor bearing were flooded, while water was present in the lubricating oil drain-tanks. Water was pouring through the starboard engine clutch and was lapping the starboard main motor casing. Mr Dodsworth, the engineer-officer, considered that it would still be possible to carry out repairs, given sufficient time, on the main engines to enable at least one of them to be used. It was thought likely that if the submarine remained dived much longer the main motors would be out of action.

By this time I had formed the opinion that there was no likelihood of the enemy leaving the vicinity in the near future. After weighing up the situation, and having received full reports from the first lieutenant and engineer-officer on the state of their departments, I decided that the best hope, although a slight one, of successful evasion lay in surfacing and attempting to slip away in the darkness. It was estimated that the enemy craft were lying at a distance of 7 to 8 cables. Under the circumstances, offensive action was impossible.

At 1815 lifebelts were issued and the after escape hatch rigged as a precautionary measure. At 1820 the order to surface was given. The submarine came up stern-first at a very heavy angle, and appeared to hang there as I passed the word aft to open the after escape hatch. A few moments later, however, the bows broke out and the boat assumed a normal angle. I proceeded on deck through the engine room hatch. On each side of the boat at a distance of some 50 yards was a lit buoy. I went up to the bridge and at this moment the enemy, who were lying on each bow at a range of about 1,200 yards, illuminated us with searchlights. A few minutes later they opened fire with a machine gun, firing a short burst wide of the bridge.

I ordered Mr Dodsworth to go below and flood main ballast one side only, and Lieutenant Wardle to throw the CB [Confidential Books] chest over the side. The latter was soon done and Mr Dodsworth, working under great difficulties, managed to open number four starboard main vent, and also the 4-inch flood valve on the main line. The boat listed very heavily and water started lapping through the engine room hatch. As the boat listed I had given the order to abandon ship, considering it was wise for the crew to be clear. As the submarine did not sink immediately, some of the men climbed back on board, while others were picked up by the minesweeper.

LIEUTENANT T. A. TURNER, *STARFISH*'S CO

Starfish's survivors became prisoners-of-war. Ten months later, Wardle, the Torpedo Officer, was in Colditz where he became known as 'Stooge' Wardle, for his skill in organising the 'stooges', who stood on watch and gave warning of the approach of any German guard 'goons' whilst escape activity was going on.

*

The Skagerrak in the summer of 1940 was a nightmare place for a submarine on patrol; the shallow sea depth, the sudden fresh-water layers, the interminable hours of daylight, and the almost continuous surveillance from the air meant that submarines could only stay in the area for short periods and were relieved every four days. In June HMS/M Sealion *was there on what her captain called*

My Worst Patrol

Shark was going to relieve us next day and I decided that I must tell her to keep out; this meant relaying the message home because only Rugby could transmit to a submerged submarine. The skies clouded over, low cloud, but at last there was no aircraft in sight. It might only be because they were behind cloud cover, but we had to charge batteries and we had to get a signal through to *Shark*. It was a risk we had to take.

We surfaced with just enough buoyancy to bring out the conning-tower hatch and I scrambled through as it came clear. I was half out when I saw the aircraft; it came out from behind a cloud straight at us. I pressed the hooter, slammed shut the hatch and down we went; two depth-charges straddled us as we went down. Steering, hydro-planes and gyro compass went off the board, some of the lights went and more paint rained down. This time there were no surface craft to follow up, we got things under control and working again, and soon after midnight I decided to have another shot. Somehow we had got to tell *Shark* to keep out. The heavens remained black, one could not see what was behind the clouds. Unless we could charge batteries we were impotent; we could not get away from Stavanger submerged and we would have to run for it on the surface.

Once again our conning tower broke surface. This time I had hardly opened the hatch when there was a roar; a Heinkel came out of a cloud so close that she did not have time to bomb. I pulled the hatch shut and down we went again; we were clear of the position before the depth-charges came down and they did no damage.

Now we had to consider things carefully. The air was foul and we were already panting – one always did as the carbon dioxide collected. The conning tower had not been open for more than a few seconds during either of our attempts to surface and no fresh air had reached the boat. The battery was practically flat – another crash-dive would finish it; the enemy knew where we were; we could not get away submerged and equally we could not surface. The only thing was to sit it out submerged and hope that we would be able to last out till they gave up. We found a water layer to sit on; stopped the motors; switched out practically every light and settled down to wait.

From time to time we renewed the trays of soda lime which were laid out throughout the boat. They were meant to absorb the carbon dioxide, and so, after a fashion, they did, but without proper air-conditioning plant to force the foul air through the absorbent it could only be partially effective. We could still receive routine signals from Rugby and from time to time we came off our layer to have a look round, but there was always a hunter in sight. The damage was made good and everybody, except those on watch, lay down to conserrve the air. The hours dragged by, everyone had headaches, sleep was impossible, one's body felt cold and clammy. I had always imagined that if one got stuck in a submarine and ran out of air one would fall into a stupefying doze and just not wake up. It would seem that this is not so, one cannot sleep. Some cold food was served out with lime juice to drink, but no one seemed interested in the food.

Then we got an enemy report; a ship was coming our way. She would have to come to us. There was still enough life in the battery to turn the boat around, but there was no question of our moving to intercept her. We brought the boat back to periscope depth; the T.I. checked over his tubes and waited. Panting was getting heavier; it was obvious that we were fairly near our limit, but still the sweeping A/S forces were in sight. They were farther off now, but too near to get away on the surface. I decided to try our small store of oxygen.

When experience of long dives indicated that air was a major problem the medicos were called in; they provided us with the carbon-dioxide absorbent, but pronounced that there was no need to provide oxygen since there was enough oxygen available to last us far longer than all the carbon-dioxide absorbent we could carry. I knew the Germans, or at least one German U-boat, had carried oxygen in World War I. Years before during my training class I had heard a story in the mess of how a surrendered U-boat, which had no high-pressure air left had blown her tanks by connecting up the oxygen cylinders she carried. Whilst I believed the experts, I still felt that the Germans had not carried the oxygen for nothing, for space and stowage is very precious in a submarine. On the principle of taking no chances, I had secured some cylinders of oxygen, and a reducing valve, just before this patrol.

Everyone was pretty sick by this time and at least it could not do any harm. It was beginning to become doubtful whether, if the reported ship did come past us, we could make much of a show of attacking her. The oxygen was switched on, a gentle hissing in the silent boat; conversation except for an occasional order had long since ceased. It is not easy to talk when panting. Some of the men said they felt better; I knew that it must be imagination, but at least it was good to think you feel better.

The long-awaited ship did not come past us; it was probably just as well, but a bit disappointing at the time. We sank back to our layer and waited. The oxygen ran out; the hours dragged past; the headaches nagged. Just before midnight on the second day the sea and sky seemed clear. Men moved to their diving stations and the tanks were blown. I went up through the conning tower; this time all was clear. Then I leaned over the side of the bridge and was sick; not having eaten for some thirty hours, this was not particularly satisfactory, but it helped. The look-outs came up and they too were sick.

Down below they were trying to start the diesels; but it was some time after the fans had been running before they would fire. Diesels are more particular about the quality of air than humans.

Some time later further investigation by the medicos established that the oxygen was absolutely essential in such circumstances. My cautions, belt-and-braces philosophy had paid a dividend.

I have said that all was clear, but over towards the landward horizon something was going on. It was twilight, the nearest we ever got to darkness in those latitudes, but one could see tracer bullets and flashes. We tried again to get our signal through to *Shark*. But it was too late; we were watching *Shark* fighting her last action. The hunt had changed their foxes; she was being sunk whilst we lay sick and helpless, unable to go to her assistance.

It took three or four hours for the headaches to wear off; after everything was settled down, and we had cleared the coast, I went down below. I was feeling rather despondent; *Salmon* was overdue, *Shark* had gone, two of the four boats which had formed our division before the war. The war was going badly and one felt very alone on patrol; it seemed that the war depended upon you personally and I had missed the convoy and nearly lost the boat; I felt that I had let down the crew.

I wandered for'ard where men off watch were sleeping on the deck, covered with their oilskins to catch the drips, and suddenly the atmosphere of unworried serenity passed from them to me. I realised that they would go into action on the morrow without backward thoughts, that with crews such as I was privileged to command we could not be beaten; the depression left me.

REAR-ADMIRAL BEN BRYANT CB, DSO** DSC

*

Fingernails

By now subconscious forces began to affect the bodies as well as the minds of submarine captains. I was sitting in the mess waiting for patrol orders when our doctor asked casually, 'Let's have a look at your fingernails'. Each one showed a series of concentric half-moon ridges from base to tip. 'Interesting stigmata' he said. 'If you break off patrols for a refit you'll find a gap corresponding to the time spent in harbour. Each ridge is a patrol. They occur in *all* commanding officers of submarines, in most of their subordinate officers and in a small proportion of responsible ratings – purely psychological.'

COMMANDER WILLIAM KING DSO* DSC RN
(THEN CAPTAIN OF HMS/M *SNAPPER*)

*

Twelve Little S-Boats

One of the most remarkable characters in *Sealion* was the Chief
E.R.A. 'Skips' Marriott, a tall, saturnine submarine E.R.A. of the
old school, with a highly developed sardonic humour. At sea he
wore a peculiar headgear of his own invention, a long oblong of
cardboard twisted into strange shapes and stuffed into a dirty old
navy-blue balaclava, and when he walked through the control-
room on his way to the engine-room, with his loping gait and eyes
twinkling in a dead-pan face, he might have been a crafty old
monk straight out of the pages of Boccaccio. Sometimes in harbour
when it was my turn to be duty officer in the boat, I would join
the E.R.A.s in their mess so that I could listen to some of old
Skip's yarns. I have brought him in here because many months later,
glancing through his rough Engine-Room Register, I came across
several verses scrawled on the oil-smudged pages in his firm bold
hand, and among them the following lines, which tell the tragic
story of the S-boats in the early months of the war better than I
can:

> Twelve little S-boats 'go to it' like Bevin,
> *Starfish* goes a bit too far – then there were eleven.
>
> Eleven watchful S-boats doing fine and then
> *Seahorse* fails to answer – so there are ten.
>
> Ten stocky S-boats in a ragged line,
> *Sterlet* drops and stops out – leaving us nine.

Nine plucky S-boats all pursuing Fate,
Shark is overtaken – now we are eight.

Eight sturdy S-boats – men from Hants and Devon,
Salmon now is overdue – and so the number's seven.

Seven gallant S-boats trying all their tricks,
Spearfish tries a newer one – down we come to six.

Six tireless S-boats fighting to survive,
No reply from *Swordfish* – so we tally five.

Five scrubby S-boats patrolling close inshore,
Snapper takes a short cut – now we are four.

Four fearless S-boats too far out to sea,
Sunfish bombed and scrap-heaped – we are only three.

Three threadbare S-boats patrolling o'er the blue,
....

Two ice-bound S-boats ....
....

One lonely S-boat ....
....

His completion of the list, leaving the blanks to be filled in later (I am glad to say it was not necessary: *Sealion*, *Seawolf* and *Sturgeon* survived to the end of the war), is an example of the buoyant sense of humour, fatalistic but far from defeatist, which inspired most of *Sealion*'s crew. Contact with men who had soldiered on through hard fighting and seen their 'chummy boats' go down one after another was the best possible antidote to my state of nerves.

COMMANDER EDWARD YOUNG DSO DSC RNVR

Edward Young was the first RNVR officer to command an operational submarine.

STARFISH – Depth-charged in Heligoland Bight, January 9, 1940. Crew survived and were taken P.o.W.

SEAHORSE – Depth-charged in Heligoland Bight, January 7, 1940. Crew of 39 lost.

STERLET – Depth-charged, Skagerrak, April 18, 1940. Crew of 41 lost.

SHARK – Attacked off Norway by aircraft of Luftwaffe. Sunk while being towed by German trawler, July 6, 1940. Survivors were taken P.o.W. (there were two killed and 19 injured).

SALMON – Lost off Norway during July, 1940, probably mined. All 41 crew lost.

SPEARFISH – Sunk by torpedo fired by U34 on August 1, 1940. One survivor, who was taken P.o.W.

SWORDFISH – Mined South of the Isle of Wight with the loss of all 37 crew, November, 1940.

SNAPPER – Lost off Brest, February, 1941, with the loss of all 42 crew. Cause of loss not known.

SUNFISH – After being transferred to the Russian Navy, Sunfish was bombed in error by the R.A.F. while en route to Russia. Full crew and British liaison staff all lost.

*

On 29 April, 1940, the large 2,000-ton minelaying submarine Seal *(Lt.-Cdr. R. P. Lonsdale) sailed from Immingham to lay mines in*

the Kattegat. She rounded the Skaw, the northernmost tip of Den-
mark, and entered the Kattegat in the early hours of 4 May. She
was attacked by an aircraft and had to dive at 2.30 a.m. The mine-lay
was completed by 9.45 that forenoon but there were German anti-
submarine trawlers in the area which Lonsdale had to try and avoid.
At about 7 p.m. Seal was shaken by a tremendous explosion aft.
She had touched off a mine, and sank to the seabed, starting the
train of events which led to

The Surrender of *Seal*

In 1958 the Captain of the *Seal* wrote to the author of this book a
very generous letter setting out the salient facts of what he called
'the most momentous days in his life'. In this letter he recalled how
his damaged ship went to the bottom of the Kattegat at about
6.30 p.m. on 4th May, 1941, and how he had to wait until it became
dark at about 11 p.m. before trying to bring her to the surface again.
As the next day would begin to break at 3 a.m. he knew that he
had not more than four hours of night time in which to make good
his escape. 'For the next 2½ hours,' he wrote, 'we tried everything
that I or anyone else could think of to get to the surface, but without
success. At 1.30 a.m. I therefore called the whole crew into the
Control Room to say prayers before we made our final attempt. We
had no new ideas to try, and I myself could not see any reason why
we should be more successful than before; but in the back of my
mind was the thought, 'with God all things are possible.' Then,
after I had said prayers, a new idea came to me. We were lying with
our bows inclined 30 degrees upwards, and it occurred to me that
if I could get more weight it might succeed in breaking our stern
out of the muddy bottom. We therefore rigged a handline from the

torpedo compartment to the control room, and all men who could be spared from other duties hauled themselves right forward along the line. Then we made our final effort and, as you know, at once came to the surface. Our small Faith had been answered in a way that, to many of us, seemed miraculous. When we opened the conning tower hatch we found our bows were pointing directly towards the Danish coast, which had just been occupied by the Germans. I did all I could to turn her towards Gothenburg in Sweden, which I hoped to reach, but she obstinately refused to point in any direction except Denmark. It was my Coxswain, Joe Higgins, who jocularly suggested that we might get to Sweden stern first. Higgins was one of the finest men who ever lived – always cheerful and efficient, and his spirit rose above every difficulty. During the next five years in prisoner-of-war camps his example of moral courage and cheerfulness was worth more to those around him than man can measure, he was a humble man, but a very great one. When last I heard from him he was working for Gamages.

'I do not expect,' Lonsdale continued in his letter, 'ever to forget the shock which I experienced a few days after my capture when out for a walk under guard at Kiel, I saw the *Seal* being towed into port; nor, almost worse, when on leaving Kiel for the prison camp I caught sight of her in dry dock. Later on we read reports in German papers about how she was helping our enemies; and it was indeed an immense relief to find out after the war that those reports were not true . . . Looking back it is, of course, obvious that apart from what we did to minimise the consequences of the disaster, the one additional measure necessary was for me to stay behind and *see* that she was sunk by one or other of the measures we might have tried.' Even if true, that re-appraisal of his actions takes no account of the effects of the tremendous ordeal through which he and his men had just passed.

CAPTAIN S. W. ROSKILL DSC RN

The Royal Navy's first submarine, *Holland One*. Life on board her is described by her first CO, Lt. D. Arnold-Foster, seen here on the left, on p. 6.

A.7, one of the first Class of British-designed submarines.
On p. 18 Petty Officer Fred Parsons describes how joining *A.7* saved his life.

A rust-marked *C.37* arriving at Hong Kong in April 1911. An extract
from the diary kept by her CO during that epic 10,000-mile voyage
from Portsmouth begins on p. 23.

E.9 and her CO, Cdr. Max Horton (left). *E.9* sank the German cruiser *Hela* off Heligoland on 13 September 1914, thus becoming the first British submarine to sink an enemy warship. Horton's patrol report is on p. 35.

Cdr. Martin Nasmith (left), CO of *E.11*, and his First Lieutenant Guy D'Oyly Hughes. Nasmith was awarded the Victoria Cross and D'Oyly Hughes the DSC after *E.11*'s tremendous patrol in the Sea of Marmara in May and June 1915, when *E.11* sank eleven Turkish ships. D'Oyly Hughes' letter home to his family, giving his cheerfull and modest view of events, is on p. 47.

The unlucky steam-driven *K.13*, seen on the morning of 29 January 1917, the day she foundered during her trials in the Gareloch. Lt.-Cdr. Kenneth Michell, CO of *E.50*, also doing trials that day, was on the spot. His account begins on p. 57.

Turks examining the wreck of E.14, shelled and abandoned while attempting a penetration of the Dardanelles in January 1918, when her CO, Lt.-Cdr. Geoffrey White, was awarded a posthumous Victoria Cross. A letter from a Turkish PoW camp by Petty Officer R. A. Perkins, one of only seven survivors, describing *E.14*'s last moments, is on p. 66.

The ship's company of the giant 12-inch gun armed *M.1*. Cdr. C. G. Brodie (seated, centre), does some confidence boosting eaves-dropping after taking command, on p. 73.

Lt. John Murray, First Lieutenant of *K.5*, was there, in 'Hic Jacet', p. 76.

LOST. THE SUBMARINE-CRUISER K 5. JAN. 20ᵗʰ-1921

Never bronze, nor slab of stone,
  May their sepulchre denote,
Nor their burial place alone,
  Shall the shifting seaweed float.

Not for *them* the quiet grave
  Underneath the daisied turf,
They sleep beneath the surging wave
  They lie beneath the ceaseless surf

And each idle wave that breaks
  Henceforth on each stormy shore
Shall be nobler for their sakes,
  Shall be holy evermore.

SUBMARINE L24 SUNK IN CHANNEL WITH CREW OF 43

Collision in Fog with H.M.S. Resolution After Fleet Had Left Portland.

10. JANUARY, 1924

LIST OF CREW.

The Admiralty issued last night the following list of names of those on the vessel:

Lieut.-Commander Paul Leathley Eddis.
Lieut. Donald Howell Barton.
Lieut. Hugh Donald Nixon Gray, M.B.E.
Sub-Lieut. Eric Alfred Stedall.
Warrant-Engineer John Byren.
Chief Petty Officer Elijah Frederick Buck.
Petty Officer William John Wiss.
Petty Officer John Wilson.
Petty Officer Sidney Frank Bennett.
Leading Seaman Harold John Balbeck.
Leading Seaman Joseph Benjamin Stapleton.

Able Seaman George Henry Waterfield
Able Seaman Arthur Reginald Lawley.
Able Seaman Alfred John Mead France
Able Seaman Thomas Henry Quantock.
Able Seaman Hugh Lamberton Donald.
Able Seaman Frederick Charles Ignatius Lough.
Able Seaman William John Garrish.
Stoker Petty Officer Edward James Hillman.
Leading Stoker Edwin George Johnson.
Leading Stoker George James Niven Tippen.
Acting Leading Stoker Headley Cann.
Stoker First Class Edmund Lyons.
Stoker First Class Sidney Rowland Ballard.
Stoker First Class William Walker.
Stoker First Class Sidney Frank Phillips.
Stoker First Class Ernest Percy Victor

Stoker First Class Bertie Wennell Flanigan.
Stoker First Class Edward Newinn.
Stoker First Class George William Stewart.
Stoker First Class Alfred John Grigg.
Stoker First Class George William Frederick Green.
Stoker David William Crumbie.
Leading Signalman Harold Pielder Chavis.
Signalman Allan Smith.
Petty Officer Telegraphist Thomas Milner James Parkhurst.
Telegraphist James Mitchell.
Chief Engine-Room Artificer 2nd Class Andrew Chalmers Wallace.
Engine-Room Artificer David Kirwin Fletcher.
Engine-Room Artificer 2nd Class Charles Matthew.
Engine-Room Artificer 2nd Class Percy Lane.

Two of Sub-Lt. Sherwood's submarine training class were lost in *L.24*. He could so easily have been one of them, on p. 82.

Desperate attempts to rescue the men in *Thetis* in Liverpool Bay in June 1939. But of the 103 on board, only four escaped, including Captain 'Joe' Oram, on p. 89.

Sealion. Lt.-Cdr. Ben Bryant (inset), one of the most successful British submarine COs of World War Two, describes his 'Worst Patrol' in *Sealion* in the Skagerrak in June 1940, on p. 103.

Seal being towed to Kiel after her surrender to a German aircraft, May 1940. Her CO, Lt.-Cdr. Rupert Lonsdale (inset), tells the story of her fight for survival on p. 111.

Lt.-Cdr. Malcolm Wanklyn (left, with beard), CO of *Upholder*, being
congratulated on his Victoria Cross by his First Lieutenant,
James Drummond, December 1941.

Seal *eventually struggled to the surface at 1.30 a.m. on 5 May,
having been dived for twenty-three hours, and was again attacked
by aircraft. Unable to dive or move, with her guns jammed, deep
in hostile waters, and slowly sinking,* Seal *was in dire trouble. Lonsdale now decided that he could not risk the lives of his men any
further and he must surrender. The German anti-submarine vessel
UJ.128 came alongside and sent a boarding officer and prize crew
on board. An Arado seaplane took Lonsdale ashore. He and his
crew became prisoners-of-war. When he returned in 1945, he was
court-martialled for losing his ship, according to the custom of
the Service, but was honourably acquitted. Rupert Lonsdale was
ordained Priest in the Church of England in 1948.*

*

*One of the most intense and, despite severe losses, ultimately most
successful submarine campaigns of the war was fought by the small
(540-ton) but handy 'U' Class boats of the 10th Flotilla, known as
'the Fighting Tenth', based in Malta. One of the highest-scoring
boats was*

Upholder

Went to Barrow-in-Furness to stand by submarine *Upholder* on
about September 22, 1940. She was in the final stages of her building
at this time. Commissioned on October 16 and went to Scotland
for trials.

Did our trials in Loch Long and visited a few other places around
there, our depot ship during this time being H.M.S. *Forth*, which
was moored off Dunoon. Left Scotland for Portsmouth and there
had foreign service leave.

Sailed from U.K. and arrived in Gibraltar just before the New Year, spending Christmas at sea. In Gibraltar for a while, then we sailed for Malta, arriving about three weeks later.

Our first sinking, just off Tripoli, Tuesday, January 28, 1941 at 1427. We fired two fish from Nos. 1 and 2 tubes at a convoy and scored one hit on a cargo ship of about 5,000 tons. She took a long while to go down but eventually went bows first.

Thursday, January 30, off Tripoli, time 1619, we fired two more fish, from tubes three and four, at an escorted convoy. One hit on an 8,000-ton supply ship. We received 32 depth-charges pretty close but managed to get away under cover of darkness.

As we came off patrol we had some torpedoes fired at us by an enemy submarine but we dived out of the way.

About April 10 we fired our fish in two salvoes at a convoy. These were our last torpedoes and it was starting to get dark so we surfaced and warned Base of the position of the convoy but it must have altered course because our aircraft couldn't find it.

We saw a convoy on the following night just as it was getting dark but having no torpedoes left we surfaced and fired star shells over the convoy to give away their position to any of our aircraft that may have been about. We expected a few depth-charges in exchange but were pleasantly disappointed. A flotilla of destroyers later wiped out that convoy.

On Friday April 25, 1941, off Tripoli at 1531 we fired at a convoy getting one hit, a cargo ship of about 7,900 tons.

Saturday April 26, west of Tripoli at 2030 we went alongside the *Arta*, an Italian supply ship wiped up by destroyers. We sent a boarding party aboard but all they found was a good few German soldiers and a good stink coming from them. On blowing the safe they set fire to the ship but did manage to get her papers all right. They had to come off quickly as the ship began to blaze up but they did bring with them a few tommy guns, a few tin hats, a Nazi ensign and a lot of other junk. The ship was last seen blazing on the horizon.

Sunday April 27, we tried to get alongside a destroyer wiped out in the same convoy, but ran aground before we could do so and had to put the blower on all tanks to get her off again.

We came off that patrol with a guard of honour on the fore casing wearing German tin hats, carrying German tommy guns and flying the German ensign.

Thursday May 1, at 1146 we fired at a convoy getting three hits on three separate targets – a destroyer, a 4,000-ton supply ship and a 10,000-ton supply ship. The first two sank and the third came to a standstill. Another destroyer crept up to the 10,000-tonner in the hope of towing her off so at 1901 we slammed two more fish into the supply ship, which was last seen upside down on the surface before she sank. We could not stop to see her sink as we were too busy dodging depth-charges.

Saturday, May 24, 1941. As it was getting dark we sighted a liner with an escort of three cruisers and an uncountable number of destroyers at about 2025.

2030 Diving Stations

2045 Fired two fish, 1 and 4 tubes.

2046 Flood Q, 150 feet.

As we dived we heard both torpedoes explode on target. Depth-charges started dropping after the torpedoes exploded. Thirty-three were dropped on us, very close. Destroyers passed right overhead twice. I was pretty shaky, could not stop legs from shaking, but did not let anybody notice it.

2126 Depth-charges stopped.

2140 Came up to 70 feet.

2145 Watch diving.

2238 Diving Stations.

2247 Surface, terrible smell of oil fuel on surface when I went up as lookout. We had scored two hits on a liner of about 18,000 tons carrying 4,000 troops.

Thursday, July 3, we sighted a small convoy and at 1142 we fired 2 and 4 tubes at a timber ship of some 6,000 tons. We got one hit on the target and had 19 charges dropped but not too close.

Thursday, July 24, 1345, sighted an Italian destroyer and a 6,000-ton merchant ship.

1412 Standby.

1416 Fire a salvo of three from tubes 1, 2, and 3.

One hit on the merchantman. At 1530 she was seen to be down by the stern. We got 18 depth-charges, which they continued to drop until pretty late when we were well away from the spot.

Monday, July 28, we sighted a convoy at 1951 firing a salvo of four and getting two hits on a cruiser of 7,280 tons. We received 42 charges very near. Indeed, once, when we were expecting to hear the next one explode we heard one of the destroyers pass right overhead and, boy, we had our hearts in our mouths. The cruiser was of the D'Aosta class. We had one torpedo left and later went back and fired on the convoy but missed.

We came back through the minefield of Wednesday, July 30.

August 5, sent to prison for 30 days for losing my temper with a colonel in the Army and insulting a petty officer.

September 1, my day of freedom, got drafted to spare crew.

October 17, drafted to SM *Ursula*.

October 18, 1941, on our way to southern Italy, at 0616 we sighted a convoy of four cargo ships with a three-ship destroyer escort. At 0801 we fired 1, 2, 3 and 4 tubes and got hits on two ships of about 6,000 and 7,000 tons. In return we received five depth-charges.

October 23, at 1345 we surfaced and fired 87 rounds at a railway bridge. We did considerable damage to the bridge, but had to break off and dive out of the way owing to the breech jamming. Their coastal defence opened up at us but only with a machine gun that simply made a few dents in the control tower.

Sunday, November 30, we set out for home. Will be glad to see the folks at home.

AUTHOR'S NAME UNKNOWN

The attack described on 24 May 1941 was actually on a heavily escorted convoy of four large ocean liners – Conte Rosso, Marco Polo, Victoria *and* Esperia – *all packed with troop reinforcements for Rommel's Afrika Korps in Libya.* Upholder *sank* Conte Rosso *and it was this exploit which was later picked out for the award of the Victoria Cross to* Upholder's *CO, Lt.-Cdr. Malcolm Wanklyn. Wanklyn already had the DSO, but his VC, gazetted in December 1941, made him a naval celebrity and the subject of a visit by the Navy's most prominent war correspondent, who wrote an account of*

A Patrol in *Upholder* with Lt.-Cdr. Wanklyn VC DSO, 1942

'When I first arrived at the submarine depot ship – in this particular case a ship in name only, as the submariners live in barracks ashore while in harbour – a number of submariners were berthed alongside the jetties. From close-up one could just make out their names beneath the war-paint. Famous names which, during the last eighteen months, have made submarine history.

'One of them, recently in from patrol, was still flying the Jolly Roger, a black flag with white skull and crossbones in the centre and, on either side, various devices denoting her successes.

'There were a number of white bars, for instance, for enemy ships sunk. Two were clean and new, proud evidence that she'd sunk a couple during this last trip! But the thing which intrigued me most was a bar much larger than any of the others. I could hardly wait until I'd found her captain and discovered what it meant.

'"Why is this bar so much larger than the others – does it mean a battleship or a battle-cruiser, or what?"

'"No, just an ordinary tanker. But they'd put on a whopping great bar, because it had been such a whopping great fluke."

'And that, d'you know, was very typical of the light-hearted, happy-go-lucky way in which these lads fight their grim war under the Mediterranean.

'They talk very little about their experiences. Once in harbour and ashore they rather naturally prefer to forget all about them. I'd rather expected to go into the wardroom and be told with pride of their various achievements.

'But not a bit of it. The pride of the mess – as far as they were concerned – was Snow White and the Seven Dwarfs. Snow White is an enormous sow, the Dwarfs her piglets.

'From Snow White I was introduced to two more litters, whose prolific parents had aptly been christened Mare and Nostrum. From inside the sty there appeared a massive bearded figure. On his chest was the ribbon of the Distinguished Service Cross, and he had many an enemy ship to his credit. Be that as it may, his main claim to fame, for the moment, lay in the fact that he was the officer-in-charge of pigs.

'A few hours later I went to sea on an urgent patrol. As we steamed out of harbour, Snow White and her Seven Dwarfs grunted a farewell from the beach and, from outside the operations room, a solitary figure waved "good luck". This was the captain (S), the man who commands the submarine flotilla and operates them from the depot ship. Of all naval commands, that of a captain (S) is one of the toughest and most nerve-racking. They are invariably submariners themselves, and as they watch their boats leave harbour they realise all too well, from personal experience, the many dangers which lie ahead.

'Those weeks while his submarines are at sea are long and anxious. On the days when they are due to return you'll find him standing there, smoking rather too many cigarettes, and searching the harbour entrance through the first streaks of dawn.

'Sometimes there's an agonising twenty-four or even forty-eight hours when, for some reason or other, a boat has been delayed. Sometimes it's even longer, and eventually you'll read a short paragraph in your papers: "The Admiralty regrets to announce that one of our submarines is overdue and must be considered lost."

'It's a terrible strain on those captains of submarine flotillas, made doubly so because they must never "let up", never reveal their true feelings. For on their example – their attitude to life – depend absolutely the morale and high spirits of those grand lads who go out on the job.

'The captain of our particular submarine was a young lieutenant-commander, with a certain 14,000 tons of enemy shipping to his credit and probably a good deal more. He was tall and lanky, with a keen, studious face and a rather untidy black beard, which gave him a definitely biblical appearance. At sea he wore one of the most disreputable uniforms I've ever seen; torn and patched and with only a few wisps of what had once been gold lace hanging from his sleeves. He wore no medal ribbons, but on his smarter harbour uniform he had worn the DSO for some time. Now there was an additional ribbon, a crimson one with a small bronze cross in the centre – the VC.

'His name was Wanklyn, and it will always be one of my proudest memories that I have been out on the job with Wanklyn and his crew, who – in their submarine *Upholder* – have written such a glorious page in naval history.

'Once at sea we soon went to "diving stations". All on the bridge, with the exception of Wanklyn and one signalman, disappeared down the conning-tower hatch and, in doing so, said good-bye to daylight for many days. From now on we'd be cooped up in a steel shell with a cross-section about that of a London tube. But here most of the space is taken up by engines, torpedoes, periscopes, pipe lines, dials, valves, and so on. In *Upholder* the only reliefs from this maze of machinery – the only human reminders of the outside world – were two very lovely signed photos . . . of the King and Queen.

'At the moment it was all rather noisy and confused. Being still on the surface, the diesel engines were at "full ahead" and the boat was pitching into the swell. Various orders were being shouted, and then suddenly, above the general din, there was a hoot from the diving klaxon. In a flash the whole atmosphere changed. The noise and vibration of the diesels stopped and gave way to the quiet hum of the electric motors. The only sound to be heard was the first lieutenant giving his trimming orders . . . 'Pump on A . . . Stop the pump. Flood Z . . . Shut Z,' and so on. As the needles of the depth gauges passed the twenty foot mark, we lost the effect of the surface swell. The boat stopped creaking and settled down to her steady underwater course. The sudden silence was quite uncanny.

'For the first few days, while on passage to the pre-arranged position, there is little excitement to break the monotony. The crew work in three watches. Two hours on, and four off. In most surface warships they work four-hour tricks, but in a submarine the job is too concentrated for a man to do more than two hours at a stretch. Besides, the comparatively short time off does not allow him to get too deep a sleep in case of an emergency.

'The routine seldom varies: sleep – eat – a spell on duty – sleep and eat. The only differences between day and night are that during the daytime, while you're running submerged and clear of the effect of waves, it's all very still and quiet. At night, when you surface under cover of darkness to charge the batteries, you're rolling and pitching to the sea. There is the noise and vibration of the diesels; and, the conning-tower hatch being open, you can smoke!

'The amount of sleep you put in is quite amazing – it's largely the lack of oxygen when submerged. You don't notice it much at the time, but if you strike a match towards the end of the day you'll find that it just flickers and goes out. There is, of course, no exercise to be had in the terribly cramped quarters, and during the twenty-four hours you'll probably only move a few paces – and yet you're always tired and always hungry. And, oddly enough, by the end of a patrol you've probably lost weight.

'The whole business of submarine attack is rather like stalking big game, only about a hundred times more exciting. Sound travels a long way under water, and in one corner of the control room an operator is rotating a dial and listening out for enemy ships. He suddenly concentrates on one bearing, then raps out a report: 'Ships bearing Green 20.' The captain immediately decides to have a look and motions to the first lieutenant to take her up to periscope depth. A few sharp orders and the boat starts to rise. When nearing the depth at which the top lens of the periscope when fully extended will break surface, the captain orders 'Up periscope'. A slight swishing noise, and the periscope shoots upwards. The captain bends double, meets the eye-pieces as they rise between his feet and straightens up with his eyes glued to them and his hands grasping the handles on either side. At a flick of his fingers the periscope stops dead with its top lens just clear of the surface. A quick glance round for aircraft and then he searches the surface. As he concentrates on Green 20, he clasps the two handles just a little tighter. His back suddenly stiffens . . . yes, there it is. Smoke on the horizon.

'That's all he wants to know for the moment, and he's not going to stay up a second longer than necessary. 'Down periscope . . . 50 feet.'

'For a moment the captain considers his plan and glances at the compass. His hand reaches out to a buzzer. 'Action stations'.

'That buzzer starts the quickest move I've ever seen. There's no noise, no scramble. The men just appear. Many of them were fast asleep, but before you can say "knife" they're at their stations and there's never a yawn or a rubbing of eyes. They know that buzzer, and they know that when the captain presses it he means business.

'By now it's time for another look. A nod to the first lieutenant – a few quiet orders as tanks are blown, a nod to the periscope operator, and again that lanky figure is uncoiling himself as the periscope rises.

'A quick glance round for aircraft and he swings on to the target. Then, with the quiet confidence of the expert, he raps out the details – course, speed, bearing, range.

'At each report another officer sets various dials on a large box attached to the bulkhead. Finally he pulls a handle at the side which co-ordinates all these settings, and produces the vitally important answer – the "torpedo-firing angle". Needless to say, this box is known as the "fruit machine".'

'By now they're down deep again, and the captain discloses the good news of what he alone has seen. 'Two transports . . . four destroyers'.

'Meanwhile, the captain has finally decided on his plan of attack. As the enemy draws closer he has just one more look through the periscope to check his bearing and make sure that they haven't zig-zagged off their course.

'No, everything's going according to plan. The leading destroyers are drawing near by now and he decides to dive underneath and get a close shot on the important targets – the transports.

'Down periscope – 100 feet.' Once settled at the depth, there's a tense silence. A distant rumble heralds the approach of the destroyers; it grows louder and louder until, with a deafening din, like the roar of an express train, their propellers go racing overhead.

'The captain is a picture of cool confidence. He's got every move fixed in that clear, calculating brain, and nothing is going to deter him. Neither is there a sign of anxiety amongst the officers or crew. They know that this is the big moment, but they've got complete confidence in one another and particularly in the man in command.

'At exactly the moment when he's calculated that he's clear of the enemy destroyer screen and almost in the firing position, he gives the familiar sign – back swings the depth needle . . . 80, 70, 60, 50. . . . This time he's almost flat on his stomach as the eye-pieces come up. There's no time to swing round the horizon now. Anyhow, his periscope is set at the firing angle and he's only waiting for the target to come into view. For a moment it's an empty horizon, and then suddenly there comes into his field of vision . . . a transporter's bow. As it passes the centre wire her foremast is coming in . . . "Stand by" . . . "Fire one" . . . A fraction's pause and then a slight jolt of recoil as the torpedo leaves the tube. "Fire two" . . . "Fire Three" . . . there's no hesitation about his next order . . . "Down periscope – go deep." This time the needle fairly races round.

'The captain is eyeing his watch closely. From the range he can estimate almost exactly when his torpedoes will cross the enemy's track. Those two or three minutes put years on his life. The suspense of whether he's hit or missed is the worst part of the whole business. Fifteen seconds to go . . . ten . . . five . . . He's missed! Something must have gone wrong . . . the gyros must have failed. . . . The . . . Suddenly there's a crash which shakes the whole boat and sends a couple of light brackets clattering down.

'It's an unmistakable sound when a "fish" hits. There's a distinct metallic ping of impact, followed immediately by the explosion.

'A few seconds later, there's another. Then silence. Two hits, that should be enough to do the trick. But there's no cheering, no whoop of joy – only grins and rubbing of hands and dead silence, except for a whispered remark from the first lieutenant. "Nice work, sir".

'Silence is essential at this moment. From now on they are no longer the hunters, they're the hunted. Sound travels fast and loud under water, and the dropping of a spanner or anything like that might easily spell disaster.

'Crash! There come the depth charges – one, two, three, four, five. The petty officer telegraphist is jotting them down in his log as casually as a grocer checking the empties.

'As they get closer the submarine is shaken more and more violently. It's a terrific noise. One that gets you not so much in the ears, but in the pit of the stomach. The hunt may last for half an hour, an hour, and often much longer, but when it eventually dies away, and the captain is reasonably satisfied that it's over, he'll return to periscope depth to have a look at the damage and the possibility of other targets. Very often, of course, the torpedoed ship will have sunk by now, but if she hasn't yet foundered and there's no danger around, he lets some of his crew have a look through the periscope before she goes. Should it happen to be anyone's birthday, it's his privilege to have the first 'decco'.

'And so the patrol goes on – blank, boring days; desperately exciting days; and tense snooping days, creeping round the enemy's coast, watching him through that little eye above the surface until it's time to go home and refuel. On reaching harbour the crew are fallen in on the fore and after casings. As they pass and salute the other ships, the side is piped and they come smartly to attention with all the pomp and ceremony of peacetime.

'But if you look closer you'll notice that the men's long white submarine sweaters are grimed and dirty; their chins carry many a day's growth of beard; their eyes are heavy, and blurred at the unaccustomed glare of daylight, and on the stump mast above the conning-tower flies the 'Jolly Roger'.

'When we came in, Snow White and the Seven Dwarfs were the first to grunt a welcome home.

'The first man on board was the captain (S), to hear our news and tell us that of the outside world. As we were talking, a dilapidated motor-van pulled up on the roadway above, and a massive bearded figure leant out from the driver's seat. It was the officer-in-charge of pigs on his way to the slaughter house to put an end to half a dozen of the fattest. He wasn't looking forward to that at all.

'Odd, because only a few days before he'd sunk a transport and put an end to any number of Huns ... and he'd had no qualms about that!'

CAPTAIN ANTHONY KIMMINS

Wanklyn developed into one of the deadliest killers the Submarine Service had ever seen, and won two Bars to his DSO. By the end, he had made thirty-six attacks, of which twenty-three were successful, and sank nearly 140,000 tons of enemy shipping, including a destroyer, the Italian U-boats Ammiraglio St Bon *and* Tricheco, *and over a dozen assorted troopships, tankers, supply and store ships.*

Upholder *sailed from Malta for her twenty-fifth patrol, and her last before she was due to go home for refit, on 6 April 1942. She successfully landed a clandestine agent on the North African coast and kept a rendezvous with* Unbeaten *on the 11th. On the 14th* Urge *heard heavy prolonged depth-charging from the area off Tripoli where* Upholder *should have been. On the 18th the Italians claimed that one of their torpedo boats had sunk a British submarine.* Upholder *was overdue, presumed lost. It had been her first and only commission. Wanklyn had been her first and only commander.*

Whilst admitting that 'it was seldom proper to draw distinction between different services rendered in the course of naval duty' the Admiralty ended their statement of 22 August 1942, announcing the loss. 'The ship and her company are gone, but the example and the inspiration remain'.

*

Submariners had their own delicacies, such as

Cheese Oosh

This is a British submarine delicacy second only to Train Smash (scrambled powdered eggs, canned tomatoes and canned bacon, preferably eaten as an early breakfast while the boat is still in red lighting to preserve night vision). Cheese Oosh is distantly related to a Cheese Soufflé but, traditionally, it should be flat, heavy and more like Yorkshire pudding. Reduced to family proportion, you require:

1 pint of milk
8oz grated Cheddar cheese
4 eggs (powdered or frozen are acceptable)
1/2 teaspoon of mustard
Seasoning
1 tomato (sliced)

Beat the eggs until light and frothy. Add the pint of milk to the mixture. Add the cheese and mustard and the seasoning. Stir together. Pour into a buttered baking dish and cook in a moderate oven until golden brown and set. Garnish with sliced tomato and serve.

In wartime, submarines usually turned night into day as far as meals were concerned so that cooking could be done on the surface. Typical menus for Allied submarines operating from Malta in 1941 were

	Breakfast	Lunch	Tea	Dinner or supper
Monday	(before diving)	(submerged)	(submerged)	(surface)
	Grapefruit ½	Tinned soup ½	Jam 1oz	Pea soup
	Fried fresh fish	Tomato &		Roast Beef (5oz)
		Beetroot		Roast potatoes
		Salad (fresh)		(12oz)
		Orange (1)		Cabbage (12oz)
				Fruit pudding,
				custard
Tuesday	Grapefruit	Tinned soup	Marmite (4oz)	Lentil soup
	Pork sausages (2)	Cold beef		Beef Steak pudding
	Marmalade	(2oz cooked)		(5oz)
		Fresh tomatoes		Boiled potatoes
		(4oz)		Tinned carrots, ¼
		Cheese (2oz)		Tinned fruit, ¼
		Biscuits (2oz)		& custard
		Tangerine (1)		
Wednesday	Cornflakes, ½	Tinned soup	Meat paste ½oz	Oxtail soup
	Bacon (2oz)	Tinned lobster ½		Roast mutton
	Eggs (2)	Mayonnaise		leg (5oz)
		Potato salad (4oz)		Roast potatoes
		Orange		Braised onions
				Rice pudding
				(1½oz)
Thursday	Grapefruit	Tinned soup	Honey, jam or	Scotch broth
	Cornflakes	Cold ham (3oz)	syrup	Veal (4oz) & ham
	Buttered eggs	Fresh tomatoes		(1oz)
		Cold boiled		Boiled potatoes
		potatoes		Tinned runner
		Tangerine		beans ¼
				Pineapple &
				custard
Friday	Grapefruit	Tinned soup	Boiled eggs (2)	Pea soup
	Bacon (1oz)	Corned beef (3oz)		Roast chicken
	Liver (2oz)	Pickles (1oz)		(12oz)
		Baked beans (¼)		Tinned cauli-
		Cheese & biscuits		flower (¼)
				Boiled jam roll
Saturday	Grapefruit	Tinned soup	Marmite	Pea soup
	Fried cod	Cold hard boiled		Roast veal (5oz)
	fillets (4oz)	eggs		Roast potatoes
		Potato salad		Tinned cabbage
		Tinned pears		Boiled rice
				Tinned apricot

In July 1941, Umpire (Lt. M. R. G. Wingfield) left Chatham dockyard which had built her and joined the northbound East Coast convoy EC4, intending to go north-about around Scotland to the Clyde to undergo trials and training with the 3rd Flotilla at Dunoon.

At about midnight on 19 July, EC4 met the southbound convoy FS44 off the Wash. The usual procedure was for convoys to keep to the starboard side of the swept channel and pass each other port side to port. Wingfield, on Umpire's bridge, was therefore surprised to see the unlit shapes of the oncoming southbound convoy to starboard of him. He could not alter course to starboard because of the line of ships in the southbound convoy, so he ordered hard-a-port. At the same time, Peter Hendriks, a trawler in the southbound convoy, must have caught sight of Umpire directly ahead of her and altered to starboard. She struck Umpire on her starboard bow, tearing a large hole in her pressure hull. Wingfield clutched the trawler's side as it swung in towards him and shouted furiously

'You Bloody Bastard, You've Sunk a British Submarine!'

When the Captain left the wardroom to go up on the bridge in response to Tony's [Tony Godden, the Navigating Officer] message about the approaching convoy, Peter Bannister [the First Lieutenant] and I were sitting at the wardroom table, decoding a routine wireless signal that had been passed to us by the telegraphist on watch.

The wardroom was divided from the control-room only by a thin steel partition, and by curtains from the passage-way; at sea these curtains were drawn back, and Peter and I could hear the helmsman repeat the orders which came to him down the voice-pipe from the bridge.

When we heard him repeat the Captain's emergency order, 'Hard-a-port' we pushed back our chairs and stood up, our eyes meeting in question and alarm. We stumbled out into the passage-way, and Peter at once gave the order to 'Shut water-tight doors!' Almost immediately we heard another urgent yell down the voice-pipe, but before this last order from the bridge could be repeated by the helmsman there was a violent crash for'ard in the torpedo-stowage compartment, followed by the blue-white flare and muffled thump of an electrical explosion. The boat rocked to port, stayed there a few seconds, and then slid drunkenly forward and over to starboard as she began her plunge to the bottom. If the water were deep here, its weight would crush us like an egg-shell. Most of the lights had gone out. Then men were running past us from the next compartment. Peter was yelling 'Shut that door!' and I had my hand on it, letting the men run through, disobeying Peter because I hadn't the courage to deny any of them a chance so long as the water was not yet actually at their heels. Somehow the further door to the damaged compartment had shut, whether blown to by the explosion or deliberately shut from the inside by a last nameless act of self-sacrifice as the sea came flooding in, we shall never know. 'Shut that bloody door!' repeated Peter in a fury, but by now all the men from the intervening compartment were through. With some difficulty, because of the angle of the boat, I pulled the door up towards me and clamped it shut.

I turned, and struggled up the tilting deck into the control-room. The boat was listing to starboard and sloping forward at an angle of about ten degrees. Water was pouring in from what seemed to be a hundred places. Peter was struggling with the outboard battery-ventilation-valve overhead, desperately seeking an explanation for this inrush of water, and acutely aware of the fatal danger of chlorine gas if the sea-water should find its way into the battery cell under the deck. I reached up to help him, glad in my numbed state of something positive to do. But the valve was already shut, as we knew it should have been, and we must look elsewhere for the breach in our defences. To my paralysed brain it seemed that the shock of the collision had cracked the hull and started rivets along the whole length of the ship. Surprisingly enough, no water was coming down the conning-tower; presumably the upper hatch had fallen shut when the boat took on a list immediately before she went under.

Peter was now calling for more light, and one or two of the men searched about for the emergency head-lamps. I remembered that I had a torch in my drawer in the wardroom, so I traced my steps, moving with difficulty down the wet and sloping deck. In the passage-way the water was already knee-deep. I sloshed through it and pulled myself up in the ward-room. Streams of ice-green water were cascading from somewhere overhead, drenching the beautiful new curtains and bunks in a universal deluge. If I had brought a conscious intelligence to bear on the source of this waterfall I should have hit on something that ought to have been obvious to all of us. But not until the whole thing was over did I realise that all this water must have been coming from the *ventilation shaft*, now open to sea pressure through the damaged torpedo-stowage compartment. By reaching up my hand over the Captain's bunk I could have shut the valve on the bulkhead quite easily, and the flow of water would have stopped. But my brain, as though stunned by the catastrophe, had become incapable of constructive thought.

I found the torch and splashed my way back to the control-room. As I did so, it occurred to me to wonder what depth we were at. I shone the torch on the depth-gauges and found, to my surprise, that they were both reading only a little over 60 feet. This meant we were in very shallow water, with the bow presumably resting on the bottom at something like 80 feet. I asked Peter whether it was possible to *blow* her up. It seemed unlikely, since we had been at full buoyancy at the time of the collision, and a vast quantity of water must have entered for'ard to have overcome that buoyancy so suddenly. It was obvious that a large gash had been torn at the top of the pressure hull in the torpedo-stowage compartment, and that the compartment had filled up in a matter of seconds. We should never get her up with all that weight of water in her. However, Peter thought it would do no harm to try, so one by one he opened up the valves of the high-pressure air-panel until all five ballast tanks and the two main internal tanks were blowing. But it was no use: the depth-gauges did not even flicker.

The sea continued to pour in on us, with a terrible and relentless noise, and the water in the compartment grew deeper every minute. As the level crept up the starboard side, live electrical contacts began spitting venomously, with little lightning flashes. Vaguely I wondered if we were all going to be electrocuted.

In the half-darkness the men had become anonymous groping figures, desperately coming and going. There was no panic, but most of us, I think, were suffering from a sort of mental concussion. I discovered one man trying to force open the water-tight door that I had shut earlier. 'My pal's in there,' he was moaning, 'my pal's in there.' 'It's no good,' I told him; 'she's filled right up for'ard and there's no one left alive on the other side of that door.' He turned away sobbing a little.

For some reason we decided it would be useful if we could find more torches. I knew there must be one or two other somewhere in the wardroom, so I made yet another expedition down the slope, wading through the pool that was now waist-deep and already covering the lower tiers of drawer under our bunks. I spent some time in the wardroom, shivering with fear and cold, ransacking every drawer and cupboard, pushing aside the forsaken paraphernalia of personal belongings – under-clothes, razors, pipes, photographs of wives and girl-friends. But I could find only one torch that was still dry and working. Holding it clear of the water, I returned to the control-room.

It was deserted.

The door into the engine-room was shut. Had I spent longer in the wardroom than I thought? Perhaps they had all escaped from the engine-room escape-hatch, without realising that I had been left behind. Even if they had not yet left the submarine, they might already have started flooding the compartment in preparation for an escape, and if the flooding had gone beyond a certain point it would be impossible to get that door open again. I listened, but could hear nothing beyond the monotonous, pitiless sound of pouring water. In this terrible moment I must have come very near to panic.

I could at least try hammering on the engine-room door. Looking round for a heavy instrument, I found a valve spanner and began moving aft towards the door. As I did so I heard a voice quite close to me say, 'Christ, who's that?' I looked up and found I was standing under the conning-tower. In it, to my infinite relief, I saw Peter with an able seaman and one of the E.R.A.'s. 'Where the hell have you come from?' said Peter. 'Where the hell's everybody gone?' I retorted. 'Any room for me up there?' 'We ought to be able to squeeze you in. The others are going to escape from the engine-room.'

I climbed up through the lower hatch, grateful as never before for the company of my fellow-creatures. Four of us in the tiny space made a tight squeeze, Peter at the top of the ladder with his head jammed up against the upper hatch, the A.B. half-way up the ladder with his bottom wedged against the side of the tower, leaving just room for me and the E.R.A. standing at the foot of the tower, with our feet on the edge of the lower hatch-opening. The E.R.A. was in a bad way, vomiting continuously and hardly able to stand.

In the centre of the upper hatch was a small port, or round window, made of glass thick enough to withstand tremendous pressure. Number One said that he could see a glimmer of light through it, and supposed it to be caused by a searchlight from some vessel waiting overhead. This encouraged him to think we ought to be able to swim to the surface and be picked up without much difficulty. We knew the control-room depth-gauges were reading just over 60 feet; the upper hatch was something like 15 feet higher than the normal surface water-line (the point of reference for the depth-gauges) and was therefore probably only about 45 feet from the surface, say the height of eight men standing on top of each other. It ought to be easy.

'Shut the lower lid,' said Peter, 'and let's just think this out'. I bent down, shut the hatch and pulled the clip over. We then discussed exactly what we were going to do. We agreed that to wear Davids escape gear would be an unnecessary complication in the confined space. One of the dangers was that on our way up we might crack our skulls on the cross-bar between the periscope standards, but we decided there was little chance of this owing to the starboard list. We hoped (vainly, as it turned out) that we might be assisted in our rise to the surface by the bubble of air which would be released from the conning-tower as the hatch opened. The drill was simple. Peter would open the hatch, and as the water came in each man would fill his lungs with air and climb out as fast as he could. Except for the poor E.R.A., who was sick beyond comfort or encouragement, we were by now quite calm, even cheerful.

How long we considered the situation I cannot remember, but at last Peter said, 'Well, the next thing is to see if we can open this hatch against the pressure.' Bracing himself against the side of the tower, he pushed upwards with all his strength. The hatch remained firmly shut. Somehow we must raise the pressure inside the tower.

It occurred to me that while we had been talking the pressure had still been building up in the control-room below us, owing to the continuing inrush of water. I eased off the clip of the hatch under my feet, and sure enough there came the sharp hiss of air forcing its way into the tower. I allowed the air to come in until, after a minute or two, I became aware of a peculiar, faint smell. Perhaps it was merely the odour of fear, but my first thought was that the sea-water had at last found its way into the batteries. 'Hullo,' I said; 'I think I can smell chlorine gas'. 'All right,' said Peter; 'shut the lid again and I'll have another shot at opening this one.' This time he managed without much effort to lift the hatch slightly off its seat, allowing a trickle of water to come through.

'O.K.,' said Peter. 'Well, boys, take your time. There's no hurry. You say when you feel ready.'

I said I was for having a go at once, before we weakened ourselves any further by breathing foul air, and the others agreed. We stripped down to vest, pants and socks.

'Ready?' asked Peter.

'Ready,' we all replied, though I think the E.R.A. had reached the point in his sickness where he wanted to die more than anything else.

'Right. Stand by,' said Peter cheerfully. 'Here we go for fourteen days' survivor's leave. We're off!' – and he pushed up the lid with all his strength.

I took as deep a breath as I could, and then the sea crashed in on us. There was a roaring in my ears, a blackness everywhere, and there was nothing for it but to fight for life with all one's primitive instincts of survival. Hauling myself up by the rungs of the ladder, I found my head obstructed by the A.B.'s bottom. With the strength of a desperate man I pushed up at him, his heel struck me in the face, I pushed again, and then we were through the hatch and clear of the submarine. I swam upwards with quick, jerky breast-strokes. It seemed a terrible distance. Time stretched out of its normal span until I thought my lungs must surely crack before I reached the surface. And then suddenly I was there, coughing, spluttering, gasping in great draughts of the sweet night air and drinking in the blessed sight of the stars shining in the immensity of space.

COMMANDER EDWARD YOUNG DSO DSC RNVR

Of the four men on Umpire's *bridge at the time of the collision, only Wingfield survived. Of the rest of* Umpire's *crew of thirty-eight, only fifteen survived, making sixteen in all. Peter Bannister reached the surface with Young and both began to swim to the nearest ship. But after a time when Young looked back, Bannister had disappeared. He was never seen again.*

*

Some submarines had pets as mascots. Unruffled, *for instance, acquired the cat*

Timoshenko

Unruffled was on her way to join the 10th Flotilla in Malta. The date was July, 1942, when she passed Gibraltar during her working-up trials. The P.O. Tel. was walking through the dockyard when he was approached by a Wren (not the feathered type, I hasten to add, but a real-live pretty girl). Thinking his luck had changed at last, he paused but had his hopes dashed when she produced this tiny bundle of fur and requested a home for it. That was how the cat joined the Royal Navy in general and *Unruffled* in particular. He was welcomed aboard by all hands, made an absolute idiot of, and named after the gallant Russian marshal Timoshenko.

If there is anything in the belief of transmigration, then Timo-shenko had been a submariner before, and an outside wrecker to boot, for he made his diving station under the control panel, where he would yawn and mew when a fish left the tube. He was quickly 'house' trained and used to do his 'georges', as the Captain (Lieut. J. Stevens) quaintly called them, in a box in the P.O.'s mess. Should he forget himself at any time, there was always a willing hand to use their heads and blow the indiscretion over the side.

Timmo, as he quickly became known, accompanied *Unruffled* on every one of her patrols and was awarded a collar with a silver plate bearing his name. It was widely recognised that most of the cat world along Gzira front owed their existence to Timmo's eye for a pretty cat. One sure thing was that on arriving in from patrol, Timmo would disappear for two or three days, returning with what one can only describe as a satisfied smirk on his face.

Timmo gave us a scare when he fell ill and we discovered it was cat flu and prepared for the worst. A vet looked him over, however, diagnosed a chill and gave me Friars Balsam and the method of treatment. This gentleman, whose name we didn't know, refused to accept a fee, but he earned forever the gratitude of *Unruffled*. Timoshenko was soon his old self again. Will anybody who saw the fight ever forget the routing of the Alsatian dog in the Lazaretto? I certainly won't. I thought our brave lad was a goner until, yelping with pain, the dog bolted, leaving the field to Timmo.

Came the day when we were due to leave for patrol. No cat – panic stations. Searches revealed nothing! Captain (S) ordered that *Unruffled* was not to sail without her cat and a search of all boats was instituted. He was found in the P.O.'s mess of a boat that shall be nameless. Suffice it to say they were just passing through and not of the 10th Flotilla.

Our spell of duty over, we headed west and Timmo found himself back in the land of his birth. He developed a daily routine during our stay in Gibraltar. After breakfast he would go ashore and not be seen again until about 1700, when he would settle down for the night. Our final departure from Gib was timed for 1300 so it was plain that if we couldn't keep him on the boat we would lose him. The First Lieutenant (Lieut. O. Lascelles) suggested that we secure him to the gun and this was done. A miserable creature of a killick L.T.O. said that was no way to treat a cat and set him loose. Goodbye, Timoshenko. I think I can paraphrase the poet and say:

> Hail to thee, Blithe Spirit,
> Cat thou never were!

He was succeeded by Timoshenko II and III but neither of these approached the Master and I'm sure all old Unruffleds will agree with me when I say: 'No cat ever will.'

PO TD. JOE LEWIS DS19

*

On 26 November 1941, Perseus (Lt.-Cdr. E. C. F. Nicolay), sailed from Malta for Alexandria, carrying out a patrol off the Greek coast on the way. On the night of 6 December, she struck a mine on her starboard side forward and sank in 270 feet of water. All her complement of fifty-six were lost, but one stoker, taking passage to rejoin his own submarine Thrasher *in Alexandria, became incredibly, the*

Sole Survivor

Suddenly a devastating explosion rocked the boat from stem to stern. My makeshift bed reared up throwing me in a complete somersault on to the deck ... or what I thought to be the deck. The lights went out but not before I realised that the real deck was standing up and that I had been tossed on the forward bulkhead, normally a vertical wall of steel. I knew that *Perseus* was plunging to the bottom in a nose dive.

The bows hit the bottom with a nerve shattering jolt, the boat hung poised for a moment, standing on her head. Then the stern, where I was, fell back settling on the sea bed, possibly forever. Finally, the boat lay stretched on the uneven sea bed, listing almost 30 degrees on the starboard side, the stern was now lower than the bows.

I guessed we had hit a mine, but by some miracle the after compartments were not yet flooded, and by another miracle, I was still alive, although the thump of hitting the bulkhead on my backside was very painful. No time for pains now. How about the chaps in the engine room? I groped for the torch near the escape hatch, 'Thank Heaven', I thought, it was in its position, and it worked! The powerful rays pierced the dank foggy air already beginning to stink of paint pouring from an upturned drum. The bulkhead on which I was tossed was more or less vertical again.

Through the watertight door, I went forrard, searching the stokers mess deck, then the bulkhead to the motor room. Electricians had apparently been killed by falling on live switches. As the rays fingered through the gloom of the engine room they revealed a ghastly sight, half of the cylinder heads at the front end of the engines had sheared off from the studs, with the operation gear hurled against the engine room forrard, thrown there by the sudden jerk of the last dive.

Beyond them was the bulkhead door, shut . . . but not by human hands. No clips had been secured. It must have been slammed by the first blast of the explosion, and was now held in place by water . . . crushing on the other side. It was creaking under the great pressure. Jets and trickles from the rubber joint seeped through. That door saved me and the three injured men I found alive in the debris. Our plight was one of vital horror. The water was rising in the engine room bilges and we were surrounded by the mangled bodies of a dozen dead. *Perseus* had become a cold steel tomb surrounded by the relentless sea.

With the cold already gnawing into me I thought of the rum in my blitz bottle. That would warm us up all right. I nipped back aft, had a stiff livener and handed the bottle round for a swift pick-me-up. I didn't dwell on the very doubtful chance of escape. So far so good. I was still alive in one piece. My immediate thought was to help the others. One by one I guided them to the stern compartment. No time to be fussy about wounds. There was only one thing to do . . . to get out. The next problem was somehow to flood up the after compartment and get the men through to the surface, if by luck nothing had fallen on the escape hatch to jam it.

Willing or not, in pain or no, I dragged them aft to the escape hatch. Had the explosion warped it? Would the heavy list of the boat prevent it opening? I didn't know, but would jolly soon find out. The depth gauge, if still functioning, showed a little over two seventy feet, that had to be overcome anyhow. No one as far as I knew, had ever attempted anything like it. I didn't give it further thought. If death was going to claim me it would not be without a fight.

It took half an hour to drag three wounded shipmates to the after escape compartment. By the light of my torch I gave them another noggin of rum each and had two myself. Liquor at least kept out the damp cold for the moment. The boat was leaking and would soon be flooded through-out. No time to waste. I shut the after water-tight door, isolating us in the stern compartment. I broke the seals of the four lockers and strapped the rubber escape sets on my companions. This device consists of a rubber lung, worn on the chest, a small bottle of high pressure oxygen across the stomach, a nose clip, goggles and a tightly fitting mouthpiece with adjustable rubber band around the neck, securing fairly comfortably. I soon had our sets in place. The atmosphere in this small space was becoming foul. I lowered the collapsible canvas trunk from a recess fitted around the escape hatch, and secured it by lashings to the deck. At the top of the trunk inside was the escape hatch, with four nuts holding four large clips securing the hatch firmly on the rubber seating joints all round the rim.

Reminding them of the drill, I found the valve in the most suitable position to flood the compartment from sea. I knew the water would rise around the escape trunk, leaving a small space of air considerably compressed. This would stop the water rising further. Then we would have to insert our mouthpieces, duck down under the water coming up into the trunk and then out into the open sea through the escape hatch. The first job was to open the hatch, then return to the compartment to see the lads out. I found the valve in starboard bilge, but the spindle was bent and immovable, we were trapped. If I could not move it, no one could. Was there an alternative?

If there was it had to be found quickly before we were all frozen to death. Torpedo tubes? Could I flood them into the compartment by opening the front and back doors? I pondered but decided that as the hydraulic tele-motor system had lost all pressure this would be impossible. What else then? The under water gun! That was it. Thank god we were in the compartment with the gun in position in the lowest part of the compartment. This was normally used to send smoke signals to the surface for instruction purposes. It had a four inch bore for rapid flooding. I knew the drill book advised us to avoid rapid flooding so we would have time to get used to the pressure gradually, but I had to chance it, we were waist deep now and the water was rising steadily, the only chance was to flood quickly, release the hatch and leave without a minute's delay. I splashed down to the gun and opened the breech, I tried the sluice valve gently and could feel the thrust of water entering. It increased to a steady whirl as the sea gushed in and then steadied, the air space round the hatch diminished rapidly. Here it came . . . the sea that would save us, drown us or freeze us to death.

Almost three hundred feet above, a strong wind was passing over a short choppy sea. As the water swirled around us almost chest high, a thick oily scum of paint spread itself across the dark swell in the small confined space. We still breathed this putrid air, slightly warmer from its own compression. I swiftly fitted my mouthpiece, settled on the nose clip and manipulated the needle valve on the oxygen bottle, flat across my stomach. I opened the mouthpiece cock and oxygen flowed into my lungs. Oxygen, the life saver, and at the same time, a killer. To breathe this gas under a pressure of fifteen atmospheres was risking oxygen poisoning in a matter of a few minutes.

Breathing painfully, I ducked down through the paint scum, groped for the bottom rim of the escape trunk, braced myself against the slippery angle of the deck and dragged myself upwards. Suddenly I found my head above water in the little pocket of air in the air lock below the hatch itself. I stretched out a hand and unscrewed the small vent cock in the centre of the steel lid. The air whistled out to sea above, the slimy water rose above my face. My teeth were chattering, I realised the oxygen would not give me long . . . I had much to do still. Using all my weight, I put my remaining strength on the tommy bar in the tube spanner to undo the dog nuts. Fortunately they were not corroded with salt and came away without difficulty. The vital moment came as the last nut dropped below me as I gave a mighty heave. The hatch flew wide open, a giant bubble of air escaped. I clung to the top rungs and rim of the hatch. I was free to ascend. I lost my mouthpiece, but managed to recover it and stuffed it back. Breath came again, and a few bubbles from the lung streamed upward.

The battle was almost won. I pulled myself back down, bobbed out from under the bottom of the trunk and poked my head into the foul air still trapped in the roof of the compartment. . . . My torch showed the other to be still breathing. . . . Quick now – first one bobbed down and out, next one, and a third, all gone. All now on their way to the surface, rising slowly through the freezing black water. Not too quickly or lungs would burst. I rubbed my goggles and dipped into the trunk for the last time. On coming out of the hatch, I felt overhead for the jumping wire, it had apparently snapped and fallen away. I flashed the torch around but was unable to see further than a few feet of rear casing steel deck, this was my last glimpse of the valiant *Perseus*.

I let go, the buoyant oxygen lifted me quickly upward. Suddenly I was alone in the middle of the great ocean with only a torch . . . that faithful steel torch . . . to make a friendly glimmer on the scene. The pain became frantic, my lungs and whole body were fit to burst apart. Agony made me dizzy. I realised I was coming up too quickly, so I unrolled the small apron and held it out in front of me, designed to act like a parachute in reverse. Theoretically, it was supposed to trap the water and slow the ascent, in fact all it did was to unbalance me and tip me head over heels.

I let go and became upright again. The torch illuminated dirty looking wires, one brushed close, I passed a large cylindrical object. Wires hanging from it were caught in the light of my torch. I tried to hold my breath, but felt like a balloon about to burst. Dear God! How long can I last? A prayer was a natural suffix. With the suddenness of certainty, I burst to the surface and wallowed in a slight swell with whitecaps here and there. Had I returned to the land of the living? But where was this land?

CHIEF STOKER JOHN H. CAPES BEM

There was no sign of any other survivors. Despite the injury to his buttocks, John Capes swam some five to six miles to the shore of Cephalonia, where Greek villagers, though at first suspicious that he was a German spy, gave him dry clothing and brought a doctor to treat him. During the next eighteen months, John Capes was hidden and well-cared for in different villages, at a considerable risk to the Greeks. Eventually, on 30 May 1943, he was taken down to a small bay where a caique came in and picked him up. Because of the extraordinary depth he seemed to have escaped from, and the distance he claimed to have swum, in the Mediterranean in December, there were those who doubted Capes' entire story, saying he could never have been in Perseus *at all, and must have fabricated his fantastic experience. But some years after the war, divers discovered the wreck of* Perseus, *with the after hatch still open, just as he had described it. Capes was awarded the BEM for his escape and subsequent adventures. He was a most unusual man, an ex-public school boy (he went to Dulwich College), who joined the Navy as a stoker. He retired from the Navy as a Chief Stoker in the 1950s.*

✻

Tempest (Lt.-Cdr. W. A. K. N. Cavaye) left Malta on 10 February 1942 for a patrol in the Gulf of Taranto. At 3 a.m. on 13th, while on the surface, she was jumped by the Italian torpedo-boat, Circe:

The Loss of *Tempest*

She had seen us and was coming straight at us – to ram.

It was a crash-dive. It had to be. We went down steeply and heard the thumping of his engines. He was on us. My stomach went cold.

Then I almost gasped with sudden intense relief as I heard the noise dying away again. He had missed us on the first pass.

Action always gave me an uneasy lurch in the pit of my stomach. I had it now all right. That destroyer was really going for us, no doubt about that. We were in for a very bad time.

It would be the first time for most of our green ship's company. Those kids must have had that sick feeling, that thumping heart I knew so well, but if they had they certainly did not show it as they went quietly and smoothly about their jobs like veterans. Of course, they didn't know what was coming. Being depth-charged is something which cannot be imagined. It is a terror which has to be experienced. Any minute now we were going to get it, and when we did it wouldn't be just the distant booming of a formal search. That Eyetie knew exactly where we were. There he is now – on top of us. My heart bumped as I watched the depth-gauge, sitting in my action station, at the after hydroplanes.

The captain gave an order.

'One hundred and fifty feet.'

I turned the wheel. Rapidly we gained depth. I thought that first pattern will be keeping us company.

I had my eyes on the pointer. It was passing fifty feet. We'd never do it. . . . The dial shook and the pointer danced before my eyes. There was a tremendous, gathering surge of clanging thunder . . . seat, wheel, hands, brain, dials, deck, bulkhead, deckhead, everything shook like an earthquake shock as if every atom in the ship's company were splitting. Then it was dark, nearly all the lights gave out. Instruments were shattered, wheels locked, glass tinkled over the deck.

We were still going down. I watched the pointer . . . 150 . . . 155 . . . 160 . . . 165. . . . We were out of control.

We fought her, second cox'n Burns and I. The pointer reached 350 feet. There, at last, we steadied her and managed to bring her back to 150 feet.

Swiftly the damage reports came in. Nearly all the instruments and lights throughout the boat had been put out of action. The fore hydroplanes and hydrophones were damaged beyond repair. Worst of all, one of the propeller shafts had shifted in its housing. That accounted for the loud continuous knocking sound we could hear. We had had trouble with this shaft before leaving England and it had been put right. Now the depth-charging had thrown it out of true again. The boat was trimmed at 150 feet and we maintained her level in the stop position with just the slightest movement of the motor or adjustment of the ballast. All ship's company not actually needed now were told to lie down at their station and to move as little as possible so as to conserve the limited oxygen supply in the boat and reduce telltale noise to try to cheat his hydrophones.

That was the only 'evasive action' we could take now. Asdics and hydrophones were out of action, so we had no means of finding the bearing of our attacker. We didn't know where he was coming from next and we couldn't dodge what he was throwing at us. We just had to sit and take what was coming – until he finished us off for good and all. I began to get that this can't be happening to me feeling. So many times I had seen shipmates and chummy ships go out and never return – just, unbelievably, cease to exist, as if atomised into nothing. Failed to return from patrol. That was the official phrase. Wives and mothers sat at home and heard it over the BBC. Now our wives and mothers were going to hear it . . . 'The Admiralty regret to announce that His Majesty's submarine *Tempest* has failed to return from patrol . . .' Now it was our turn.

But after the first pattern had done its worst my stomach settled down and we carried on as if all this were just a practice run. There were no more explosions for the moment. The moments lengthened and still we went free. After a little while the cook made some tea and cocoa, and this hot brew, with biscuits, was passed round the boat. It made us all feel a lot better, even though we could hear that destroyer's engines as he passed and re-passed above us, stalking us still, hour after hour.

But they dropped no more depth-charges. In fact by 7 a.m. we were beginning to have hopes that they had really lost us when we heard engines very close overhead once more and then another series of shattering crashes as a pattern went off right alongside us. After that they came again and again, dropping pattern on pattern and all of them so close you could smell them. Dazed and shaken and scared, we hung on and hoped against hope. You couldn't tell where he was coming from until you actually heard him.

The master gyroscope was smashed and we had to rely on our magnetic compass. One oil-fuel bulkhead connection in the control-room was damaged, and oil fuel poured into the boat. The chief stoker, George Spowart, and his men got to it quickly and soon stopped the flood. The electrical artificer, John Winrow, slaved to put the gyro right, but it was past all hope of repair and we had to give it up. The fore hydroplanes were out of action and the boat was being controlled for depth by the after planes.

We were at the mercy of that destroyer. At regular intervals we heard her rumble over us. We could hear the Asdic 'pinging' us, the sound wave stinging our quivering steel flanks like an invisible whiplash, but never knew exactly where she was. Each time she turned and came back to try again. Each run did more damage than the last.

For a time the submarine was kept under perfect control. Then the ring main shorted on the pressure hull, blowing the main fuses. This put the ballast pumps out of action. This meant that the compensating tanks and auxiliary tanks had to be trimmed by using our compressed-air supply, when air was priceless to us. The boat was forced down willy-nilly to 500 feet completely out of control. I was helpless on the planes. There wasn't a thing I could do to stop her.

The position was so desperate that we had to bring her to rest finally by trimming her on the main ballast tanks. To lighten the boat these main ballast tanks had to be trimmed either by venting the air into them, or blowing water out by means of compressed air. This was a far from satisfactory method of trimming and we were particularly reluctant to resort to it because it was very noisy at a time when silence was vital to give us any chance of surviving at all.

This started us on our way up again and to check the rate of rise we had quickly to flood the main ballast tanks again. All the time the sudden extra noise was playing right into the hands of our attacker. With deadly regularity she passed overhead, each time laying her eggs. They burst all round us as we sat and shook in the semi-darkness, with only the secondary lighting flickering palely like candles guttering in a dark tomb and the ship lurching and wallowing between 100 and 500 feet and things breaking loose and crashing about us. *Tempest* was a strong boat and she was withstanding a pounding that would have completely shattered a less well-found ship, but nevertheless the strain was beginning to show in the state of her machinery and on the faces and movements of her crew.

We went on steering blindly at any old depth between 100 and 500 feet. Bulkhead fixtures and spare parts were torn from their housing, and hurled across the narrow spaces. The boat was continually either bow up or bow down, and the angle was so acute at times that the bubble in the fore-and-aft spirit-level would disappear completely.

In the engine-room heavy spares like the big breech-ends from the diesels, each weighing half a ton, were sliding dangerously up and down the steel deck at each plunge and lurch. It was quite impossible to stop them, much less secure them again.

To make matters worse we were carrying a big load of extra spares for the submarines based at Alexandria – not to mention sack-loads of mail for the Fleet – and all these broke loose and started to smash about through the boat. All the time, as the relentless depth-charging went on, the always dim emergency lighting burned lower and lower until it was hardly more than a faint glow.

The position inside *Tempest* steadily worsened as more and more fittings were shaken loose. The earthings of the main electric cable against the hull increased the danger of fire and electrocution.

This hell went on until 10 a.m. Then, miraculously, unbelievably, there was a definite lull. We blinked, breathed again and looked around us to take stock of our position.

John Winrow, creeping through the submarine on the track of some electrical repair, accidentally kicked a bucket which clattered with a deafening noise along the deck.

'I'll have that man shot!' shouted the captain. It nearly made us jump out of our skins.

Then the attack began again. Again I thought this is not happening to me. I suppose many of us felt that. I know that no one, least of all the young submariners who had been civilians only a few months before, showed the slightest sign of panic or fear. They all behaved splendidly.

About 10.30 a.m. the battery securing boards showed signs of lifting. A closer inspection showed that salt-water had got into the battery compartment and several containers, with sulphuric acid in them were broken.

When salt-water and sulphuric acid mix they give off chlorine gas. That is the ultimate horror of all submariners.

The boat started to fill with it. One whole battery was flooded now. We had reached the end. The boat was just a pitch-dark, gas-filled shambles, flooding at the after end, with no instrument working except 'faithful Freddie' the magnetic compass. What use was a compass now? *Tempest* had nowhere to go any more, except to the bottom. At last, to save us from going with her, the captain decided to abandon ship.

Quietly the ship's company were told to put on Davis escape gear. Without any fuss everybody buckled the gear on. Then the order was passed for everyone except men at key positions needed to maintain the trim of the boat to muster in the control-room.

Then the captain gave the order 'Abandon ship'.

CHIEF PETTY OFFICER CHARLES ANSCOMB DSM BEM, *TEMPEST*'S
COXSWAIN

The submarine surfaced and the twenty-three survivors of a ship's company of sixty-two were picked up by the Italians.

*

In the first four months of 1942, the Luftwaffe's bombing offensive against Malta intensified. There were 263 raids in January, 236 in February, 275 in March and 282 in April. It reached the stage where submarines in Malta had to dive, and stay on the bottom of the harbour during daylight hours. The submarines which did not dive were bombed where they lay, as in

The Last Voyage of *Pandora*

Just before the completion of our refit at the submarine base at Portland, Maine, along with *Truant*, our skipper J. W. Linton was relieved by R. L. Alexander, 'Tubby' Linton taking over *Turbulent*. We left the U.S.A. but had to put in to Bermuda owing to the loss of lubricating oil. We left Bermuda and crossed the Atlantic to tie up alongside the *Maidstone* at Gib in March 1942. *Parthian* was also there but left on March 13–14. We loaded two of our fuel groups with petrol, ammunition and supplies, then left for Malta.

On the third day out something scraped along our starboard saddle tank – we were dived at the time. We arrived at Malta on April 1 and tied up at the jetty. Our skipper had gone ashore to make his report and we discharged our load of petrol. In the meantime, a number of our crew had gone over to the dockyard to stand by and unload the rest of our cargo. Speed was essential owing to the heavy air raids. We were going across the harbour on our motors and a number of us decided to have a breather on the casing.

Seven of us went up through the after hatch and there were eight on the bridge, including our engineer, Hickman. We were nearly across the harbour when an air raid started. We managed to tie up port side alongside the dockside.

The raid was now intense and everyone on shore had gone into the shelters. Someone in our bunch shouted that he was going down below (to dodge bomb splinters). As I was the first on the casing I was the last to go down when I noticed that no one was firing any gun from our bridge. By this time I could have almost hit a plane with a potato. I had reached the conning-tower casing and the last rungs to the bridge when we received a direct hit. Some soldiers on a gunsight stated that a flame shot up the conning tower like a blow torch and later it was stated that parts of the engine-room were found ashore in the dockyard. I don't remember anything after the explosion until I came to in St Patrick's Hospital at 0300. *Pandora* had been hit almost 12 hours earlier at 1345. I was lucky only to be suffering from shock and blast injuries to my left hand. I had been in the water but who fished me out and how I got to hospital I don't know. I tried to find out later but failed.

I joined the base at Manoel and joined working parties. One job we got was to get the 'tacks' and toilet out of *P39*, who had broken her back and was on a sand bar. At that time we lost *Upholder* and *Urge*. By a twist of fate quite a few of us took passage on the *Clyde* to Gibraltar. They had emptied one battery space for that purpose.

I've often wondered if any of the crew of the *Pandora* who were not on her when she was hit, took passage on the *Olympus* when she hit a mine. I had a chat with my mate Banjo Best, who was S.P.O. of *Olympus* just before they left Malta for Gib. He went down with her.

G. JENKINS

Pandora *was lost, with twenty-seven of her people. Her CO, 'Robbie' Alexander, happened to be ashore, being briefed about his next patrol, due to start that night, when she was bombed. In 1957, as a Captain, he commanded the destroyer* Solebay *and the 1st Destroyer Squadron, serving in the Mediterranean, where he was able to perform one last service for* Pandora *and the men who died in her. She had been raised, the bodies recovered and her hull beached as a total loss in 1943. In June 1957, when the shipbreakers' torches went to work on her, two skeletons were found in a small compartment where they had lain for fifteen years. Alexander read a prayer as the coffins of his two former shipmates were committed to the deep from the gun platform of the submarine* Tudor, *at sea off Malta on 1 July.*

*

In June, 1942, Rommel's Afrika Korps reached El Alamein, only seventy miles from Alexandria. This resulted in what became known as 'The Flap' – wholesale destruction of papers and equipment, and a mass evacuation ('flight' would be a better word) of personnel. Amongst the ships moved from Alexandria, to set up a new base at Haifa, was the submarine depot ship, HMS Medway. *Unlike many so-called 'depot ships', converted with varying degrees of success from other roles,* Medway *was specifically designed and built for her purpose. She was so successful that the sailors thought the*

Admiralty must have slipped up. Her loss, when she was torpedoed and sunk by U.372 off Port Said on 30 June 1942, was one of the most grievous blows to the Submarine Service of the whole war.

HMS *Medway*

The Submarine Service believed that *Medway* was the biggest mistake the Admiralty had ever made. Even today, a decade and a half after she was sunk by the enemy, she is still acclaimed as the most comfortable, easy to work, and accommodating parent-ship ever entered in the Navy List. She was, of course, built as a parent-ship and not converted. She knew what submariners wanted and how they liked to live – well – and she had the right sort of welcome for them when they returned to her.

She was genuinely thought of as 'Home'. There was a warmth about her sides that welcomed you as your boat nudged under her protection. The easy manner of her mess-decks (seamen and stokers were separated), the palatial space allotted to each submarine, the generous locker accommodation, the almost opulent washing and toilet facilities, and above all the tradition of 'submarines first' that was so often lacking in other depot ships: all went to make up perfection. When the sad news of the demise of 'Mother Medway' reached Blockhouse there was great sorrow. The lower deck knew that Admiralty would never make such a mistake twice; and, as one may still be told, they have been proved right.

C.E.T. WARREN AND JAMES BENSON

Early in her first commission in 1942, Sybil carried out a clandestine operation which gave her the nickname of

The 'Scarlet Pimpernel' Boat

She was built at Birkenhead by Cammell Lairds and when completed left on 12th August 1942 for the Clyde. We arrived at Holy Loch where we tied up alongside the depot ship H.M.S. *Forth*. For the next four weeks we carried out all the necessary trials and working up practices. On the 13th September, we left the *Forth* for our first shake-down patrol in the North Sea off the coast of Norway where it was hoped to find U-boats leaving and returning from patrol. This proved uneventful and we returned to Holy Loch on 26th September.

After 72 hours leave each watch we left Holy Loch on passage to Gibraltar in company with two other submarines. H.M.S. *Splendid* and H.M.S. *Unique* on 31st October. This proved a bit more eventful. On the 9th a U-boat was sighted too near to make a torpedo attack so an attempt to ram was made but the U-boat dived and we ran over the top of her. On the 10th we were in position off Ferrol to intercept a blockade runner that was due to leave. Just after 2130 hours she was sighted and we made a surface attack on her. This proved a bit hair-raising as two of our torpedoes started circling and we had to make a hurried dive which was just as well as one of them passed across the top of us. Needless to say, the blockade runner made a run for it and managed to avoid the other two submarines that were with us.

On 12th October, we left the patrol area for Gibraltar where we arrived on the 15th October and tied up alongside H.M.S. *Maidstone*. Unfortunately the *Unique* never made it. On the 15th November we left Gibraltar for a patrol area off Toulon arriving there on the 5th. This was with the company of other submarines, to keep an eye on the French Fleet in case it put to sea to interfere with the invasion of North Africa which was due to take place.

Within a few days on the 8th, we were ordered to a beach off Cap D'Antibes to pick up a party of General Giraud's staff. On arriving there we went within three hundred yards of the shore and then about 1220 hours a small boat was seen coming towards us. The skipper, Lieut. Turner, asked for the password and was surprised to hear a woman's voice answer 'They seek him here they seek him there, those Frenchies seek him everywhere. Is he in Heaven or is he in hell? that damned elusive Pimpernel!' She proved to be an Englishwoman married to a French Officer who had been picked up the day before with General Giraud by H.M.S. *Seraph* and was now on his way to Gibraltar.

In all we picked up six men and one woman, two men and another woman had been arrested a few hours earlier by the French police. We left straight away for Algiers arriving there on the 11th where we disembarked our honoured passengers.

LEADING STOKER BILL BRITTON

*

Round Trip

When the second stick of depth charges exploded around H.M. Submarine *Shark* off Skudesnes Fjord, south-west of Norway, on the evening of July 6, 1940, she floundered to the surface at an incredible angle. The lights were out, the starboard main motor was stopped, a fire was blazing behind it and water was pouring in through a leak. As the rudder was jammed hard-a-port, *Shark* could only go round in circles. A jury aerial was rigged and Lieut. Commander P. N. Buckley, R.N., sent off the message 'Unable to dive; 58-51 N 04-50 E; need assistance,' but he knew there was little hope of it reaching them in time.

After running submerged all day ready to surface and flash instant warning if a German invasion fleet sailed from Stavanger, *Shark* had been spotted by a German plane when she surfaced at 2230 to try to charge batteries. She had been seen all too clearly in the half light which persists during the summer months off Norway. For more than three hours the submariners fought back gallantly and even raised a cheer when one of their three-inch shells sent a Heinkel seaplane limping away with sparks shooting out of its tail, but then four ME109 fighters poured a hail of fire into the decks and conning tower. Two of the crew were killed and 19 others, including the captain, were wounded.

Fifteen minutes later the submarine ran out of ammunition and the captain, himself wounded in the head and leg, reluctantly decided to break off the action. The crew of the first seaplane to board the *Shark* were left stranded when their plane sank through a riddled float. While a second seaplane alighted and took off the captain, the First Lieutenant, Lieut, D. H. B. Barratt, R.N., completed scuttling preparations. When three armed trawlers arrived, took off the crew and the airmen, and tried to tow *Shark* away, she sank suddenly. Her bow hit the propeller of one of the trawlers and the vessel had to be towed back to base.

So Lieut. Commander Buckley, his officers and the crew of the *Shark* passed into German captivity. The submariners were at various camps. One was Engine Room Artificer (E.R.A.) Frederick William Edmond Hammond, R.N., who was determined to escape. In the spring of 1942 he was at Marlag Nord, Sandbostel, near Hamburg. Here he became friends with Donald Lister, a fellow E.R.A. from submarines and a kindred spirit. Hammond, short, thickset, neat and sharp-eyed, was known to everyone as Wally.

Lister, taller, stouter, easy going with a lively sense of humour, was universally known as Tubby. He had been a prisoner since May, 1940, from the submarine *Seal* which had hit a mine in the Kattegat after laying mines of her own and had lain on the seabed for many hours. She had struggled to the surface with a sick and exhausted crew and was further damaged by German planes while Lieut. Commander R. P. Lonsdale was trying to reach Sweden. With all her secret papers and gear destroyed, the partly flooded *Seal* had been boarded by the Germans but British and Germans soon abandoned the boat and left her to sink. Though heeled over far to port and heavily down by the stern, *Seal* stayed afloat and so just reached Denmark on the end of a German towline. The Germans repaired the boat but learned little from her and were never able to make much use of her.

In April, 1942, the two E.R.A.s tunnelled out of Sandbostel, but were caught at Hamburg. Sent to the fortress prison in Colditz Castle, south of Leipzig in Saxony (now East Germany), they got out of Oflag IVc by 'complaining' of being put in an officers' camp, and by getting the officers to complain of other ranks being put in with them. As other ranks the E.R.A.s agreed vaguely to 'work for Germany' and the gates of Colditz eventually opened. Meanwhile the very officers who had 'complained' forged identity papers, provided money and briefed the E.R.A.s with all available information. The escapers were to be Flemish diesel engineers working as collaborators in Germany. They were eventually to head for the Swiss border by a route followed by other Colditz escapers.

Transferred to Stalag VIIIb at Lamsdorf, near Breslau Gas Works, in Silesia, the escapers got an R.S.M. Sheriff to draft them to work in the gas works sidings. A Sergeant Brown obtained clothes, and enough food was found for the escapers to take with them. Leaving a dummy grave of coal slack in the yard, surmounted by a wooden cross marked 'Adolf R.I.P.', the escapers prepared to vanish into the night of December 12, 1942.

When a sentry appeared at the escape position, Hammond and Lister gave out that the escape was off, then volunteered to wash up the Sunday soup cauldrons in the wash house. Hiding their civilian clothes in the cauldrons they changed in the wash house and slipped out through the gas works manager's garden. In a suitcase and a briefcase they carried food, shaving gear, mending things and bottle of mixture for Hammond's smoker's cough.

They travelled by tram to Breslau station, then by train to join the Colditz escape route at Dresden, smoking meerschaum pipes and showing German cigarettes. They passed through all police checks quickly, except when one officer lingered over checking their papers 'because two prisoners had escaped'. Going via Nuremburg they continued to Ulm, accepting a drink from a German soldier along the way. They were diesel engineers called to Rottweil to repair an engine while they were returning to Belgium for Christmas. All travellers to Rottweil had to change trains at Tuttlingen, which was only 15 miles from the Swiss border.

Getting to Ulm on Tuesday night, they found there was no train until morning. There was sleet and rain, but the escapers could not stay in the railway station. After trying to walk about the countryside they got a room at a cheap hotel in Ulm. The only other language which the manager spoke was English so they 'understood a little bit of this,' and checked that the Rottweil train left at 10 a.m. After breakfasting on their own bread, margarine and sugar they could not resist pouring water into a German officer's jackboots standing outside another room. On the train to Tuttlingen they returned the stares of an inquisitive German woman until she got off the train in embarrassment.

Walking half a mile from Tuttlingen station at 4 p.m., they were stopped by a police patrol. The officer was not entirely satisfied by their story that they had left the station to stretch their legs and get a drink while waiting for the Rottweil train. While he searched their briefcase, wallets and pockets, they told him to phone the factory at Rottweil. Waiting pensively at a tavern while the officer phoned the factory, the escapers were blissfully relieved when someone confirmed the story! Perhaps whoever had answered the phone had been too busy to check.

Laughing and drinking with a stranger who told them a long incomprehensible story in Flemish, the E.R.A.s soon slipped out of the beer house, down the road and into a wood. Working their way towards the Swiss border by compass they lay up in woods during the day. Early next morning they pulled tiles off the low roof of a woodman's hut in a clearing and dropped inside. Hammond pulled the lock off the door and kept it shut with a piece of string. Lister cut knots out of wood for spy holes. Eating the rest of their food, they waited for dusk. They had a good all-round view in case they had to retreat in a hurry.

A road passed within half a mile of the border. Beyond the road was a marshy field of grass, then fields down to a wood, which was in Switzerland. Leaving five marks under the broken lock the escapers walked off into rising mist. They knew motor-cyclists patrolled the road. Following the railway line west they then tramped south alongside the wood until they heard traffic on the border road. Five miles west of Singen they lay down, checking patrols. They waited as a motor-cycle roared up the road, headlamp flashing. Three minutes later they crossed the road and plunged into the marshy grass. After tramping on for 25 minutes they knew they must almost be in Switzerland. 'Halt! Wer Da?' (Halt, who is there?) The sentry had glimpsed only a dark shadow. While Hammond showed himself in the beam of the torch, the taller Lister crept round the sentry. With Lister rising out of the darkness Hammond suddenly saw moonlight glinting on the Swiss Cross of a greatcoat button. He yelled 'No Tubby . . . he's Swiss.' Twisting the knife away Lister fell limply against the man. Laughing and joking they identified themselves and waited while the sentry shouted to a fellow soldier. At the village of Ramsden they swallowed hot Army soup then slept soundly under warm blankets. Later they held a great Christmas party with other escapers from Colditz.

The German occupation of southern France in November, 1942, disrupted arrangements for passing Allied escapers. While the E.R.A.s waited in Switzerland the London Gazette of May 11, 1942, announced the award of the British Empire Medal to them both 'for bravery and enterprise'.

When finally they left Switzerland, they were taken through France by the French Resistance, smuggled over the Pyrenees into Spain, and passed on to Gibraltar. So it was, some four years after leaving their submarine bases, that the two E.R.A.s returned to Britain. Other submariners got back to Britain before them, in exchanges of wounded and disabled prisoners, but Engine Room Artificers Hammond and Lister remain the only British submariners who ever broke out of German prison camps during the Second World War and actually got back to Britain.

*

Rum, Tobacco and Satisfaction

Our skipper was a heavy smoker. Normally in subs, there were no restrictions on smoking with the boat on the surface except for a period during charging of the batteries, and then only in certain places. Whilst dived, however, smoking was strictly taboo. With Bennington in *Porpoise*, and later in *Tally-ho*, he always allowed a smoke about noon and again just before surfacing at dusk. Word would be passed by Tannoy: 'One each apiece all round'. The air would become blue but very soon would be filtered through our lungs. Such a break was a Godsend and we blessed 'Old Benny' for his consideration. The highlight of the day was, of course, when we surfaced at dusk with an empty sea. We could breathe the cool air as it was dragged down the conning tower hatch by the main engines and we could light up and smoke at will. The rum store would be opened and the coxswain would serve out the rum issue – an eighth of a pint. Several of the junior lads had no taste for the stuff, which was probably just as well. To bottle it was a breach of naval regulations but this was more or less condoned in subs as being the lesser of two evils. On arrival in harbour this liquor would pay large dividends: repayment of debts, getting jobs done, etc. I'm afraid I never had any run to barter with. As a matter of fact, I more often than not had more than one tot per day. On more than one occasion after a severe depth-charge attack 'Benny' would say to the Cox'n 'What's the state of the rum jars, Cox'n?' Ginger Ridley would then report: 'Two jars cracked, sir, and will have to be written off'. This, of course meant an unofficial 'splicing of the main brace'. Benny could consume and hold large quantities of liquor at the right time and place but at sea there was strictly *no drinking* in the wardroom, except for a glass of sherry for some special celebration. Once aboard the Depot Ship, however, the officers were free to make whoopee, and did!

As for food, we always had a well stocked refrigerator. In the larger sub, before we went to sea, bags of spuds, oranges or any fruit available were stacked, mainly in the fore-ends. There were plenty of tinned foods. In fact, with a good cook, such as the one we had in *Porpoise* (Fred Crossley), we had very good menus. Of course, under the stresses and strains of our particular way of life, appetites were rarely hearty. One great problem was the shortage of drinking water. Any thoughts of a daily wash had to go by the board. Twice a day, I filled a milk tin with water. This was for cleaning the teeth and, after rinsing out the mouth, it was used to saturate a sweat rag which gave me a refreshing wipe down. Likewise, the cook could not be too fussy when preparing food. I remember settling down one night to a meal of rabbit, all nicely cooked. The Chief Stoker was praising the cook for the quality of the stuffing. The cook modestly accepted the praise. It turned out that the stuffing represented the last meal the rabbit had enjoyed on this earth, but it never lived to digest it! Most of us (all those served with a portion of the body), found that we had been served with stuffing.

Another problem was constipation. Apart from the lack of normal exercise to keep the bowels 'regular' there was always a reluctance to use the 'heads' in a sub, as the effect of a blow-back could be very unpleasant. In a large sub there were usually four heads – one for the officers, one for the Chiefs and POs and one each for the seamen and engine room ratings. In the up-to-date boats, these tiny compartments were about the size of a sentry box. In the H & L Class subs there was no privacy at all, and the seat was established between the diesel engines and, during his session on the 'throne' the patient would most likely be disturbed many times to allow one of the crew to get past. In the more up-to-date L class, the 'throne' was still among the engines but not directly in the gangway. In the later boats, however, there were these tiny cubicles with a door and a grill at the bottom so one could tell at a glance whether it was occupied or not. Before using the heads at sea, permission had to be obtained from the OOW. The need for this in war time will, of course, be obvious as the discharge was blown out of the boat by high pressure air which gave rise to bubbles on the surface. Inside this tiny compartment (measuring only thirty inches by twenty-four inches), the main furniture was a shallow pan with the usual baker-lite seat and flap. (It was always a mystery why the pan was so shallow. It was certainly a hazard for the hanging members of the anatomy). At the bottom of the pan was a water tight flap and, below that, a tank which would hold about one and a half gallons. Above the seat were pressure gauges, valves and an air bottle. By the side of the seat was a lever about eighteen inches long with a handle. This was held in the rest position by a flap. The operation of the system was as follows: The patient would ask the OOW for permission to use the heads. This being granted, he being a wise and experienced person, would check that the previous occupant of the cubicle had left everything as it should have been left. Having entered the cubicle and used the seat and the pan in the normal manner, he would then lower the flap on the seat. He would then open two valves (one, a non-return type) which connected the tank under the pan to the pressure hull and the sea. The next operation was to charge the air bottle with high pressure air so that the pressure in the bottle was about two or three pounds per square inch greater than the external sea pressure. Next, the operator, being experienced, would leave the flap on top of the seat and place his foot upon it. The next move was to grasp the operating lever (having released the retaining flap) and move the lever down to the first position. This opened the flap at the bottom of the pan. It was this movement which could be disastrous for, if the previous user had *not* carried out the proper procedure and vented the air pressure, the contents of the pan would be blown back inboard when the flap at the bottom of the pan was opened. Hence the reason for placing the foot on top of the seat cover! The lever was then moved to the second position. This allowed sea water to flush the contents of the pan into the tank. The lever was then moved to the third position. This movement shut the flap at the bottom of the pan and admitted high pressure air to blow the contents of the tank overboard. The next movement of the lever, to the fourth position, vented the air from the tank. *This was most important*, as any air left in the tank would cause a blow-back for the next user. The lever was then returned to the central position and the operation was completed.

CHIEF TORPEDO GUNNER'S MATE JOE BRIGHTON DSM AND BAR

Taurus Versus Bulgars on Horseback

One patrol in 1943 we found ourselves in the North Aegean near the Greek-Bulgarian frontier, not far from the Dardanelles. We decided to have a look at a small port called Neo Playa which we entered on the surface as it was much too shallow to dive. The harbour was full and our trusty gun-layer Ldg. Sea. Starbuck soon sank half a dozen ships. (We always called them 'ships' if they were not actually rowing). The range was very short and Starbuck could put a row of hits along the water-line without much trouble. The Gunnery Officer, Lieut. Gibson, R.N.V.R. gave the usual spotting orders – 'Up 200, Right 4, Down 100' etc. but I don't think his contribution was very effective. I'm almost sure I heard Starbuck say 'Why don't you shut up'.

We had almost completed sending the local merchant navy to permanent diving stations when we were surprised to hear a clatter of hooves. Coming down the mountainside in a cloud of dust was a squadron of cavalry in dress uniform with pennons flying and lances at the ready. When they reached the quayside the Bulgarian Life Guards, for such they were, unloaded Point 5 machine-guns from the animals' backsides and opened fire, much to our consternation. Soon the air was full of flying lead making those 'Whipp' noises which means they have missed you.

At the charge of the Light Brigade Lord Cardigan found himself alone and surrounded by Russians who attacked him fiercely. In his memoirs he writes 'It being no part of the duties of a General to cross swords with private soldiers, I turned my horse and left the battlefield.'

It occurred to me that it was no part of the duty of a submarine to fight with horsed cavalry, so I turned sea-ward and rang down full speed.

Abaft the bridge on the T-class there was a 20mm. Oerlikon, which had been firing steadily at the Household Cavalry. (This was one of the few occasions when this quick-firing gun did not jamb after a few rounds).

But suddenly our firing ceased. I was surprised to see our Oerlikon gunner coming forward on to the bridge. I asked him what he was doing and he replied 'I am wounded and I am going to see the Coxswain'. I pointed out that he was not wounded very badly and one wasn't supposed to leave one's gun in the middle of a battle. He insisted that he was entitled to have his wound dressed.

There was some surprise when he arrived in the control-room and I am told that the comments of the crew were critical to say the least of it.

By this time we had sustained a number of half-inch holes in the upperworks. Personally I was all right as I was standing behind the forward periscope. The OOW, Lieut. Gibson, who was slimmer than me was sheltering behind the after periscope. I told him to take over the Oerlikon. With no more protest than 'Who *me*, sir?' he took his seat at the gun. Taking careful aim he put half a pan into the first floor windows of the Grand Hotel. Soon we were out of range of the horsemen and when we were in deep enough water we dived.

It was my custom after a successful action to take a day's holiday at 100 feet. This appeared in the log as 'Continued patrol, nothing sighted.' It also gave time for our knees to stop knocking together. The coxswain had his own ritual. 'Complaints about rum again, Sir. I think you ought to taste it.' A couple of inches of 'neaters' tasted pretty good to me.

But what, you will ask, about our wounded gunner? He certainly had a bullet in his foot, so the first thing to do was to inspect the damage which we did on the wardroom table. The lad was in some pain and the coxswain had already given him a tot. I suggested that he should have another one, and that the operating team should have one too to steady their nerves at this testing time.

The medical kit supplied to H.M.S./Ms contains a number of lancets and scalpels, also a saw similar to, but rather smaller than that on view in H.M.S. *Victory*. I hacked away at the foot but the knives were extremely blunt and would not cut the flesh satisfactorily. Sterner measures were clearly necessary so I got a Gillette razor blade (a new one, of course – nothing unhygienic about *Taurus*) and made a series of longitudinal cuts down the foot avoiding the metatarsal bones as far as possible. We got the bullet out in the end with a pair of pliers and bound up the wound with an ample dose of M & B 293, now known as penicillin.

The patient was by now making loud protests as the rum had not completely dulled his senses. He was also worried by what his messmates were saying. 'Left your gun in action', 'Cowardice in the face of the enemy' and 'I expect the Captain will shoot you in the morning' were some of their remarks.

We put him in his bunk and I had some discussion with the coxswain as to the proper course of action. He was in favour of a Court Martial quoting the case of Dunbar-Nasmith in the Dardanelles in 1915 who had in fact condemned a man to death for some dereliction of duty. 'You put the prisoner on the casing in front of the gun-platform and then have four men with rifles only one of which has a live bullet in it, the rest are blank. So nobody knows who fires the fatal shot'.

We decided to defer a decision till morning. One poor wounded man had a bad night and was much taunted by the crew with blood-curdling accounts of the fate in store for him. In fact he was in such a state of nerves that we all decided that he had had enough. The coxswain told him he was lucky and the Captain had decided to spare his life.

We eventually got him to hospital where he made a good recovery, but the doctor said that it was a curious wound. He couldn't understand how the man got all those long cuts down his foot.

Much of our time in the Aegean was spent in sinking caiques. These picturesque vessels were used for shipping stores to the enemy garrisons on the different islands and were usually under sail. They were legitimate targets but it was disagreeable work. We sank one once off Mitylene which according to the chart was 'formerly Lesbos'. We took three of the crew on board and set course for our base. I made the usual 'requirements on arrival' signal concluding with 'Request accommodation for three Lesbian survivors'.

CAPTAIN M. R. G. WINGFIELD DSO DSC* RN

*

Submarine Sketches

The doctor had run over me, the ear specialist and the X-ray expert had all had their turn, I was ready for the tank where all the submariners learn how to escape.

A happy, husky chief petty officer took me in charge and gave me a lecture on DSEA – Davis Submarine Escape Apparatus. Valve locks and other gadgets were all taken down and explained in a most thorough way, occasionally interrupted by the annoying phone that insisted on breaking in and destroying the continuity of the memorising.

Suddenly, to my horror, the chief said 'Right, sir! We have just time to try you out before lunch.'

With very mixed emotions I undressed and got into a pair of swimming trunks. The set was strapped across my chest and I lowered myself into the tank. When the outlet valve got below water I turned it on and took another step down.

With the rubber mouthpiece between my lips, the nose clip on, water trickling into my goggles, and the set around my chest – not to mention the business of breathing oxygen through the mouth – I realised with some shock my utter dependence on the apparatus.

Down the iron steps I went, pausing opposite a notice marked 'Clear Your Ears'. Obediently I squeezed my nose and with the other hand gripped the air tube, blowing meanwhile, to put inside pressure on the ear drums, which by now, were becoming very heavy. All this accomplished, I reached the bottom, where my instructor was waiting to make sure all was well.

It was a weird feeling, standing just off the bottom, learning to regulate the flow of oxygen in sufficient quantities to keep down and not shoot to the surface – the slightest misjudgement would send one shooting ignominiously up.

Then on the signal, I switched on the air supply, and with my hands crossed behind my back, shot up to the surface, where the temptation to swim was quickly checked by the instructor, who ordered, 'Lie on your back and let the set take charge'.

I let in more air until some began to escape through the outlet valve, then switched off. Blowing hard on my mouthpiece I put more air into the buoyancy bag and found myself floating nicely on my back. Taking care to switch off the mouthpiece lever and clearing myself of oxygen, I at last took the mouthpiece off, and breathed fresh air with a sigh of relief.

After lunch came the actual escape routine, when for the first time I was to realise what it felt to be imprisoned under water.

In all my life I had never known such fear. The strong, almost overwhelming desire to pull off the set and strike out, was only kept in check by the knowledge that I was bottled up in a flooded iron submarine chamber and utterly dependent on keeping my head and following implicitly the instructions I had received. I got in through a round safe-like door, then the water was flooded in and the door closed. The level rose higher and higher and at last reached my chest, then I had to switch on the outlet valve and give the 'Thumbs up' signal as the level of water passed my eyes. Soft green light flooded through the port and the noise of flowing water drummed on my ears. Soon the pressure became offensive to my ear drums and water seemed to be dribbling between my lips and down the air pipe. I did not realise that I had forgotten to keep the bag supplied with air, and felt my last second had come.

I tried to steady myself, but water still came in and a dreadful surge of panic to add to all my other unpleasant sensations was rushing up inside me. I tried to remember all the instructions, but there had been so many. Then on a last hope, I accidentally did the right thing – though I did not know it even then: I gave more air to the bag. Now, instead of water getting in, air bubbled out, which was equally alarming to me in my ignorance of the apparatus.

It was a dreadful moment. I felt I was completely helpless in a flooded tank with all bulkheads closed, entirely dependent on myself – I did not learn until later, that the instructor could have emptied the chamber in a few seconds. I was biting the mouthpiece and had stopped breathing for a second or two which seemed like aeons of time. But at long last things straightened themselves out and a lever clanged at my feet – a reminder for me to pull it and open the hatch above my head.

I let in more air and, with my arms above me, felt for the escape hatch which was heavy and would not at first yield. Putting more pressure, I felt it give slowly. At last it opened and fell back with a clang and I shot through to the surface.

The sensation of escape was indescribable. For the first time in my life I had felt trapped. In the back of my mind the thought, 'You're finished, you really are drowning,' had surged forward in spite of all my efforts to be calm. In those few minutes I knew exactly what death below water was like; the past did not come racing forward to entertain me, there was only the stark present. I cursed myself alternately for going into this thing and for being so easily panicked. Never in so short a space of time have I said so many contradictory things to myself as I did at the bottom of that tank. There seemed to be two very forceful characters inside my brain, one driving me on to do the right thing and the other like some little black dog, snapping and tearing at the little morale I had left.

The feeling of panic had so completely gripped me, that I couldn't remember what I had done below. Spluttering breathlessly I pushed my goggles off and looked up into the faces of my instructors, now leaning calmly over the small iron rail. They were almost in darkness against the bright sunlight that shone through the great glass dome above.

What a lovely feeling to be back in a world of humans again! And then the thought, 'I wonder if they had seen how scared I had been?'

The instructor's 'All right, sir?' jarred on my throbbing ear drums. I nodded. 'Carry on down again, sir.' And down I went again below the surface.

'Keep calm you fool,' I kept telling myself. 'Keep calm!' As I reached the hatch, water again came in through my mouthpiece, but thoughts of fear crushed in on me again, and I flashed back to the surface. It was no good: my nerves were getting the better of me.

Up in God's good air I took off the mouthpiece and got to grips with myself. This would not do at all.

'What's up, sir?' asked the instructor.

In a choked sort of voice I said, 'How do you stop the water leaking down the ruddy pipe?' He told me and down I went once more. But immediately an indescribable dreadful fear took hold and everything seemed to be going round. His last words had been,

'Remember your drill sir! You did all right this morning. This is just the same.'

As I reached the hatch, 'Remember your drill! Remember your drill!' seemed to keep time with my beating eardrums.

I pulled myself through and heard the trap door clang shut above me. New directions were chalked up on a slate and held outside the tank, in front of the glass. But now there was another complication – my goggles had misted up and flooded. I thought back over his instructions. There were several handles and wheels to turn; the outlet valve had to be opened and the compressed air lever switched on. What next? What a fool I was.

In what order I carried out the drill, I do not know, but the pressure became terrific and my head felt as if it would explode, added to which, the nose of air being forced out and the continuous hissing made me feel that at any moment my eardrums would give out. What *was* happening? What should I do next? Suddenly I found that all was well. The water level sank to my chest, and I took my mouthpiece off when it fell below the entrance door. When I switched off and turned the flood shut, pressure on the equalising cock gradually lessened, the hissing stopped and the door opened; I was back in my own element again and relief was intense.

Psychologically, this had been an awful business for me – my first real encounter with fear. I'd always been at home in the water; in fact I could swim almost as soon as I could walk. I had been buffeted about by formidable Pacific surf before I was a yard high; I had been dared to swim in a dark deep mountain pool in Java, among the unpleasant goggle-eyed carp of pugnacious mien, when not much bigger than they; and had shot on a banana leaf down the sliding rock of an almost perpendicular waterfall in a Malayan jungle, not much later. And of course, there had been other thrills in various countries, which had all given me some heart beat, but those qualms had been exhilarating – I had known I could be saved if anything went wrong.

Down in the submarine tank with hatch closed, I was alone, shut in and entirely dependent on, not only doing the right thing in the right way at the right moment, but on a number of very urgent things that were indispensable to the smooth running of the apparatus – and to my very breathing. There were many exigent gadgets that demanded a cool head.

The awful sensation of claustrophobia that seemed to take charge of my senses – clouding my power of thought and making my heart beat heavily – as soon as the trap door shut me in, was overwhelming and had to be mastered. I knew at once that if I did not go through the whole ruddy business again, I never would. I had reached a crossroads with myself and knew with absolute certainty that if I did not take charge of my mental forces, and master my panic once and for all, I was lost and would have to get out of submarines.

'Do you mind if I do it once more, chief?' I asked. 'See if I can't do it without a muck-up this time.'

'O.K., sir,' he answered. 'But you don't *have* to you know!'

But I knew better – so down I went again and all went well that time. I now knew my stuff. I felt a changed person when I went in to dinner that night.

LIEUT. HENTY HENTY-CREER RNVR

*

The German battleship Tirpitz, *lurking in her northern Norwegian fjord, affected the movements of Allied warships all over the world, merely by her existence. Several attempts were made to sink or disable her, all unsuccessful until the attack by X-craft midget submarines in September 1943. X-craft were fifty-one feet long, and weighed thirty-five tons. They could make about six-and-a-half knots on the surface, and five knots dived, and could dive to 300 feet. Their operational range was limited by the physical endurance of their crews, of three officers and one engine-room artificer (ERA). Their weapons consisted of two detachable charges, each containing two tons of explosive, which could be dropped on the sea-bed under the target and then fired by clockwork time-fuses.*

Six X-craft were built and two crews – a 'passage' crew and an operational crew – were specially trained for each craft. For this attack – Operation 'Source' – they were allocated targets: X5 (Lieutenant H. Henty-Creer RNVR), X6 (Lieutenant D. Cameron RNR) and X7 (Lieutenant B. C. G. Place RN) – Tirpitz, in Kaafjord; X9 and X10 (Lieutenant K. R. Hudspeth RANVR) – Scharnhorst, also in Kaafjord; X8 – Lutzow, in Langefjord. The X-craft left their depot ship HMS Bonaventure *in Loch Cairnbawn on 11th September 1943, and were towed by 'orthodox' submarines to their slipping points off the Norwegian coast. X9 (Sub-Lieutenant E. Kearon RNVR) was lost with all hands on passage, and X8 (Lieutenant B. M. MacFarlane RAN) had to be scuttled because of defects. X7's captain describes*

The Midget Attack on *Tirpitz*

On the evening of the 18th, although the weather left much to be desired, we decided to change crews. The actual change-over was satisfactory, but when *Stubborn* got under way again it seemed to me, on the casing of X7, that the tow was extremely long – it was, it had parted again. We only had two rope tows with us, so we were forced to use the last resort, a two-and-a-half inch wire. It was no joke securing this in the sea conditions that prevailed, and Bill

Whittam* and I – secured by lines to the boat against being washed overboard – spent three exhausting hours on the casing before X7 was finally in tow again. We were neither of us dry nor in good humour when we went below, but the orderliness within was a delight to be seen. One would hardly have known that three men had spent a week in this confined space, and the mechanical efficiency of the machinery was in keeping – the passage crew could not have done their job better.

The next day was a lazy one – on these occasions the human being seems to develop an almost infinite capacity for sleep, uncomfortable as his bed may be.

The only excitement before we slipped was Minerva. By that night, the 19th, we were within twenty miles of the slipping position and the weather had cleared completely. X7 was on the surface and charging to full capacity. Bill Whittam was keeping a lookout through the night periscope and the rest of us were having supper.

'*Stubborn*'s flashing and there is something bumping up against the bow' he announced. I looked through the periscope. There was something bumping against the bow, but I couldn't make out what.

'I'll go and have a look,' I said, and Bill went back to the periscope. 'You'd better hurry – it's a mine.'

I did. It was a German one, whose broken mooring had half-hitched itself round the tow and come to rest against X7's bow. I noticed it was painted green and black, that it was obviously freshly laid and that one horn had already been broken, but I didn't wait to examine it closely; keeping it off with my foot gingerly placed on its shell I loosed its mooring wire from the tow and breathed more deeply as it floated astern.

When I got below I thought a tot wouldn't do us any harm, so

---

* Lieutenant L. B. Whittam RNVR

we toasted the Geneva Convention and Minerva – the mine with the crumpled horn.

The night of the 20th was beautifully calm with only a gentle swell from the west. We slipped at 2000, exchanged a few comments on this and that with *Stubborn* and set course for Stjernsund. During the night we saw one other X-craft, I think X5, but otherwise nothing. The internal exhaust pipe from the engine split just before dawn, so the fumes had to be extracted by the air compressor and X7 dived, rather later than had been intended, at 0145. At 0230 we came up to periscope depth and were able to identify the entrance to Stjernsund. (Times in this narrative are GMT – the sun rising at about 0200 and setting at 1900).

The day, calm and peaceful, was spent mostly at ninety feet, coming to periscope depth to fix our position every hour or so. In Stjernsund the water was like a sheet of turquoise stained glass, the steep sides of the fjord luxurious in browns and greens emphasised by the bright sunlight and the Norwegian fishing-boats, picturesque enough for even the most blasé traveller. There were occasional patches of snow on the higher ground, but the water – clear as a mountain stream – did not appear to be very cold.

At 1230 we entered Altenfjord proper, where there was sufficient lop on the surface to allow us to raise the induction trunk and release the excess of pressure within the boat that five hours with the oxygen switched on had caused.

At 1945 we surfaced, and Whitley* immediately started to fit the spare for the broken section of the exhaust-pipe – regrettably without success; however, canvas bandages and spun yarn made the fracture reasonably gas-tight and the charge was started about an hour after surfacing. The boat was cleaned up generally and empty tins, used protosorb and the used oxygen bottles were thrown overboard.

* E. R. A. Whitley

Rafsbotm itself was the anchorage for German fleet auxiliaries, so the charge and the tidying up had to be stopped for short periods from time to time when small craft appeared to be leading our way and it was thought wiser to dive out of sight, but the weather was in our favour – overcast and enough wind to cover the noise of our engine. Not long after the charge had been started searchlights and starshell were seen to the northward, near the top of Altenfjord – at first it was feared that an X-craft had been located, but it was probably the *Scharnhorst* on night exercises. (She had been sighted anchored south of Arnöy Island when we went by that afternoon: a sitting target, but we were after larger fish.)

At 0100 on the 22nd the charge was stopped, the few engine fumes that had escaped extracted by the compressor, and X7 dived to make her way for the entrance of Kaafjord.

Before 0400 the gap in the anti-submarine nets at the entrance had been located (it was over a hundred yards wide and had no way of shutting it) but we waited for a minesweeper to come out before entering – her ensign was the first I had seen worn by an enemy ship in commission. To avoid any close watch there might be at the entrance (the day was calm and clear with only a slight surface ruffle) X7 entered at forty feet, but on coming to periscope depth inside had to be taken down again immediately to avoid a small motor-boat. Somewhat uncertain of our position relative to the ships and net defences inside, X7 was brought up again as soon as seemed reasonable, but at thirty feet the boat ran into an anti-torpedo net – the water was clear enough to see it and it appeared as the most formidable-looking underwater defence I had seen. The wire of which it was constructed was thin, not more than an inch in circumference, but was meshed into squares less than six inches across and there seemed to be at least two such thicknesses, presenting a baffling jazz pattern to the observer. X7 was stuck, she did not 'fall out' when the motor was stopped, nor when the slow astern speeds were tried. (High speeds were considered unwise lest the disturbance of the buoys on the surface betray our presence.) The internal tanks were flooded in the hope that the boat would 'fall out' with the increased weight but this had no effect and the pump was run to get back to normal trim. After ten minutes it was apparent that this pump was not sucking out any water. We tried the other pump, with almost laughable results – there was a single spark from the commutator casing of its motor but other wise no movement. No. 2 main ballast was blown right out but X7 did not float out of the net. Finally, all main ballast tanks were blown, and the main motor run for two minutes full ahead and then put full astern, so that X7 could gather as much way as the slack in the nets would allow. She came clear – all main ballast tanks were vented but the boat did break surface before going to the bottom like a stone, more than half a ton heavy. We thought this escapade would be certain to invoke some attention even if we ourselves had not been seen. I felt they could not fail to notice the bubbles from the vented main ballast tanks.

We waited on the bottom for about twenty minutes to give the gyro a chance to steady (we had already been an hour in the net) then blew No. 2 main ballast tank gently – when it was right we still had not left the bottom and I noticed that a large wire (presumably a wire securing the nets we had recently been in) was across our periscope standard. However, a burst of full speed and a little air in 1 and 3 was enough to clear us, and we immediately left that unpleasant spot.

Trimming by air was not easy in these craft, but without pumps there was no choice. When we left the bottom this time we did, admittedly, break surface for a second or two, but subsequently Whittam managed it perfectly, using Q and 2MB for bodily weight and moving Aitken* (who, unfortunate individual, had no job during an attack).

---

* Sub-Lieutenant R. Aitken RNVR

At 0640, when X7 was close to the northward of a tanker of the *Altmark*-class, the *Tirpitz* was sighted for the first time at a range of about a mile.

My intention for the attack was to go deep at a range of 500 yards, pass under the anti-torpedo nets at seventy feet and run down the length of the target from bow to stern, letting go one charge under the bridge, the other well aft and altering to port to escape under the nets of the *Tirpitz*'s starboard side.

At 0705 X7 was taken to seventy feet for the attack but stuck in the net instead of passing underneath. This time I had no intention of staying there. By similar tactics to those that extricated us before, but without breaking surface, we came out and tried again at ninety feet, this time getting more firmly stuck. On occasions when the craft is being navigated blind, it is extremely difficult to know one's position to within a hundred yards – in this case the *Tirpitz*, the nets and the shore were all within a circle of that diameter, and the gyro had again gone off the board with the excessive angles the boat had taken. Thus when X7 next came clear and started rising, the motor was stopped lest she run up the beach or on to the top of the nets and fall into enemy hands. When she broke surface I saw we were inside the close-net defences (how we got underneath, I have no idea) about thirty yards from the *Tirpitz*'s port beam – 'group up, full ahead, forty feet'.

We actually hit the target's side obliquely at twenty feet and slid underneath, swinging our fore-and-aft line to the line of her keel. The first charge was let go – as I estimated, under the *Tirpitz*'s bridge – and X7 was taken about 200 feet astern to drop the other charge under the after turrets. The time was 0720. It was just as we were letting go the second charge that we heard the first signs of enemy counter-attack – but oddly enough, we were wrong in assuming they were meant for us.

In X7 we had to guess a course that we hoped would take us

back to that lucky spot where we had got under the nets on our way in; but we were not lucky. We tried many places within a few feet of the bottom, but in vain, and rapidly lost all sense of our exact position. The gyro was still chasing its tail and the magnetic compass could not be raised for fear it foul some wire or a portion of a net; we did use the course indicator (a form of compass that remains steady during alterations of course but does indicate true position) but the noise it made was most tiresome so we switched it off again.

The next three-quarters of an hour were very trying; exactly what track X7 made I have no idea, but we tried most places along the bottom of those nets, passing under the *Tirpitz* again more than once, and even breaking surface at times, but nowhere could we find a way out. We had to blow each time we got into the nets and the HP air was getting down to a dangerously low level – but bull-in-a-china-shop tactics were essential as our charges had been set with only an hour's delay – and those of others might go up at any time after eight o'clock. The small charges that were periodically dropped by the Germans were not likely to do us any harm and, when we were on the surface, no guns larger than light automatic weapons which caused no damage could be brought to bear – but we were sceptical about our chances against at least four tons of torpex exploding within a hundred yards. But the luck that had recently deserted us came back for a few minutes shortly after eight. We came to the surface – an original method, but we were halfway across before I realised what was happening. On the other side we dived to the bottom and at once started to get under way again to put as much distance as possible between us and the coming explosion. Sticking again in a net at sixty feet was the limit, as this confounded my estimate of our position relative to the nets. But we were not here long before the explosion came – a continuous roar that seemed to last whole minutes. The damage it caused X7 was really surprisingly small – depth-gauges, trimming bubble and some lights broken; considerable but no catastrophic leaks at most hull glands; the gyro spinning with almost the speed of its rotor – but the hull was still complete. An incidental effect of the explosion was to shake us out of the net, so we sat at the bottom to review our position. We had no pumps that would work; the HP air bottles were empty, but internal venting where possible had increased the air pressure within the boat and the compressor was still working. The leaks were not immediately dangerous, but, as we had no way of pumping them out, we could not afford to delay. So we set off again, aiming at taking advantage of the confusion to get a good check on our position (I was not really certain we were even out of the nets) and then lying up and refitting on the bottom in shallow water. Nos. 1 and 3 MB tanks had to be blown to get us off bottom and with air in these open-bottom tanks, depth-keeping was impossible – we could choose only between surface and bottom. Nor was I correct in thinking we would be able to fix our position when we were on the surface (it was provoking to see the *Tirpitz* still on the surface, but that was about all that could be seen). We did another of these hops to the surface and this time the night periscope was hit; as it was probable we had only enough air for one more surface and there was no chance of getting away, we decided to abandon ship. DSEA escape was considered, but we were not keen to risk depth-charges that were being dropped, so it was decided to try a surface surrender first. If firing did not stop at the showing of a white sweater, we could always try DSEA from the bottom after a delay to allow enemy activity to die down.

X7 was surfaced and I gingerly, I must confess, opened the fore hatch just enough to allow the waving of a white sweater. Firing did immediately stop, so I came outside and waved the sweater more vigorously.

The Germans had put a battle-practise target some 500 yards off the starboard bow of the *Tirpitz* – probably an attempt to obscure other attacking craft's view of their target – and X7 hit this just after I came on the casing, with her extremely low buoyancy forward – one main ballast tank had presumably been hit – the curved side of this was sufficient to force the bow down so that water went into the wet-and-dry before I could shut the hatch. From Aitken's description this was probably not more than thirty gallons, but it was sufficient to send X7 to the bottom again – I was left on the battle-practise target.

From Aitken's description of subsequent events inside X7 it is clear that Whittam managed everything with great calm and skill. A DSEA escape was planned and a certain amount of wrecking of more secret machinery carried out. They waited more than an hour and then decided to make their escape. From this depth – 120 feet – the oxygen in a DSEA set lasts very little time, so it is imperative that the boat is flooded as quickly as possible until the pressure within is the same as that outside and the hatches can be opened; also those escaping must breathe the air in the boat until the batteries are flooded and the air foul with gas. In this case the drill was perfect, but only one small hull valve can be opened for the flooding up – all others were tried and why they had jammed is impossible to say – perhaps the explosion was the cause. Thus it was that only Aitken managed to conserve his oxygen long enough for a successful escape – he gave the other two their emergency supply when they had already lost consciousness but they did not revive, and Aitken himself was picked up on the surface in a coma-tose condition.

I can only voice my disappointment that all my crew were not successful at this last hazard. When X7 went down I thought they would be, but perhaps we had already had more than our fair share of naturals. Whittam – six foot five of English public school with stories as tall as himself; Whitley – older than any of us, a gay lad whose father was waiting for him to take over his engineering works in the Midlands.

For my own part I felt ridiculous walking on to the quarter-deck of a Fleet flagship wearing vest, pants, sea-boot stockings and army boots size twelve. When I was told that I would be shot if I did not state where I had laid my mines (this much, at least, they now knew by sunrise) I stated I was an English naval officer and as such demanded the courtesy entitled to my rank. (I didn't say what rank – I had a fleeting vision of Gabby, the town crier in Max Fleischer's cartoon of *Gulliver's Travels*, shouting, 'You can't do this to me, you can't do this to me – I've a wife and kids, millions of kids.')

CAPTAIN GODFREY PLACE VC DSC VM RN

Charges from X6 *and* X7 *exploded at 0800 on 22nd damaging* Tirpitz *so badly she was unable to move from her anchorage until April 1944; she was finally destroyed by RAF bombers at Tromso in November. Nothing definite was ever seen nor heard of* X5 *after the author's sighting on the evening of the 20th.* X10's *target* Scharnhorst *had left her anchorage; after many defects and delays,* X10 *eventually abandoned the operation and was picked up in tow by HMS/M* Stubborn *on 28th. The author and Cameron were both awarded the Victoria Cross.*

*

The experience of being stuck on the seabed was one that any submariner could have done without. It carried its own special fears. In May 1944, the newly-refitted Seraph *left Chatham for routine diving trials in the Western Approaches. On arrival, early on May 14, she signalled goodbye to her trawler escort and dived to carry out trials and tests in preparation for her third operational commission.*

At the sacred hour of eleven, tot time, in the Royal Navy, I was in the Tiffies' [Artificers] mess waiting for our stoker messman to pour out my tot when the boat suddenly took a nose down angle which became more and more pronounced.

As the Chief Engine Room Artificer of the boat, I was close at hand to deal with what was obviously a major problem, and I was on my feet in a second. Loose gear had already started to slide down the passage and I had a glimpse of the chef, still clutching a large frying pan in both hands, sliding past the mess.

I scrambled forward into the torpedo stowage compartment where the seamen lived, to see tables, lockers, boxes of food, bedding, knives, forks, spoons, potatoes, cups, saucers and seamen all in one great melange on the deck.

I have vivid recollections of Kellogg's cornflakes crunching under my feet, one rating with his blitz bottle to his mouth, and a startled face peering at me from a hammock overhead. Many submarine ratings never drank their rum at sea and collected it in a bottle for celebrating after a patrol, but when being hunted or depth charged, it would be drunk from the blitz bottle out of sight of the officers.

In the torpedo stowage compartment, the duty seaman stood looking at the water pouring in through the inboard vent of A trimming tank, unable to react to the emergency. I shoved him aside and, knee deep in water, shut the vent. Normally an open vent would have caused no problems, but it was later discovered that a piece of zinc had fallen off the hull and jammed the kingston valve in the bottom of the tank, permitting the sea to flow straight in.

On our way to the seabed, the main ballast tanks had been blown and the propellers reversed to no avail, and we went gently into what must have been a muddy bottom. I was not worried because the S boats had a safe diving depth of 300 feet, and the ballast pump would soon get rid of excess water so that we could carry on our trials. But on arrival in the crowded control room, I saw that the needle of the deep diving gauge had gone past 500 feet and was resting on the stop, indicating that we were below 500 feet and likely to be crushed flat by the terrific sea pressure.

As I moved aft to the engine room, two grease nipples gave way under pressure and shot across the control room, followed by jets of water. I stumbled over the legs of a senior rating who was on his knees, crying and praying to a photograph of his girl friend, which he had propped up on a valve. I kicked him and told him he was a submariner, not a soldier, and to get back on his feet.

As I climbed through the engine room bulkhead door, I heard a loud thump and could hear water rushing in, so I quickly squeezed behind the port engine and shut off the valve which admitted water to a four-inch water cooling hose. No sooner had I done this than there was an ominous creaking sound and as I watched, the pressure hull itself split, admitting a very fine spray into the engine room.

At that moment I thought that *Seraph*'s motto, 'I follow on wings', was most appropriate! But there was work to do, and soon water was being passed in buckets along a human chain from forward to aft to be poured in the engine room bilges to distribute the weight. This done, 'Diving stations' were ordered, followed by 'Stand by to surface. Blow main ballast. Slow astern together'.

Relief showed in every face as the familiar orders were rapped out that would mean us being reunited with the world again, but the needle on the diving gauge remained adamantly stuck against the stop, and sickening despair could almost be felt. *Seraph* appeared to be held fast in mud which would never let her go.

I heard 'Lord Louis' Stevenson, our warrant engineer, immaculate as ever in white overalls, silk scarf and gloves, give his opinion that we had to 'go for broke', as he quaintly put it, because there was little high pressure air left and the electrical systems were badly damaged. If we did not get off the bottom this time, we would stay there.

Fingers were crossed as air thudded into the tanks once again and the amps poured into the electric motors as 'Full astern' was ordered. At first the needle remained stuck but as fuses blew and the smell of electrical burning filled the boat, she started to move. The *Seraph*, beautiful *Seraph*, took to her wings and shot upward and backwards to the surface to remain rolling gently in the swell without any engine or electrical power and finished as an operational boat, but alive and basking in the daylight.

Mud covered her hull as far back as the gun, so she had been well and truly embedded in the seabed. Our happiness was tempered by the knowledge that we had to face an enemy more feared by British submarines than the enemy or the sea – the Royal Air Force. *Seraph*, like many of her sisters, had been attacked on several occasions by them, but this time we had endured enough, luck was with us and we returned to Plymouth safely.

There was one sad note about this incident. When I returned to our snug little mess more than ready for my tot of rum, which I had had to leave so precipitously, I found the messman asleep on my bunk clutching the E.R.A.'s rum bottle, which he had emptied. When he woke up to find himself still alive, in my bunk and having drunk the Tiffies rum, terror – for the second time in 24 hours – appeared in his eyes!

LIEUTENANT 'MICKY' BUDD DSM RN

✳

Skull and Crossbones

The use of the 'Jolly Roger' flag to denote success against the enemy is now universal in submarine flotillas, and the 'heraldry' has become more or less standardised. Some remarks on the composition of these flags and generally accepted rules governing their display may be of interest.

As far as can be discovered Jolly Rogers were not flown by our submarines in the last war, but the connection between submarine warfare and piracy certainly started then. Both were unrestricted and illegal.

In this war the Germans announced unrestricted submarine warfare from the start. We did not follow suit until some time later, after some very worth-while targets had got away.

One of these was the liner *Bremen*. Commander Bickford, in the *Salmon*, was in a good position for torpedoing her, but according to the rules and his orders at the time he had to see the crew in a place of safety before sinking the ship, He tried to achieve this by means of a surface attack with his guns, but the air escort forced him to dive again immediately, and this valuable ship passed unmolested.

As a matter of fact, even if there had been no air escort, Commander Bickford would have been lucky if his plan had succeeded. The *Bremen* had only to turn away at full speed and the *Salmon*'s gun would have been very unlikely to have damaged her during the short time she would have been in range. It requires many well placed hits with a submarine's small gun to sink even a moderate-sized ship, let alone a 52,000-ton job.

Fortunately the distinction between combatants and non-combatants at sea was eventually abandoned by us, and our submarines were left free (like our aircraft) to operate in the only way they can with any hope of success, i.e. without restriction.

The first Jolly Roger seen this war was probably that presented by the Captain (S) commanding the First Flotilla at Alexandria, some time early in 1941. The practice soon spread to Malta and the home flotillas. Now each new or newly commissioned boat starts its own Jolly Roger when it scores its first success.

The flag is flown, usually from one of the periscopes, as the submarine enters harbour, and is left flying for the rest of that day. It is eagerly watched for from the signal bridge of the depot ship, as it is often the first news that Captain (S) has that one of his boats has had a bit of luck. It is also flown on that great day when the submarine steams into her home port after a foreign commission. The White Ensign is, of course, always flown as well.

The different devices on the flag must be well known by now, since so many photographs have appeared in the Press. Warships sunk are represented by red bars, merchant ships by white bars. For a U-boat the sign is a red bar with the letter 'U' super-imposed. (Yes, it does happen, despite the official doctrine that the submarine is *not* the answer to the submarine.)

Occasionally, when very large ships have been sunk, an extra thick bar has been put up. One submarine explained that one of their bars was very large because it had been such a colossal fluke hitting the ship. One or two odd coloured bars have also been seen at various times. The boat which accounted for a floating dock used a green bar, while another boat which, by mistake, sank a ship which he should have allowed to pass, decided that yellow was the appropriate colour.

Small ships are usually sunk by gunfire for the sake of economy, and also because they are difficult to hit with a torpedo. They can, however, also be dealt with by a demolition charge or by ramming, but the latter is not recommended. Apart from the risk of damaging the submarine, it is quite easy to misjudge the angle so that the target slides off unhurt. Needless to say this never happens when a slight error of judgement in coming alongside causes the submarine's bows to come into momentary contact with another ship's side. Then the damage is always spectacular and widespread.

All gun actions are shown on the Jolly Roger by stars over crossed guns. Each action rates one star only, even if several ships are sunk at the same time, as often happened in raids on the harbours of the Aegean. Red stars indicate gun actions with warships. Sensible people avoid these if they can, but sometimes they occur either by mistake or as a last resort. The submarine should be very careful not to get hit. It does not require a very big hole in the pressure hull to prevent it from diving.

One of our boats in the Mediterranean mistook an Italian destroyer for a U-boat one dark night a couple of years ago. He opened fire and scored some hits before the destroyer turned to ram and he realised what he was attacking. It was then too late to dive, so he turned exactly end on and neatly sliced open the whole side of the destroyer with his fore hydroplanes as it swept past. We probably know now whether it sank or not, but it was considered a 'probable' at the time.

Bombardments of ports and specific objectives are quite good fun, and earn a white star as well. Even if there is an airfield quite near, there is an interval of at least ten minutes before the arrival of the first aircraft, which can be well employed. It is unwise to do a bombardment from too near a shore battery. But even then it is surprising how long it takes them to realise what is going on.

'Mines are laid in enemy water' quite frequently by our submarines, although it is not considered necessary to announce the fact on the nine o'clock news. But if the reader sees a horned mine with the figure, say 458, alongside it on some submarine's Jolly Roger, he is entitled to draw his own conclusions.

The daggers which appear on most of the flags of the boats returning from abroad may cause speculation. They are copied from the Commando fighting knife and are awarded for 'Special Operations'. Without delving too deeply into this subject, it may be said that the transportation of General Giraud and his staff from France to North Africa was a special operation which entitled the British submarine which carried it out to add a dagger to its already impressive flag. A curious fact about this romantic operation was that for political reasons the submarine flew the United States ensign and was technically under the command of an American naval captain. This officer took no part, of course, in the handling of the ship. It is circumstances like this which are apt to muddle historians.

Various senior officers have objected to submarines flying Jolly Rogers; but their use has never been officially proscribed, so it is probable that they have come to stay. They may also be dangerous from a security point of view, but evidently not sufficiently so to warrant their abolition. If *The Naval Review* is read in the Wilhelmstrasse this article may clear up any doubtful points.

The story of Jolly Rogers is the story of our submarines in this war. Some of that story will remain on the Most Secret list for ever. Much of it will have to wait till after the war for publication. But it is to be hoped that it is being written now before memories fade and time colours recollection. It will be worth reading.

*

D-Day June 1944 – Operation 'Gambit'

It was the successful attack by Italian frogmen on HMS *Queen Elizabeth* and HMS *Valiant* in Alexandria Harbour on December 19/20th 1941 that first pointed me in the direction of the D-Day Beaches.

At that time in 1941/42, I was serving in the Western Desert. In March 1942 a signal (instigated by Winston Churchill) was sent by Flag Officer Submarines asking for volunteers for 'hazardous and secret operations involving vigorous underwater training'. I submitted my name and in July 1942 was ordered to return to the UK.

On arrival in England, I spent some days at HMS *Dolphin* at Gosport, the home of submarines, undergoing underwater tests. Having passed these successfully, I was sent to HMS *Varbel* at Rothesay, the Headquarters of the 12th Submarine Flotilla.

After a concentrated course – covering electrics, diesel engines, navigation, and the never to be forgotten diving (very cold in the Scottish lochs), we were all frogmen . . . trained to leave the X craft to cut nets and attach limpet mines.

Following this course, I was lucky enough to get command of X4, one of the two prototype X craft and, as her sister ship, X3, had sunk and was now under refit, X4 took the brunt of the training programme.

In early 1944 I was appointed in command of X23, a new craft under construction at Markhams in Chesterfield.

By this time it had been decided that two craft (X20 and X23) were to be detached from the 12th Flotilla, to act as navigational beacons off the D-Day beaches, and to be based at HMS *Dolphin* Gosport to train and make ready for the day.

These craft were 52 ft long, 6 ft in circumference with a range of 1000 miles. A surface speed of a maximum of 7 knots could be achieved (submerged 3–3½ knots). Normally they would carry a crew of four, but for this special operation this was increased to five, three X craft crew and two members of the C.O.P.P. (Combined Operations Pilotage Party). Our task was to cross the Channel submerged and undetected to our marking position approximately 1 mile off Ouistreham, surface before dawn on D-Day and erect an

18 ft telescopic mast showing a green light to seaward together with other navigational aids.

We sailed from HMS *Dolphin* on the evening of Friday 2nd June, escorted by trawlers to a position beyond the Isle of Wight. From then on we carried on alone, running submerged across the Channel for the 90 odd miles to the French coast. We passed through the mine barrier in the Baye de la Seine reaching the French coast by dawn on Sunday 4th June. We were able to fix our position by periscope, this was made easier by the low level aerial photographs supplied by the R.A.F. clearly showing Churches and other prominent buildings. A light was still showing at the mouth of the Orne Canal.

Having fixed our position, we bottomed and waited until after dark to surface again and set up our wireless. We simply received a message that the landings had been postponed, which was not surprising as the weather was very rough. We took the opportunity to drop our anchor, to ensure we kept our marking position and returned to the bottom to wait for darkness the next night (Monday).

During all this time submerged we had been on oxygen. This was fed to us from air bottles taken, incidentally, from German Luftwaffe bombers, they being the lightest bottles available at the time. We had no idea how long the postponement was to be and our oxygen supply was limited. . . .

On the Monday night we once again surfaced when it was dark and received the signal stating that the invasion would start at first light on Tuesday, 6th June.

Once again we bottomed until just before dawn on the Tuesday. At 0445 we surfaced, it was still rough which made entry and exit through the hatch difficult, but we set up our 18 ft mast and commenced flashing as a navigational beacon at 0506. At sunrise a D-Flag was substituted for the lamp.

One of the main objects of our operation was to mark the limited beaches where the DD swimming tanks could emerge from the sea, after they had been launched from the landing craft and had proceeded to the beaches under their own power.

As dawn broke there were ships of all sizes passing us and approaching the shore, from battleships to the smallest landing craft. The shore installations were under bombardment from both sea and air.

Once the tanks and commandos had landed, our job was done. We cut the anchor rope (we were too exhausted to pull it up) and reported to the Headquarters Ship, HMS *Largs*, at 0935.

We then proceeded back across the Channel to our base at Gosport to be greeted in the traditional way after a successful operation.

The operation had covered a period of 72 hours during which we had been submerged for 64 of them.

We were especially relieved to return safely, as we had looked up the definition of our Code word, 'Gambit' in the dictionary. It was defined as 'the pawn you throw away before a big move in chess'.

LT.-CDR. GEORGE HONOUR DSC VRD RNVR

Honour was awarded his DSC for 'Gambit'. X20, the other X craft, was commanded by Lt. Kenneth Hudspeth RANVR, who was awarded a second Bar to his DSC for 'Gambit'.

*

George Luck DSM was the youngest seaman Chief Petty Officer in the Royal Navy and the youngest submarine Coxswain when he joined Taurus *at Algiers in February 1943, one month before his 21st birthday, having risen from Boy 1st Class to Chief Petty Officer in a little less than three years. But the hero of his story was two years younger.*

Young Murray

It all began 40 years ago. Young Murray had been conscripted into the Navy, and, after basic training followed by a course in radar, was sent via the Submarine Training School to his first sea-going vessel – a T class submarine of which I was then Coxswain. He was just a month or two past his 19th birthday, a little Scots laddie that you just had to like. He was just five feet one and a quarter in seaboots and weighed around seven stone.

Small though he was, Murray was Mobile Nautical Disaster Area – the proverbial accident looking for somewhere to happen. It eventually reached the point when even the Captain, on occasion, would say, 'Cox'n, find out what Murray is up to – and *stop him*.'

Radar in those days was not the exact science it appears to be today and frequently, after a sharp-eyed lookout had been observing a ship for some considerable time, the radar operator's Scottish voice would issue forth from the bridge voicepipe and proudly explain that on a certain bearing there could be seen 'an object, sir.'

Perhaps Murray's not quite all-seeing eye got him off to an undeservedly poor start. But before long we realised that things happened sooner or later when Murray was around. We coped quite well with the Germans, the Italians and the Japanese, who were more predictable in their habits. But with Young Murray – well, perhaps a few examples will help to explain the problem.

Once, we were patrolling off Toulon when he took over the helm for a spell. I had been listening purposely while the necessary information was turned over to him by the man he was relieving and I noticed a puzzled look on Young Murray's face. Here I should explain that the compass repeater the helmsman had to watch continually, and which indicated our course, was the usual endless tape marked in degrees – o representing north, o90 east, 180 south, 270 west, and back to o.

Young Murray duly took over and the routine settled down. A little while later, the officer of the watch, a young sub-lieutenant (who was later to be knighted and become the Second Sea Lord) asked in a quiet but distinctly ominous voice if I would find out what on earth Young Murray was supposed to be doing. Going over to the wheel, I saw the young stalwart sitting back in his seat reading a book and happily humming to himself. Gently (as submarine Cox'ns are wont to do in such circumstances) I politely suggested that he might care to attend to his steering.

Looking hurt, Young Murray asked, 'what are we stopped for 'Swain?' Furiously I pointed to the telegraph repeaters and the revolution counter which showed half ahead and a healthy 300 revolutions respectively. His reply was to indicate the zero on the gyro repeater and say, 'if we're nay stopped, why are no goin' anywhere the noo?'

We just happened to be steering due north! (Murray came off the wheel).

There was another jolly little happening soon afterwards. When the Captain deemed it safe to do so, to save precious time in harbour, we would top up the batteries with distilled water while returning submerged from patrol. This entailed lifting the deckplates covering the batteries, an operation carried out by the Petty Officer LTO and his electrical team. In the past I had sent Young Murray to assist various heads of departments if they had a spot of work to do like this. The usual response was a jocular, 'thanks a lot, what have you got against me?'

This time it was the turn of the POLTO to be 'assisted'. Young Murray had been given a dustpan and brush to clean the airtight seals around the deckplates. Surely, we thought, he was capable of doing that quite safely. Unfortunately, we overlooked the fact that in those days dustpans were made of metal so when our young friend nonchalantly placed his dustpan across the terminals of a battery cell it produced a flash, a bang and a cloud of smoke and fumes which scared the wits out of everybody. Young Murray looked at the mangled remains and complained bitterly that no-one had told him 'yon battery was switched on'.

Fortunately nobody was hurt but it was a close shave.

Then came the frolic in Trincomalee harbour. A strong wind was making it difficult for us to secure to a buoy prior to swinging compasses. It was customary, when carrying out this normally simple little evolution, for a man to mount the heavy wire, an evolution known as 'jumping the buoy'. After a couple of futile attempts, frustrated by the wind, the Captain at last succeeded in manoeuvring the boat somewhere near striking distance. It was now or never. Glaring at me he ordered 'get down there and get someone on that buoy immediately'.

I hurried to the fore-casing, saw Young Murray standing spare and ordered, 'jump the buoy. Do you know what you have to do?' Something told me I had not made a wise choice when he replied all too confidently, 'och, that's nae problem at all.'

Scarcely reassured I sped back to the bridge. Young Murray thought a bit, turned to the bridge and shouted, 'Right then, let's be havin' ye.'

The Captain's next remark was 'all right Cox'n. You put him there, let's find out what he wants.'

And so, with shouts of 'up a bit . . . back a bit . . .' enough arm waving for a battleship's farewell and a final 'whoa . . . hold her there!' from the prospective buoy-jumper, we got within about 15 feet of the buoy. Motioning everyone to one side and fully in command of the situation, Young Murray secured one end of the heaving line around his midriff, the other end to our capstan and faced forward. From a standing start he hurtled along the casing and, like

a Grand National winner at Aintree, literally took off, clearing
the buoy with feet to spare. Spluttering, he surfaced and somehow
managed to clamber onto the buoy, untie the flimsy heaving line
from around his waist and secure it to the huge steel ring. Well
satisfied he then faced the bridge smartly and called out trium-
phantly, as the line tautened and threatened to part, 'all secured up
forrard the noo, sir. Ye can relax.'

Gravely the Captain turned to me, 'thank you very much, Cox'n.
We must do that again sometime. Captain (S) must be very
impressed.' As all the foregoing had been witnessed by an interested
depot ship and three or four other submarines, I don't think he
meant it.

But my fondest memory is of Murray's amorous interlude at
Colombo. To appreciate this you must visualise a tropical beach,
palm trees, the whisper of the surf on silver sand, a big yellow moon
– a typical Hollywood movie scene. With some messmates I was
relaxing on the beach with a few bottles of canteen beer. The atmosphere was tranquil and peaceful. I think it was the Stoker PO who
spoke first, 'blimey, take a look at this'.

'This' was Young Murray. He was rigged out in Empire Builder's
shorts, pusser's boots, long black stockings (around his ankles), a
white jumper (at least ten sizes too large) and, of all things, the
biggest pith helmet imaginable. The sight of his diminutive figure
inside this lot was arresting to say the least. However, Murray's
companion was even more startling. She was a veritable amazon of
a woman – all of six feet with long blond hair and a 44-24-36 figure.
She was wearing, barely, a bikini which would have failed the Trades
Description Act if it had been in force in those days. She sinuated
over towards us while Young Murray stomped alongside her through
the soft sand. As the strangely assorted pair passed our group the
face beneath the pith helmet grinned and chuckled something about,
'all right the noo.' His companion haughtily peered down at us over

the starboard half of her 44, tossed her long tresses and glided on. A little further along the beach they selected a spot for themselves and Young Murray dutifully scooped out a hollow into which they both snuggled. Soon there came little squeaks, giggles and other rapturous sounds. To say that we were dumbstruck is an understatement. And then it happened: *Swipe!* We all winced in sympathy and watched as the voluptuous amazon leapt to her feet. Everything trembled as she brushed off the sand and steamed off down the beach like the *Ark Royal* which also overhung at both ends.

Eventually Young Murray came over looking quite shattered. I naturally asked what had upset the fair damsel and, visibly affected, he said, 'och. 'Swain, there's no pleasin' yon big lassie. I've taken her for a taxi ride, we've had big eats, I've bought her sun glasses and lots more besides, then she said, "let's go down to the beach". I didna mind that. And then she started kissin' and cuddlin' and that was OK. Then all of a rush, she said "take me, take me". So ah said, "where the hell d'ye want tae go the noo, the pictures?" And then she belted me one.'

About three weeks later we were sitting on the bottom of the Malacca Strait off Penang, being depth-charged unmercifully, when Young Murray crawled over alongside me, forced a grin and whispered, 'Ah'm thinkin' 'Swain, if yon Japs don't get tae hell out if it soon I'll no stand much chance again with that big lassie.'

I thought that if the 'big lassie' could have seen and heard him at that moment she would not have slapped his face. As I said earlier, you couldn't help but like Young Murray.

Looking back over the years, I suppose a few grey hairs are a small price to pay for the privilege of having served with a very select band of men of whom Winston Churchill once told Parliament, 'I have often looked for an opportunity of paying tribute to our submarines. There is no branch of His Majesty's forces which in this war have suffered the same proportion of fatal losses as our

Chief Stoker John Capes BEM, the sole survivor (inset) of *Perseus* (above), mined and sunk off Cephalonia, western Greece, in December 1941. The story of his one-man escape from a depth of 300 feet – a story so incredible that some refused to believe Capes was ever on board *Perseus* – begins on p. 137. *Tempest* (below) on the surface after seven hours' depth charging by the Italian Torpedo Boat *Circe*, 13 February 1942. She later sank under tow. The terrible experience of *Tempest's* last hour is described by her Coxswain, Chief Petty Officer Charles Anscomb DSM BEM, on p. 143.

E.R.A.s Hammond (left) and Lister in Switzerland after talking their way out of Colditz. They were the only British submariners to escape from Germany and make their way back to Britain during the war. See p. 155.

Timoshenko, *Unruffled*'s ship's cat,
who sailed on 23 war patrols,
pictured ashore in Malta, 1943.

An X-craft 'midget' submarine exercising in a Scottish loch.

Lt. Henty Henty-Creer RNVR (left) overcomes his fear of submarine escape training
on p. 166 while on p. 172 Lt. Godfrey Place RN gives his account of Operation
'Source', the X-craft midget submarine attack on *Tirpitz* in September 1943, in which
Henty-Creer, CO of *X5*, was lost and Place, CO of *X7*, won the Victoria Cross.

The 'Jolly Roger' of *Safari*. The bars represent ships torpedoed; the stars, ships sunk, by gun, or gun and torpedo; the daggers for 'cloak and dagger' operations, and the lighthouse commemorates *Safari*'s acting as a navigational beacon for the invasion of Sicily. The origins of submarines' Jolly Rogers are explained in 'Skull and Crossbones', on p. 185.

X.23 coming alongside the headquarters' ship *Largs* on D-Day 6 June 1944 after acting as a navigation beacon for the landings on Sword beach. The photograph (inset) of *X.23*'s CO, Lt. George Honour RNVR, who tells his story on p. 188, was given to him so that the French Resistance could make up a false identity card for him should the Normandy landings have to be abandoned.

The survivors of *Shakespeare*, 'The Unsinkable Submarine' seen at Trincomalee in January 1945, whose extraordinary story is told by one of them, Leading Telegraphist Ken Wade DSM, on p. 209.

On p. 215 Lt. Ian Fraser RNR (left) tells the story of the midget submarine *XE.3*'s attack on the Japanese cruiser *Takao* in Singapore, in July 1945, for which he as *XE.3*'s CO and Leading Seaman James Magennis, the frogman diver, both won the Victoria Cross.

The hydrogen-peroxide powered submarine *Explorer* undergoing
speed trials. The editor explains how *Explorer* (should have been
called *Exploder*) gave him his 'Worst Hangover' on p. 239.

Dreadnought surfaces at the North Pole on p. 255.

Resolution (left), Britain's first Polaris submarine. Life with Polaris, 'Have Polaris, Will Travel' is on p. 262. The first British Polaris test firing, February 1968 (right). All did not go exactly to plan, as an eye-witness describes on p. 260.

The Happy Return. *Onyx* (above), the only diesel-electric submarine to take part in the Falklands conflict, returns home to Gosport, 18 August 1982. The report of her 116-day patrol by her CO, Lt.-Cdr. Andrew Johnson MBE (inset, at the periscope) is on p. 291.

The nuclear submarine *Conqueror* (left) comes home from the Falklands, flying her Jolly Roger. 'The sinking of the *General Belgrano*' by her CO, seen here on the right of the bridge, is on p. 279.

Submarine Service. It is the most dangerous of all services. That is perhaps the reason why the First Lord tells me that entry into it is keenly sought by officers and men. I feel sure that the House would wish to testify its gratitude and admiration to our submarine crews for their skill and devotion, which have proved of inestimable value to the life of our country.'

I don't know to this day whether Young Murray came through safely or whether he finished up worrying the Archangel Gabriel as much as he worried the ship's company of HMS *Taurus*. But I would like to think he reads these few lines and gets as much happiness as I do myself from my memories.

CHIEF PETTY OFFICER GEORGE LUCK DSM

*

In 1944 the submarine flotillas which had borne the heat and burden of the day in the Mediterranean moved to the Indian Ocean and thence to the Far East. At 0708 on 17th July 1944 Telemachus *was at periscope depth in the Malacca Straits in position 156 degrees One Fathom Bank Light seven miles. Her captain tells the story of*

A Collected Shot

I saw a sea mirror-calm, metal-still. The fingers of mist half dispersed were moving in the morning sun. My heart lightened as out of a curl of fog there burst a large Japanese U-boat. She was going top speed for home on the surface.

This was the Joker. The card you abandon the rest of the pack to get.

For twenty minutes I watched with my eyes glued to the eye-pieces.

197

There she sped. Only four miles away. Thinking herself safe. All set for Singapore – dreaming of the lights and lemonade! Strangely I could sense the mood of the captain. He was placed in a narrow channel with no room to zigzag, but batting along full of confidence, relying on his speed and the mist to keep him secure.

His look-outs would, of course, be top-line, alert. But although frightened of their captain all the crew must be thinking of the fun they were going to have in Singapore. They would be country boys with superb eyesight, unlike the Japanese student class, but the brains behind the eyes would not be concentrating on every ripple, on what might be a small black stick showing for a minute in the glistening water of this superbly lovely morning. Their thoughts seemed transmitted to me through the sunshine. How often had I raced back on the last lap just as they!

I reckoned that U-boat would pass about three-quarters of a mile off me. For a moment I contemplated speeding up to close a little, but any telltale swirl in the early stages of the attack might give us away and cause the target to dive or zig. It seemed better to get collected and keep an accurate estimate of his course and speed with the crew settled down at their action stations and the trim perfect.

Through the periscope I could not pick out any escort vessels but there might be several hidden by patches of mist. It was so still I could see flies floating on the water. In these vital moments the captain of a submarine has to keep an almost psychic relationship with the leading stoker who works the hydraulic control lever of the periscope rams. As the huge brass cylinder weighing several tons comes out of its well the captain squats down, seizes the handles in both hands, presses his face to the eye-pieces His knees straighten as the periscope ascends and by the briefest order or even the moving of a finger he dictates the control of the height of that tip showing above the water.

I concentrated on the U-boat with tiny popping-up looks. We had to estimate her speed and course very exactly for a certain hit. The course was pretty easy to work out, for she could not leave that narrow channel. Estimations of her speed could be helped by looking up intelligence reports. The third officer crouched beside me with his pile of reference books.

'What is the best speed of Jap big-class submarines?'

His fingers, probably shaking with anxiety, found it fast.

'Nineteen knots,' he replied.

We had plotted this U-boat on the chart at twenty knots, but I thought she would travel slower after a long patrol because her bottom must be fouled by marine growth. I gave her eighteen knots – it was tricky to pop up the periscope now but I risked it for one more glance.

Nearer and nearer she came. Everything was ready in *Telemachus*. The gauges showed we kept a steady thirty-two feet below the surface and I heard eager confident voices reporting the torpedo tubes ready. Something in me recorded with pleasure that my crew did not have the depth-charge-shocked tightness of earlier days.

I longed to poke the periscope higher up to examine the U-boat's bow wave and thus obtain a check on her speed, but I dared not. Above all, we must not be spotted. But when you cannot see a bow wave the target appears to move slow and I itched to reduce the estimate of her eighteen knots. Within *Telemachus* the whole action was so silent that it had a dream-like quality. Although I had done all this before it seemed strange. The tubes were ready. The crew at diving stations. Twenty minutes of careful, often-rehearsed work and now all was ready for a collected shot.

As the U-boat approached to within a mile and reached the firing point beam-on, *Telemachus* hung steady beneath the water.

There was a moment's silence in the submarine. You could hear men breathing while they waited the order. 'Stand by to fire numbers one, two, three, four, five, six tubes.'

By each tube a pin is pulled. A valve opened.

'*Fire one! Fire two! Fire three ...*'

As the torpedoes shot out at regular intervals I realised that the unbelievable was happening to us. Johnnie Pope, the competent first lieutenant, couldn't hold our submarine under water. Something had gone wrong. *Telemachus* was rising inexorably to the surface.

Periscope down, we strove by flooding, speeding up and putting planes to 'Hard adive' to keep her under water. The seconds of torpedo running time ticked by. Seventy. Eighty. Ninety. *Ninety-two*. As *Telemachus* clove the surface with her top hamper a shattering explosion rent the sea dead on the range running time.

One of our torpedoes had hit.

At the same instant the flooding of our forward tank coupled with speeding up enabled us to regain control and our submarine dived down into the sea. I shot up the periscope as we sank. Swirling water blotted out all view and we had to hope wild hopes that the U-boat had been done to death. One torpedo hit is enough to sink a submarine but the explosion *might* have been something else. Could the U-boat be waiting for us to surface in order to torpedo us in turn?

I longed to be able to tell my men we had got her but I *knew* I was right not to surface and look for an oil patch or debris. Our intelligence found out later that she had sunk with all hands.

COMMANDER WILLIAM KING DSO* DSC RN

The target was I-166, a large U-boat of the Kaigun-*class. The loss of trim after firing was caused by* Telemachus *being loaded with torpedoes carrying a heavier war-head than before; the ship's company were not informed, and therefore did not adjust the amount of compensating water for each torpedo fired.*

*

Later, in September, Storm was on patrol off the islands of the Mergui Archipelago in southern Burma. The Japanese were passing convoys of small ships along the coast from the Pakchan River northwards to the town of Mergui. After one bold but unsuccessful attack on a convoy, Storm's captain decided not to waste any more torpedoes on these small ships. Instead, he chose what is, for a submarine, a much more hazardous method.

Surface and Gun Attack

It was not until half past nine that morning that we saw the head of the convoy emerging from the inner channel exactly where I had expected. As on the previous day, it was a long time – about an hour and a half – before the slow-moving ships reached our position. In the intervals of watching them through the periscope I studied the chart and memorised the general shape of the sea's bottom so that I had a fairly accurate mental picture of the shoal dangers. I knew that once the action started there would be no opportunity of precise fixing and that this would be another case of navigating by eye.

Beyond deciding to let all the ships pass me before surfacing, hoping thus to minimise the chances of a massed ramming attack, I still could not make up my mind what tactics to adopt. Submarines had never been designed for this sort of work, and I had a strong foreboding that the odds were weighted too heavily against us. But we could not sit tamely there and watch them pass unharmed. We must *do* something.

Once again I had to contend with a sea that was as unruffled as a sheet of polished glass. It was desperate work trying to keep track of the movements of so many ships with only split-second observations through the periscope. The two escorts seemed very much aware that they were approaching a danger point, for they were moving in a rapid and continuous zigzag on the seaward beam of the convoy. However, although they passed within about 200 yards of us, they did not spot the periscope, and when the second of them was well past us we were abeam of the last coaster of the column. Now, if ever, was the moment for gun action.

When I gave the order to surface it was the first time I had ever done so without knowing exactly what I meant to do when I got to the top. Climbing the ladder to the bridge on the heels of the gun's crew, I was in a blue funk and full of a premonition of disaster.

Yet as soon as I reached the bridge and stood in the sunshine under the blue sky all my apprehensions were miraculously swept away. Every one of our guns opened fire at once without a hitch and continued firing for the next thirty-six minutes without any of the stoppages which had sometimes let us down in the past. Action, once joined, produced its own stimulus to the brain; our tactics were adapted every moment to meet the changing situation, and we were never at a loss.

1117 Opened fire at the rear ship at a range of 2,000 yards, obtaining seven or eight fairly destructive hits. She turned away and limped towards the shore. We then attacked and stopped the ship ahead of her, but both the escorts were now racing towards us, firing their machine-guns. Turned to port to bring them both on to the starboard bow, and directed the fire of all our guns on to them. In turn, they were each hit and stopped by several direct hits from the three-inch. This part of the action was most exciting, the range eventually closing to 400 yards. The enemy were very brave, and we were lucky not to suffer any casualties. Both these escorts were carrying a score or so of Japanese, presumably troops. One of them released a depth-charge (or it may have been shot over the side) when it was 500 yards away, and it went off on the bottom causing the submarine to heel slightly to starboard for a moment. One of the escorts got out of control, and eventually drove herself under, still with way on. The other remained afloat and was sunk later when things calmed down.

In the meantime, a small vessel had been sighted approaching from the northward at great speed. This looked too much like a motor torpedo-boat to be healthy, so it was the next target to be engaged. At the same time a constant-helm zigzag was maintained. Several near-misses were seen before the torpedo-boat, at a range of about 3,000 yards, turned and fired two stern torpedoes. The tracks passed about 100 yards astern of us. One definite direct hit was scored on this MTB as she was retiring, at a range of about 4,000 yards, and she took little further interest in the proceedings. I think our shooting had put her off quite effectively.

Before this, some vessel had opened up with a pompom. We traced the firing to a small ship not previously sighted which lay stopped about 4,000 yards away, and began to get uncomfortably accurate. Fortunately this fellow, probably a motor gunboat, obtained only one direct hit, which struck *Storm*'s bridge casing below the Oerlikon and caused no casualties. Neither the motor torpedo-boat nor the gunboat had been previously seen through the periscope, and it is considered that they came out from Mergui to meet the convoy.

All this time, also, there was a perpetual whine of machine-gun bullets, but it was difficult to see exactly which ships were firing. They caused no casualties. It was now decided to finish off the coaster which had been stopped earlier (the second target engaged) and also the other escort. These both sank after a few short-range waterline shots. Meanwhile, the first coaster we had attacked and severely damaged appeared to have beached herself; later, however, she seemed to be still under way and may have succeeded in proceeding with the remainder. Fire was now directed at a coaster which had stopped about 4,000 yards away. Two direct hits were obtained, and his bridge demolished.

But by this time we had fired over 150 rounds of three-inch and the barrel was so heated that the next round jammed. Moreover, the remainder of the convoy was getting out of range, we had exhausted all our pans of Oerlikon and Vickers ammunition, and I was getting anxious about the navigation. I decided to call it a day, as the situation did not justify the risk of running the submarine aground.

1153 Broke off the action and retired westward on the surface, passing through the gap north of Bentinck Island. There seemed no point in remaining in the vicinity.

The net result of the action was: two escorts and one coaster sunk, two coasters damaged, one torpedo-boat hit. Also, the last clue to the inshore convoy route had been uncovered. An interesting point was that all the survivors seen in the water were apparently Japanese. Not a single Malay or Burman was among them, though these had been plentiful in the coasters sunk on the previous patrol.

I was staggered, and profoundly thankful, that we had survived those thirty-six minutes without a single casualty. There was great elation throughout the boat at our success. The gun's crew were no doubt regaling their messmates below with vivid descriptions of the action; they had enjoyed themselves, and were only too disappointed when the engagement was broken off. Inspired by the grim determination of Taylor, the gun-layer, they had done very well, quite unperturbed by the machine-gun fire coming at us from all directions; even Greenway, now back in the gun's crew as breach-worker, was unshaken by any memories of his previous wounding in somewhat similar circumstances. My highest admiration went to Richard Blake, who as gunnery control officer, had been faced with unusually rapid decisions – for my constant shifts of target, and the wild zigzag forced on us by the threat of torpedoes from the MTB had demanded frequent and immediate corrections to range and deflection. In spite of these difficulties he had remained cool, patient and accurate. At the end both he and I were hoarse from shouting our orders above the inferno of noise. For several hours afterwards we were partially deaf, and I think it must have been on this occasion that Blake suffered the damage to his eardrums which led, five years after the end of the war, to his being invalided out of the service.

Out of the original nine ships we had sunk three and damaged two. It was better than I had hoped for when we surfaced, but I could not help remembering that if I had been quicker in the uptake on the previous day we should probably have taken a heavier toll and might even have sunk the entire convoy.

COMMANDER EDWARD YOUNG DSO DSC RNVR

*

At dawn on 22 November 1944, Stratagem (Lt. C. R. Pelly) was at periscope depth in the Malacca Strait, about four miles offshore. A Japanese destroyer could be seen patrolling closer inshore, and a Japanese float-plane was very active overhead. It is possible that Stratagem was sighted by the aircraft, in the shallow water, for at about midday a destroyer detected the submarine and severely damaged and flooded her with an accurate depth-charge attack. Stratagem was overdue on 3 December, having failed to answer signals, and was presumed lost. The story of her last moments is most movingly told by a survivor, the Torpedo Officer, Lt. D. C. Douglas.

'At approximately 1210 I was awakened by the order "Diving Stations". As soon as I arrived in the tube space the order "Shut off for depth-charging" was passed. This was carried out and a report sent to the control room. After four minutes had elapsed without any further orders coming through – nobody in the fore ends knowing what was taking place – then the thrash of the Japanese destroyer could be heard very loud as he passed overhead. Almost immediately a depth-charge exploded somewhere extremely close under us, lifting the stern and causing us to bottom hard. This charge extinguished the greater part of the lighting, although one or two of the emergency lights held. About five seconds later a second charge exploded, as far as I could calculate right amidships, extinguishing the remaining lights.

'By this time I had a torch in operation and could see water flooding through the door at the after end of the torpedo stowage compartment. Immediately I gave the order "Shut watertight doors" and turned to make sure that the three ratings in the tube space were brought out of that compartment, before the door was shut. By the time the door was shut the water was flooding very much faster and had risen above the deck boards in the torpedo stowage compartment. It was now above our knees. It was flooding through the after door so fast that the ratings were unable to shut this door. The position of the stop, retaining the door in the open position on this watertight door, was such that to move it one had to stand in the doorway, as the port-side of the door was blocked by stores. Hence, due to the furious rate of flooding, this stop could not be removed.

'According to Able Seaman Westwood, who came forward from the control room, the Captain gave the order for main ballast to be blown as soon as he found that the ship was being flooded. The valves on the panel were opened, without effect. In what appeared to be an incredibly short time, I was keeping above water by clinging on to a hammock, which was slung from the deckhead. The crew in my compartment began to sing, but I ordered this to stop and told the men to get out and put on DSEA sets. The first I managed to reach had a defective valve on the oxygen bottle and I could not move it. The second was in working order and I put this over the head of one of the older ratings, who was panicking and in tears, due to the pressure effect on his eyes. The pressure in the boat at that time was immense and the chlorine content in the air considerable. The water all around us must have been full of oil fuel as we were all drenched with it although I did not notice it at the time. The air could be heard to be escaping through the hull forward and the water was still rising fast.

'At this time, Leading Seaman Gibbs was in the escape hatch, trying to slack back the clips. He shouted to me that he could not move the third clip. Speaking was nearly impossible due to the pressure. I swung up into the trunk alongside Gibbs and tried to remove the clip. After what seemed like an hour and what I suppose was really a minute, I managed to move the clip by hammering it with my fist. By this time there was no hope of using the escape trunk as the water was already up to the metal coaming which houses the twill trunking. I took off the last clip and as I did so the hatch commenced to open. Immediately this clip was free the hatch was blown open and Leading Seaman Gibbs was shot out so suddenly that I cannot remember him going. The hatch slammed shut again and I was shot out in a bubble of air.

'Ten of the men in the compartment which contained fourteen at the time are known to have left the submarine alive, though only eight were picked up. The ship's cook was later seen to be floating face downwards on the surface but was obviously drowned. Another rating was seen while in the submarine to have on a DSEA set and apparently working it correctly. Although he was observed to leave the boat he was not seen on the surface.

'The Japanese destroyer had dropped two more charges after we were hit but these were not so close and did not seem to harm us, although they probably accelerated the flooding. Throughout the above experiences the behaviour of the crew in my compartment was magnificent. I should especially like to mention the ship's cook. Leading Cook Weatherhead, who kept up a cheerful narrative about the wonderful fruit cake which he had recently cooked and who showed great bravery and coolness throughout the dreadful experiences in the flooded submarine. This rating was responsible for the singing and by his behaviour greatly assisted in preventing panic. It is with the deepest regret that I have to report that this extremely brave rating failed to survive the ascent to the surface.

'The destroyer circled us for about three-quarters of an hour, dropping a life-belt and some baulks of timber. All of us were suffering from 'bends' and I do not know about the ratings but I myself was scared "pea-green" at the sight of the Japanese ensign flying from their masthead. This was more or less justified, as we later found out. However, I managed to overcome this somewhat by swimming round and seeing to the ratings. Able Seaman Westwood was just on the verge of sinking. His eyes were full of oil and he could hardly keep himself afloat. I fixed him into the lifebelt and then went to the assistance of Able Seaman Philips. He was in a similar plight but a puff of air into his DSEA set kept his head above water and he was all right although he was almost delirious with shock.

'The Japanese eventually lowered a cutter and picked us up, clubbing us as they hauled us into the boat. Then we were each compelled to pull an oar. This was practically impossible, due to the bends, but we reached the destroyer assisted by their clouts and unpleasantness.

'By this time another destroyer of a similar type had arrived on the scene. The Japanese were certain there was another submarine in the vicinity and got furious with us when we denied this. On being hauled on board we were bound, blind-folded and beaten. We were not given food at any time whilst on board the destroyer and spent the night on the top of the hatch which was about three feet square all bound together. We were not clothed and the night was extremely cold. The pain from the bends was now at its worst and every time someone murmured the guards would come and hit us over the head with their clubs. We were being taken to Singapore, where we arrived at about 2100 on 23 November. No food was given us and we were locked in separate cells, still bound and blind-folded. We remained in this condition for twenty-eight days, although I was allowed to remove my bonds after about ten days.'

Lt. Douglas and seven ratings were taken to Singapore. On 19 December Douglas, Leading Seaman Gibbs and A. B. Robinson were flown to Japan and taken to Ofuna, an unregistered PoW camp unknown to the Red Cross, where they endured terrible hardships before being released, suffering from beri-beri and malnutrition, by the US Navy in August 1945. These three were the only survivors of Stratagem. *The others died or were executed in captivity.*

*

On 3rd January 1945, Shakespeare *(Lt. D. Swanston) was off Port Blair in the Andaman Islands, on her first patrol in the Indian Ocean, when she missed an enemy merchant vessel with four torpedoes and so surfaced to attack with gun-fire. After about five minutes' action, a Japanese submarine chaser was seen some 9,000 yards away, and approaching. Swanston cleared the bridge and gun positions, before diving. The merchant ship was by now less than a mile away and before* Shakespeare *could dive scored a hit on the submarine's pressure hull, starboard amidships, just on the water-line. What happened next gave* Shakespeare *the nickname*

The Unsinkable Submarine

As Swanston prepared to leave the bridge *Shakespeare* rocked violently, and water cascaded down the vessel's side and the bridge was riddled with holes. A 12 pounder shell had ripped a gash approximately 10" long and 5" wide in the pressure hull, just above the water line and the sea was pouring in through the gap. The deluge flooded the auxiliary machinery space which housed the gyro and the main compass, and flooded the control room and engine room. The ballast pump which had been started to stem the flow, flooded and broke down, water poured over the wireless transmitter and put it out of action. I experienced an unplanned and unexpected takeoff while at my action station in the wireless office!

The outside ventilating trunking system to the battery had been shattered, and the engine room bulkhead door had to be left open. Efforts to seal the battery compartment were made before the sea forced through and cut off the battery supply of power. We were wallowing helplessly unable to dive, and open to attack from the Japanese ships and any aircraft that might be summoned to deal the final blow. After inspecting the damage Swanston accompanied by Sub-Lt. Morgan and Lt. Pearson RNVR went back to the bridge. *Shakespeare* was now under heavy fire from the sub-chaser, but no further damage was caused at this stage. Standing in the control room which was flooded to knee level 'Guts' Harmer and I exchanged glances and proved that mental telepathy exists and works. Without further conversation, I said 'Let's go' and we proceeded to the fore-ends, grabbed blankets, hammocks and locker cushions and went up the conning tower and sighted the hole just aft of the Oerlikon gun platform. Lying on my stomach I gripped 'Guts' who had his feet in the hole endeavouring to effect a temporary repair. Four more shots from the sub-chaser were on target and one of these ricocheted on the casing blowing off Harmer's prize boots and my shirt and shorts. His feet were burned and we both appeared to have been prepared for 'Jungle warfare' but continued our efforts on plugging the hole.

Able Seaman Frank Foster, the gun layer and Able Seaman R. Whitelaw had both been injured, and Lt. Lutley and Telegraphist Britton took their places on the 3" gun.

Swanston fired the stern torpedo which missed and after about an hour the gun's crew scored a direct hit on the merchant ship at which stage the sub-chaser withdrew to aid the damaged ship.

During the lull in the fighting a bucket-chain was established to bail out water using the officers and crews 'heads'. Able Seaman Wild produced about 20 buckets which he had 'won' prior to sailing.

As the diving compass on the bridge had been hit and the Gyro compass was flooded, we were being guided by 'Faithful Freddy' (a boat compass) which TGM Tommy Gates supported on his knees. At approximately 0900 Wt. Eng. Hodge reported the Port engine had seized and there was little hope of it functioning again, at the same time 'Guts' Harmer fell overboard and as the water had not yet reached the main motors Swanston stopped, manoeuvred and recovered him. He continued to 'gripe' over the loss of his much prized boots. Course was resumed on one engine at a speed of 7 knots. I then joined 'Guts' and we added extra strength to the bucket chain. Later 'Guts' then went onto the bridge and acted as an air lookout until dark, taking occasional bursts with a Tommy gun on very close aircraft.

At 0930 a seaplane sighted over Nankauri Strait, started a low level dive bombing attack from astern. When the range had closed sufficiently, a short burst from the starboard Vickers gun manned by P.O. Ted Jones (2nd Coxswain) caused him to release a bomb 20 yards away on the port side, and was seen to crash into the sea about 100 yards off the starboard bow. At 1000 two 'Jakes' appeared and carried out a diving low-level attack and then came in and bombed us. The splash from one bomb flooded the bridge and burst an HP airline in the bilges. There was a general feeling that we had been holed again and might have to abandon ship! Up to 1420, five more attacks by Jakes each carrying 50lb bombs were made and further subsequent attacks were diverted by Vickers gun and Oerlikon fire.

At 1420 an unidentified vessel was seen closing from the starboard quarter. On sighting this, all deciphered signals and patrol orders were burned under the guidance and authority of Sub-Lt. William Grey RNVR. The code books and silhouette photos were sacked ready for ditching, and the two torpedoes were brought to the ready. A bomber and two fighter bombers now appeared and one fighter carrying two bombs made a dive attack at an angle of 75 degrees, dropped his bombs and made a machine gun attack. The bomber came in at a height of about 3,000 ft and had a near miss with two heavy (1,000lb) bombs on the port side, seriously wounding Able Seaman T. A. Motterham who died the following day. Able Seaman G. Taylor also died from injuries sustained while in the bucket-chain.

From 1600 until just before sunset single attacks by groups of four aircraft, fighter bombers with machine guns, occurred at half hourly intervals. The Oerlikon finally jammed and could not be cleared. The 3 gun was used throughout the day. Some 200 rounds were fired, using all time fused shell, and then when these were expended changes were made to fuse other shells. At 1830 just before sunset, a bomber, two fighter bombers and a seaplane carried out attacks from the sun and were circling in and out of the clouds but no further damage was done. With darkness the air attacks ceased and it was possible to take stock of the situation below.

The ships company was then organised for the night, a chain of buckets still being necessary to deal with water entering through the damaged pressure hull.

On the morning of the 4th January the port circulator was rigged as a bilge pump, and a suction obtained in the control room. A hammock was rigged as a chute, so that the water from the hull ran into the engine room bilges. Work was started on the seized cylinder (no. 7) port engine, but the spare cylinder and piston stowed in the after end of the motor room were under water and work was therefore abandoned.

At dawn the Vickers guns were stripped and cleaned, and an

attempt was made to get the Oerlikon to work in readiness to repel another day's air attack. A heavy rainstorm obscured the eastern horizon for more than two hours after dawn. To our great relief and surprise nothing occurred throughout the day, *many agnostics were converted.* Ted Jones (2nd Cox) then went over the side and with soap and Hedley's compound improved the blanket plugging which considerably reduced the input of water. I then reminded Lt. Lutley that a signal stating that HMS/M *Stygian* was outward bound for patrol had been received the previous night, this was recovered from the W/T office and deciphered again. Course was set to place *Shakespeare* on *Stygian*'s route.

On the 5th January at 0900 it was decided to put an external patch on the hull to make it more seaworthy, using rubber insertion, soap, part of the steel bridge chart table, two McMahon spanners as strongbacks and clips and bolts from the reload torpedo safety bands. The repair was finished at 1400. This enabled speed to be increased to 8 knots. A spare semi-rotary pump was also rigged to remove water from the engine room bilges.

At 2100 it was decided to fire recognition grenades at each hour and very-lights of the same colour every half hour (to conserve grenades) and to fire a star shell every two hours through the night or until HMS/M *Stygian* challenged. The White Ensign was then laid on the fore casing, a risk if spotted by any enemy aircraft but considered an aid to our survival.

On 6th January at 0100 a light was sighted to westward and shortly after we exchanged pendants with *Stygian*. We burnt navigation lights as we were manoeuvring with difficulty. *Stygian*, suspecting a trap, in spite of correct recognition grenade, asked for the Christian name of our commanding officer's wife, as both commanding officers were personal friends. We replied the name of our commanding officer's wife is Sheila and that your wife's name is Stella. Details of damage, casualties etc., were passed for transmission.

At 0200 in company with *Stygian* course was set for Trincomalee. At 0900 both submarines stopped and *Stygian* sent over a working party of six ratings, torches, medical supplies aboard, by a Folboat, and informed us that HMS *Raider* would be meeting us about 1530. On arrival all 16 wounded and injured were transferred to her and *Stygian* proceeded for patrol.

On 7th January at 1000, water was now so low in the engine room and motor room bilges that the starboard shaft which had been cooled by it now fired up at the bulkhead gland, and the starboard engine practically stopped; then it was found the shaft had dropped. A tow was passed after some difficulty to HMS *Raider*. At 1030 towing commenced the speed working up to 15 knots in an endeavour to get in before nightfall. At 1200 the tow parted at our end owing to a break in one of the studless links adjacent to the joining shackle. At 1205 after repassing a 4" wire during which operation *Raider*'s stern swung onto our bow, and caused a neat cut in her side. At 1300 *Raider* was relieved by HMS *Whelp*. The 1st Lt. of HMS *Whelp* was HRH Prince Philip (now the Duke of Edinburgh). I recall Lt. Lutley informing me that the officer supervising the tow was a royal prince. My reply at this stage did less than justice to the monarchy which I admire and respect. At 1800 the resumed tow at *Whelp*'s end parted and with great difficulty we hauled this in sufficiently to unshackle our end of the 4" wire, this was then secured to a rope from the destroyer and after necessary adjustments was again passed to us and shackled on. During this operation *Whelp* was also holed!

On the 8th January at 0500 we passed Foul Point and assisted by a tug secured alongside HMS *Wolfe*.

LEADING TEL. KEN WADE DSM

*

The depot ship HMS Bonaventure *(Captain W. R. Fell RN) arrived in Victoria harbour, Labuan, in July 1945 with six XE-craft – improved versions of the midget submarines which attacked* Tirpitz. *Although at first it seemed that no operational use would be found for them, these craft distinguished themselves in several memorable exploits before the war ended: XE4 (Lieutenant M. H. Shean RANVR) cut submarine telegraph cable at Cap St Jacques, Saigon, on 31st July, and XE5 (Lieutenant H. P. Westmacott RN) did the same in Lamma Channel, off Hong Kong, on 1st August. Meanwhile XE1 (Lieutenant J. E. Smart RNVR) and XE3 (Lieutenant I. E. Fraser RNR) attacked shipping in Singapore harbour. XE3's target was the 9,850-ton cruiser* Takao, *which had been lying in shallow water in the Johore Straits since being damaged by USS/M Darter in the Battle of Leyte Gulf in October 1944. XE3 was towed to the entrance of the straits by HMS/M Stygian and, on 31st July, made*

The Attack on *Takao*

Excitement was betrayed in my voice. 'There she is!' I cried.

At that part of the strait where the *Takao* lay the water is shallow, with depths shown on Admiralty charts of from eleven to seventeen feet; but there is a depression in the sea-bed, which amounts to a hole, 500 feet across, 1,500 feet long, and some five feet deeper than the water around. The *Takao* lay across this depression so that the first hundred feet of her length, beginning at her bow, lay in water which dropped to less than three feet at low tide; and the same conditions occurred at her stern. It was proposed that I should pass over this shallow patch and down into the hole where I was expected to manoeuvre my boat under the ship. As I have already said, I had made it clear that I thought this feat impossible.

'Stand by for a bearing, ship's ahead, now' I ordered. Then I translated the bearing into a true bearing and laid it on the chart. The attack had started.

From that moment, until I was back on board the *Stygian*, all fear left me.

I felt only that nervous tautness that comes so often in moments of stress. I let each of the others have a quick look at the *Takao* through the periscope, and then we were ready.

It was eight minutes to two when I finally decided that the position of XE3 was right enough for us to start the actual run in. By this time the sun was high in the heavens, the sea was as placid as a Scottish loch early on a summer's day, and visibility, both above and under the water, was excellent.

Looking through the attack periscope, I could see distinctly the tall outlines of cranes in the dockyard lying behind the *Takao*, and the barrack buildings and numerous small boats making their way back and forth from the vessels anchored in midstream. I could see a small destroyer escort, and, tied up between the buoys, a ship of 7,000 or 8,000 tons, which, for a moment, I thought might be worthwhile attacking, should we get away from the *Takao* quickly. I also saw the mooring buoys of battleships lying in the channel, and always looming up I could see the *Takao* as she came closer and closer. Her three for'ard turrets stood out distinctly like Olympic winners on a rostrum, the centre one above the other two, and all three close together. The guns in 'C' turret pointed aft, unlike any other cruiser constructed at that time. Her massive bridgework was easily discernible, with the thick black-topped funnel raking astern of it. I could see the second funnel, smaller, and somewhat insignificant, stuck vertically upwards between the two tripod trellis-work masts, and on 'B', and 'X' turrets a sort of tripod framework.

From her vertical bow with the acutely curved top, stretched two anchor cables, gently rising and falling in the slowly ebbing tide. I could see the gangway on her starboard side, and, just above, a derrick used for hoisting in aircraft. I saw no aircraft.

When, during a spell on the run-in, I glanced through the night periscope, I was disturbed to find that I could see both ends of XE3 quite distinctly, showing that the underwater visibility was ten feet or more. I reconciled myself to this disadvantage by thinking that I would at least be able to keep an eye on Magennis* as he attached the limpet mines.

Later on, at eight minutes past two, the range of 2,000 yards, one mile away, about thirty degrees on our port bow.

'Four hundred and fifty revolutions, steer 218 degrees, stand by to start the attack.'

'Course 218 degrees. All ready to start the attack,' came the reply.

'Start the attack,' I ordered.

Magennis started the stop-watch, and we prepared ourselves.

'Up periscope.'

Magennis pressed the switch, the motor whirred.

'Whoa!'

The motor stopped.

'Bearing right ahead, range two degrees on her funnel – down periscope.'

Magennis changed the degrees into yards by means of the slide rule.

'Length 1,600 yards, sir,' he called.

I did not answer; there was no need to. Each of us was sweating profusely, and energy and air had to be reserved. In any case, we were doing now the thing that we had practised time and time again when stationed in the Scottish lochs and when lying off the coast of Australia.

The only sounds in the boat were the whirr of the main motor, the hiss of escaping oxygen from the cylinder in the engine-room,

* Leading Seaman J. Magennis

and an occasional scraping sound of steel on steel in the well-greased bearings when the hydroplane wheel was turned. Ten feet, forty feet. 'Up periscope', range. 'Down periscope'. So it went on until the range had narrowed to 400 yards.

'Up periscope, stand by for a last look round.'

Click! Down went the handles: I fixed my eye to the eye-piece for the hundredth time, slowly swinging to port.

'Ah, there she is, range eight degrees.'

Slowly I swung the periscope round to starboard.

'Flood "Q", down periscope, quick, thirty feet. Bloody hell! There's a boat full of Japs going ashore, she's only about forty or fifty feet away on the starboard bow. God. I hope they didn't see us!'

So close had they been that I could make out their faces quite distinctly, and even had time to notice that one of them was trailing his hand in the water. The boat, painted white, stood out clearly against the camouflaged background of the cruiser. Similar to the cutters used in the Royal Navy for taking liberty men ashore, she was packed with sailors. The helmsman stood aft, his sailor's coat and ribbon gently lifting in the breeze caused by the boat's headway. She was so close that it seemed that her bow waves almost broke over our periscope. I could see the lips of the men moving as they chatted away on the journey ashore. They should have seen us. I do not know why they did not.

'Thirty feet, sir.'

My mind re-focused.

'All right, Magennis, the range is 200 yards, we should touch bottom in a moment.'

To Smith*: 'Keep her as slow as you can.'

Followed anxious silence, then a jar and the noise of gravel scrap-

---

* Sub-Lieutenant W. J. L. Smith RNZNVR

ing along the keel as we touched bottom. Reid* had to fight hard to keep her on course as we scraped and dragged our way across the bank at depths of only fifteen feet, which means our upper deck was only ten feet below the surface.

Watching through the night periscope, I could see the surface of the water like a wrinkled window-pane above our heads, until it gradually darkened as we came into the shadow of the great ship. Something scraped down our starboard side, and then, with a reverberating crash, we hit the *Takao* a glancing blow, which stopped us. I thought we had made enough noise to awaken the dead, and I was worried in case someone above might have felt the jar.

'Stop the motor! I wonder where the hell we are?' I said. I could see nothing through the periscope to give me a clear indication of our position in relation to the enemy ship, only her dark shadow on our starboard side. Obviously I was not underneath it, as the depth on the gauge was only thirteen feet.

I began to fear that we might be much too far forward, that the ominous-sounding scraping along our side had been made by an anchor cable at the target's bows.

'We seem to be too far for'ard,' I reported. 'We'll alter course to 190 degrees and try to run down her side. Port thirty half ahead, group down.'

The motor hummed into life again, but we did not budge.

'Group up half ahead,' I called, and we tried many other movements. The motor hummed even faster, the propeller threshed, but still no sign of movement. We were jammed, and, looking back on this afterwards, I am inclined to think that as the *Takao* veered in the tideway, the slackening cable came to rest on us. Then it lifted as she veered away again, or else we were jammed for the same reason under the curve of her hull at this point. It was only after

* ERA C. Reid.

some really powerful motor movements in both directions, and ten minutes of severe strain, that we finally broke loose and dragged our way across the shingly bottom to the deeper channel.

I had attacked from too fine an angle on the bow, and after running out again I altered course and steered for a position more on the *Takao*'s beam, which would mean a longer run over the shallow bank, but I decided the risk was worth it if I were to hit the ship amidships.

At three minutes past three we were ready again, a thousand yards away. Once more we started the run-in for the attack. This time we were successful. We slid easily across the bank with the gauge at one time registering only thirteen feet, and then, blackness, as we slid into the hole and under the keel of the *Takao*. It was just as I had practised it so many times before, and I was surprised how easy it was.

The depth gauge began to indicate deeper water, fifteen feet, eighteen feet, twenty feet, and then a greying of the night periscope and upper viewing window.

'Stop the motor.'

'Full astern.'

The bottom of the *Takao* showed dimly, and then suddenly it was distinct, encrusted with thick heavy layers of weed as it fell sharply to her keel.

'Stop the motor!'

The hull stopped sliding overhead. We were under her.

We were resting on the bottom with the hull of the *Takao* only a foot above our heads. I wondered if we would be able to go straight through.

'Come and have a look at this,' I called to the crew, and they left their positions to come and see the encrusted bottom of our prize.

'What a dirty bastard!' said one of them; and I couldn't have agreed more. It would have been nice to have gone out and written my name on the years and years of growth on the keel, but time was passing, and the need for haste cut short our conversations. We were anxious to be away. The *Takao* had no interest for us, other than the need to blow her up.

'Raise the antennae,' I called.

Smith operated the lever and the two antennae came up hydraulically from their stowage positions on either side of the bow.

'It doesn't matter about the after one,' I told Smith, 'there's no point in trying to raise it.'

The after antennae, unlike the two for'ard ones, was raised by hand, and sometimes it was an awful struggle, particularly after several days at sea, to get it up, and in any case it would not have been effective owing to the sharp slope of the ship down to her keel.

Magennis was ready: he must have been stewing in his rubber suit, and I thought, momentarily forgetting the dangers, how pleasant it would be for him to get out into the cool water. He strapped on his breathing apparatus. The only instruction I could give him was to place all six limpets in the container as quickly as possible and not to make a noise. I fitted in the Perspex window, patted him on the shoulder, and into the escape compartment he went. Reid closed the door on him; the valves were opened and shut, and the pumps started. Looking through the observation window into the wet-and-dry compartment, I could see Magennis breathing steadily into the bag as the water rose around him, and then I moved over to the night periscope again, with its larger field of vision and higher magnification. I could see along the keel of the *Takao* for some fifteen yards in either direction, and it was like looking into a dark cave with XE3 lying across the centre of the sunlit entrance. I swung around on the periscope so that the keel of the enemy lay against our upper deck, just for'ard of the periscope bracket, and as the bottom rose away sloping from the keel at a fairly sharp angle the antennae stuck up from the bow like an ant's feelers. They were not resting on the *Takao*'s bottom. Huge lumps and clusters of seaweed hung down like festoons and Christmas decorations, and the faint sunlight danced between them.

Inside the boat we waited patiently. Suddenly, almost as though we hadn't expected it, the pumps stopped and the wheels controlling the valves began to move, as if controlled by a hidden power, as indeed in a sense they were. Reid again moved across from his seat by the wheel to help Magennis to shut them off, and looking through my only means of communication with the diver now that he was outside, I saw the lever which operated the clip on the hatch swing round in an arc of 120 degrees. A few bubbles of free air escaped and gyrated to the surface, wobbling and stretching as they floated through the tangled weed. I saw there was not enough room between us and the *Takao*'s bottom for the hatch to rise fully, but, fortunately, it opened enough for Magennis to squeeze through as his hands gripped the sides of the hatch: and he was safely out. He looked all right, safe and confident, and he gave the 'thumbs-up' sign. I noticed a slight leak from the joint between his oxygen cylinder and the reducing valve on his breathing set. It wasn't really big enough to cause concerns, but I imagine that to Magennis it must have seemed like a full-scale submarine venting its air. He shut the lid and disappeared over the side, and we settled down nervously to await his return.

We counted the limpets as he bumped them out of the containers and moved them one by one along the starboard side, and occasionally I caught a glimpse of him as he worked away under that hull above. Six limpets he took – three towards the for'ard end and three towards the after end. In all, the total time taken was somewhere round about thirty minutes. To me it seemed like thirty days. I cursed every little sound he made, for every little sound was magnified a thousand times by my nerves. It was a long wait. I couldn't remember if we talked or kept silent through it. I think and hope we were pretty calm superficially.

The inside of the boat was like a boiler, but we had to keep quiet. I dared not start the fan or motor. We had simply to sit still and drink tin after tin of orange juice from the Freon container.

The tide was still falling. Although the rise and fall in the Johore Strait is only eight feet, this was more than sufficient to allow the cruiser to sit on us in the shallow hole beneath her hull. High water had been at 1200 zero hour for the attack, and it was now nearly four hours later. I was very anxious to get away. Magennis still seemed to be an age, and just when I could hardly contain myself a moment longer, he appeared on the hatch. He gave the 'thumbs-up' sign again and in he jumped. I saw the lid shut and the clip go home. He was back, and now at last we could go.

Quickly, we started to release the side cargoes. The fuses on the port charge, four tons of amatol, had, like the 200lb limpets, already been set to detonate in six hours' time, so that it was only necessary for us to unscrew the small wheel which started the mechanism, and then to unscrew the larger wheel which released the charge. The first ten turns of this wheel opened a Kingston in the charge to allow water to enter the compartment, previously filled by air, and rendered the charge negatively buoyant. The last turn released the charge itself, which should have fallen away and rested on the bottom. In order to relish the full pleasure of placing four tons of high explosive under a Japanese ship, the three of us took it in turns to operate the wheels as Magennis was draining down his compartment. The port charge fell away – we heard it bump down our side, but we hung on for Magennis to re-enter the craft before finally letting the starboard limpet-carrier go. As a result of this delay, it became too heavy and would not release or slide away. Such an emergency had already been thought of by the designers of XE-craft, and an additional wheel had been provided. This operated a pusher to push the side cargo off, and between us we wound the wheel out to its limit, but with no effect. The bottom held fast. By now I felt sure that the pins at the top were holding, but I thought to myself that the movement of the craft might shake it loose. We certainly couldn't make headway very far with two tons of dead weight fast to our side.

In the meantime Magennis reported that he had found it very difficult getting the limpets into position; the work of attaching them successfully had exhausted him. I could well imagine his feelings, as, out on the lonely water with only the sound of his own breathing to accompany him, he struggled and fought, first of all to clear an area of the bottom so that the magnetic hold-fasts could be fitted against the bare plate of the ship's hull. With his diving knife he had cut away the thick weed waving like the feelers of an octopus above his head, too tough to pull away, and all the time a slow leak from his breathing set. After clearing away the weed he had to tackle the encrustation of barnacles and other shell-fish attached to the bottom. These had to be chipped off as silently as possible. The limpets themselves, clumsily designed (they were big awkward jobs to drag through the water, all angles and projections, and they caught and tangled in the weeds), had to be attached. Unfortunately, owing to the positive buoyancy of the charge itself and the angular bottom of the *Takao*, there was a tendency for the charges to break loose from the magnetic hold-fasts, which, for reasons unknown, had become very feeble, and to run up towards the surface, with Magennis chasing after them to bring them back into position in two groups of three charges. In each group he had secured the limpets some fifty to sixty feet apart – three away along the cavern to our starboard side, and three along the cavern on either side of the keel, so that they could not dislodge and slide off on to the bottom. He had set the firing mechanism working, but in his exhausted state had become unable to remove three of the counter-mining pins, which ensure that should one limpet blow up the rest will follow immediately, even if the clocks have been wound for the set delay.

The counter-mining device, which was lethal after twenty minutes, also ensured that any diver sent down by the Japanese to render the mines safe, or to remove them, would blow himself to eternity should he give the charges the slightest blow.

Looking back on the limpet-placing part of the operation, I see how wonderfully well Magennis did his work. He was the first frogman to work against an enemy from a midget submarine in the manner designed: he was the first and only frogman during the whole X-craft operations ever to leave a boat under an enemy ship and to attach limpet mines: in fact, he was the only frogman to operate from X-craft in harbour against enemy shipping.

Perhaps I had, in some undetectable way, made him aware of my own nervousness. The limpets should not have been less than sixty feet apart for successful working, but, although we should, perhaps, have moved them away a bit further, it was too late now; a final effort had now to be made to get clear of the harbour.

'Group up, half ahead – let's get the hell out of this hole!'

I gave the order with a feeling of relief.

'Main motor, half ahead, sir,' from Smith. 'May I start the fan, sir?'

'Yes, start the fan.'

Magennis began to take off his breathing set and hood.

'What is the course, sir?' asked good, calm, cheerful Reid.

'Two hundred degrees,' I answered. 'Let me know if you have any trouble keeping her on.'

I moved over to the sounding machine and switched it on, and then back to the night periscope to watch as we moved out under the vast hull which was slowly settling down upon us with the fall of the tide, and through which we hoped our charges would blow a hole big enough to sink her for good.

But although the motor had been running for several seconds there was no sign of movement.

'Full ahead,' I ordered.

Still no movement!

'Stop, full astern, group up.'

Glancing at Smith, I sincerely hoped I was not becoming hysterical. I felt certain that the *Takao* must have settled down on us, thus preventing any movement whatsoever. We couldn't go astern as the *Takao*'s keel was lower than the rear periscope standard. We must go ahead if we could go anywhere at all.

'Stop, full ahead, group up, lift the red, stop.'

This gave us maximum power, the motors whirred and we could hear the propeller thrusting hard against the water, but it was useless. We seemed to be well and truly stuck, and for a moment I thought of hanging on until half an hour before the charge was due to go off and then abandoning the ship. After all, I consoled myself, it was only 200 yards from the shore, and we might be able to hide in the swamps and forests until Singapore fell into British hands again. Our flags and emblems were going to come in useful after all!

We tried pumping the water aft and then for'ard, out and then in, and finally we even partially blew No. 2 main ballast tank to try to shake loose from what looked like *XE2*'s watery grave. I was in despair. Sweat poured into my eyes. But still that black menacing shape stood overhead. Then suddenly, with a final effort, she began to move.

'Ship's head swinging to starboard, can't control her.'

Once again Reid's quiet voice calmed my turmoil. We began to move slowly ahead, the flooded charge dragging like a broken wing on our starboard side. The black roof slid astern, and fresh pure welcome sunlight streamed through the water into my upturned eyes.

We had a bow angle on some five degrees, and slowly the needle of my depth gauge moved in an anti-clockwise direction until it steadied at seventeen feet. The weight on our right swung the ship's head round until we were parallel to the side of the *Takao*, and I reckoned some thirty feet away on her port side.

'Stop the motor, we'll have to try to release the cargo. It'll have to be very carefully done as we're only a few yards away,' I explained.

Magennis was still sweating away in his suit, and I felt he had done enough to make the operation a success. As Reid had little or no experience of underwater swimming in the frogmen gear, and Smith wasn't particularly good at this either, I considered that it was justifiable for me to take the risk of leaving the boat for a few moments, even if I was the commanding officer. Should anything happen, I had enough confidence in Smith to know that he could get her out to rejoin the *Stygian*.

'Come out of the way, Magennis, I'll go out and release it myself. Get me the spare set from the battery compartment.'

'I'll be all right in a minute, sir' said Magennis, 'just let me get my wind.'

What a wonderful lad he was! He said this with a most hurt expression on his face, quite obviously meaning that since he was the diver it was up to him to do the diving. And so we sat quietly for five minutes, and when he was ready I replaced his hood and perspex face. 'Thanks' he said, and into the wet-and-dry compartment he went for the second time.

The wheels spun, the pumps started and the water began to rise. Reid had equipped Magennis with an elephant-size spanner, and as the lid of the hatch opened, I saw this come through the opening immediately behind a mass of air bubbles, followed by Magennis. Once again I wondered what he was thinking about only thirty feet away from a Japanese cruiser in seventeen feet of clear water, his only weapon being a spanner. The bubbles released from opening the hatch were quite enough to cause me a great deal of worry. Had anybody been looking over the side of the *Takao* – perhaps a seaman gazing idly into the water with his thoughts away at home in Yokohama,

Nagasaki, or somewhere like that – he must have seen us. The water was as clear as glass, and Magennis in his green diving suit was sending out a steady stream of bubbles from the reducing valve of his set.

Inside the boat it was as quiet as death: none of us spoke. I could hear the ship's chronometer ticking away, the anxious seconds interrupted by an occasional clank as Magennis used his spanner. It took some five minutes to release the cargo – five of the most anxious minutes of my life. Watching through the periscope, I could see the position of both securing pins at which he should have been working, but for some reason or other he was out of sight. I bit my fingers, swore and cursed at him, swore and cursed at the captain and all the staff on board *Bonaventure* who had planned his operation, at the British Admiralty, and finally at myself for ever having been so stupid as to volunteer for this life, and, having volunteered, for being so stupid as to work hard enough to get myself this particular operation. I wished myself anywhere except lying on the bottom of Singapore harbour.

I don't know what Reid or Smith thought of this little display, but as far as I know they never mentioned my temporary lapse.

I had told Magennis to make no noise, but this hammering and bashing, in what I thought to be really the wrong place, was loud enough to alarm the whole Japanese Navy.

'What the bloody hell is that bloody fool doing?' I asked no one in particular. 'Why the hell doesn't he come on top of the charge? Why didn't I go out myself?' Then I saw Magennis for a moment, and at the same time the cargo came away and we were free. He gave me the 'thumbs-up' sign for the third and last time and slid feet first into the wet-and-dry compartment and closed the lid. Wheels turned, pumps started and down came the water.

Right, I thought. Then:

'Starboard twenty steer 090 degrees half ahead group up,' I ordered all in one breath.

'Aye, aye, sir.'

'Twelve hundred revolutions.'

'Aye, aye, sir.'

'O.K.,' I said. 'Home James, and don't spare the horses.'

I think we all managed a smile at that moment.

LIEUTENANT-COMMANDER IAN FRASER VC DSC RNR

Takao was badly damaged but did not sink. The author and Leading Seaman J. Magennis were both awarded the Victoria Cross. In the same operation XE1's target was the cruiser Myoko, some two miles further in the straits; XE1 was delayed by Japanese patrol boats and, time running out, added her charges to XE3's burden already under Takao. Both craft returned safely to Brunei Bay on 4th August.

Part Five:
POSTWAR

A submarine officer joined his first boat as a 'Fourth Hand', pro-
gressed to 'Third Hand', and then to First Lieutenant. The hardest
advance was from First Lieutenant to Commanding Officer. To
become a submarine CO, one had to pass the Submarine Commanding
Officers' Qualifying Course, always known as the 'Perisher'. The offi-
cer in charge of the course was known as 'Teacher'. A 'Perisher' lasted
between three and four months, in which 'Teacher' subjected candi-
dates to the most intense physical, mental and psychological pressure,
to find out if they could stand the strain of submarine command.

One submarine CO, who took the course in 1947, describes

The Perisher

There were only two others on my Submarine Commanding Officers'
Qualifying Course – to give the Perisher its proper title. John Black-
burn, who had great potential, was to lose his life in his second
command, HMS *Affray*, which took down with her not only her
ship's company of 65 men but an entire training-class of submarine
engineer officers, many of them the sons of serving officers. She had
only just come out of an extended time in dockyard hands when she

was abruptly ordered to sea, straight into the potentially dangerous procedure of snorting by night in a main shipping lane. It was not in John's nature to question his orders, no matter what misgivings he must have felt. Another Commanding Officer in a boat in a similar state of operational unreadiness flatly refused to sail on the exercise which led to the untimely end of *Affray* and her fine company. Significantly no disciplinary action was taken against him, and he was soon afterwards promoted to Commander. *Affray* lies in 250 feet of water next to the Hurd Deep, fifteen miles north-west of Alderney Harbour. The other candidate on my Perisher had an uneventful subsequent career.

So soon after the end of the war, the Submarine Command did not have to look far for the ideal person to turn a First Lieutenant into a Commanding Officer, a considerably greater step in the extra dimension of submarine warfare than in any other ships. My course was lucky to have two of the very best, with four DSO's and three DSC's between them, and assured of a place in submarine history by their exploits in the Mediterranean. We started on the Meccano-set dry attack teacher at Fort Blockhouse run by mischievous Wrens with the power to make any candidate they fancied look better than he was, literally by pulling strings and vice versa! They probably did not fool our first Teacher, Commander Hugh ('Rufus') Mackenzie, whose ready smile and infectious sense of fun concealed a shrewd observant mind. We now learnt the first of many steps in the choreography of converting data visually observed by the attacker through a World War I monocular periscope into the final solution of the velocity triangle formed by the target's course and speed and that of a 45-knot straight-running Mk 8** torpedo. The angle to be aimed off at the moment of firing was known as the Director Angle, or D.A. It was arrived at by cranking target data (course and speed from a plot of periscope ranges and bearings) into the fruit-machine – a crude mechanical angle-solver. Unlike German and American

submarines, our torpedo control angle-solver did not have its inputs
fed in directly from the periscope, nor was a running solution available allowing for the change of bearing generated between successive
periscope up-dates. The velocity triangle was frozen each time the
periscope was lowered. So if you had to go deep to run in and close
the track or to dip under the escort screen, the captain got no reliable
steer where to look when the periscope next broke surface, unless
sonar was delivering useful data.

Most captains carried an approximate running solution in their
heads, others were disorientated and swung the periscope around
frantically in search of the target. This situation was known as being
'lost in the box'. In the rapidly closing stages of an attack it often
meant the target had slipped past the firing point and the D.A. was
missed. One of my most terrifying moments in peacetime was when a
captain, who conspicuously lacked any intuitive feel for a developing
attack scene, solemnly had the periscope held on the D.A., say Green
22 (22 degrees aim-off on the starboard bow) and fired a deliberately
aimed and spread salvo of six dummy torpedoes at an aircraft carrier
whose screws were heard throughout the boat thundering over the
after ends. It can't have missed us by much, but the captain's claim
to have scored 3 'hits' was never disputed.

Apparently Rufus was satisfied with our efforts on the synthetic
nursery slopes at Fort Blockhouse, for we then went up to the Clyde
and joined the Perisher boat for honing our art in Inchmarnock
Water, starting with straight targets at moderate speeds, then gradu-
ating to dealing with high-speed Fleet destroyers escorting a zigzagging convoy, by day and night. Early on during this phase Rufus
left, later going on to greater things as a Vice Admiral in charge of the
Polaris Executive which delivered Britain's nuclear ballistic missile
submarines dead on time, after the Skybolt fiasco. He was replaced
by someone I knew well from La Maddalena, George Hunt, formerly
C.O. of *Ultor*, the top-scoring submarine of her day in the Tenth

Flotilla. He was a quiet, undemonstrative man who didn't miss a trick. Every one of the hundreds of attacks we carried out under his tutelage was patiently analysed afterwards. His stopwatch checked the duration of each periscope exposure and whether they were too frequent. But, above all, it told him the precise moment to step in and abort an attack by pressing the klaxon to flood 'Q' tank and get the boat below any risk of being rammed by a destroyer. During the later stages of the course the destroyer was allowed to turn towards and make a threatening charge at any periscope sighted or sonar contact. It was then up to the student to break off the attack under peace-time safety rules, or suffer the humiliation of having Teacher do it for him. On the other hand, pulling the plug too soon earned you an equally undesirable mark. With a destroyer turning towards at, say, 500 yards and capable of being on top of you in 30 seconds there wasn't too much time to scratch your arse and ask advice from the attack team.

The final catch was that any student enjoying a run of successful undetected attacks was cut down to size by Teacher ordering the big periscope to be raised and left waving around in the air until the destroyer's lookouts saw it.

I always felt sorry for the C.O. of the submarine in which we stumbled our way towards the required standards. He was ultimately responsible for the safety of his own submarine, yet had to stand aside and watch potentially dangerous situations deliberately contrived by Teacher. At intervals there were consecutive long days and nights intended to stretch the students and see how they reacted when fatigue blurred their judgement. Ironically, it was Teacher who visibly sagged the most. We at least only had to concentrate for one attack in three, the others being played out on the fruit-machine or the plot.

Recently a TV series was built around Perisher with all kinds of mental hangups, domestic distractions and personal defects holding centre stage. That was never the case, and I doubt if it is today. No candidate is selected for the course unless his qualities of leadership and mental equilibrium have already been proven. The most common cause of failure was for Teacher to realise early on that a student lacked 3-D vision through a periscope, not being able to size up a given situation in full perspective. Or he may lack the mental agility to cope with a rapidly developing situation. Sadly for some very fine officers, the weakness of their periscope eye is not exposed until they get out there in the Perisher boat, after years of faultless service from Fourth Hand to First Lieutenant. So they are reverted to General Service without a stain on their record, or so they are blandly assured by Flag Officer Submarines. In practice they might as well start reading the Appointments column in the *Daily Telegraph* right away.

CAPTAIN JOHN COOTE RN

*

The 'schnorkel', a Dutch invention used by German U-boats in the latter stages of the Second World War, but not by British submarines until after the war, enabled a submarine to run its main diesel engines to propel the boat and/or to charge the battery whilst submerged. It consisted of a metal mast incorporating two tubes – an inlet tube fitted with a float-controlled valve at its top, through which the engines could draw down air for combustion, while the float-controlled valve would shut off the tube if for any reason it dipped beneath the surface, and an open-ended tube through which the engines could discharge their exhaust gases against sea pressure.

The Royal Navy carried out several trials on the schnorkel. One was the tropical 'snort' cruise by Alliance *which lasted for thirty days, from 0833, 9th October, to 0900, 8th November 1947, covering a distance of 3,193 miles, the route being south-east from the Canary*

Islands to Cape Verde, then due east along the Equator, altering north-east to Cape Palmas, thence northwards up the African coast to Freetown.

The Tropical Cruise of *Alliance*

The snort exhaust valves, as expected, were a bone of contention. They proved unreliable from a watertight point of view owing to distortion, and also required constant attention to keep the operating and grinding gear from seizing up. Consequently, on more than one occasion water found its way into the (engine) cylinders when stopping the engines. Owing to this inherent defect, every effort was made to avoid shutting off both engines together in cases of emergency. The practice adhered to if the snort head dipped for a considerable period, was to shut down one engine just before 6 inches of depression was reached and to take out the engine clutch to make that motor available to regain trim. Meanwhile the exhaust valve was ground in..

This ensured that one engine was dry, and available to start, in case the second engine became flooded in the event of that also having stopped. It should be pointed out here that the exhaust from both engines marry before entering the snort mast, so that no flooding back can occur so long as one engine is running at medium speed.

The maximum depression reached during the cruise was about 8 ins. of mercury, but *Alliance* was fortunate in having fair weather all the way, so that there was very little continuous 'pumping' of the atmosphere, which can, if it goes on long enough become very demoralising. This condition is caused by successive heavy swells passing over the snort head, or more acutely by repeated loss of depth control due to bad weather. This 'pumping' did however occur for short periods, the effect of which was to lower the dew-point sufficiently to produce fogging in various parts of the boat, notably one which persisted in descending from the gun-tower into the ward-room. The tinned foods carried on board reacted noisily to the varying states of atmospheric depression (no record is held of any reaction to mental depression!) strangely enough, not always to the detriment of their contents. The coxswain's store on occasions sounded rather like a hard pressed machine gun post as the ends of the cans buckled under the fluctuating pressure. No insurmountable difficulties were experienced during night snorting. The chief diffi-culties were those of visibility, especially on moonless nights. A slightly shallower depth of 35 feet was maintained at night for this reason.

At 0900 on Saturday, 8th November, *Alliance* surfaced and both conning tower hatches were opened together for the first time in thirty days. The stench of marine life drawn down into the boat was at least a change, if unpleasant. . . .

LIEUTENANT (E) D. H. RUSSELL RN

*

The Worst Hangover

Any casual onlooker who happened to glance out into the North Channel from the Mull of Kintyre on the afternoon of Thursday, 5th October, 1961, would have seen a remarkable sight: one small black submarine, lying apparently stopped on the surface a few miles offshore, blowing off clouds of dense smoke, with her casing crowded with men huddled in blankets. Had that spectator used binoculars he would have noticed that the men were all violently coughing and retching, some of them clutching their foreheads seemingly in agony, while others were comprehensively vomiting over the side. He would, in fact, have been witnessing the aftermath of a unique submarine accident.

The submarine was HMS *Explorer*, one of the two 'E' Class submarines (the other was *Excalibur*, then undergoing refit) which were fitted with experimental hydrogen peroxide propulsion machinery. At that time, *Explorer* provided a high-speed underwater exercise target for the Third Submarine Squadron at Faslane, and for the frigates and RAF Shackletons at Londonderry. She was based at Faslane, but was normally day-running from Campbeltown. (Both submarines have now been scrapped).

Hydrogen peroxide (H_2O_2) is a most curious substance. In weak solution, it is the stuff blondes dye their hair with. In its strongest manufactured form it is known as High Test Peroxide, or HTP, which is a potent fuel used in rockets, torpedoes and submarines. HTP is a clear liquid, like water but heavier. In depth it is faintly greenish, with tiny bubbles rising to the surface. HTP decomposes continuously, giving off oxygen, and it can therefore never be kept in sealed tanks nor left trapped between two shut valves. If confined, HTP will always explode sooner or later. (A failure properly to appreciate this phenomenon contributed to the HTP torpedo explosion which led to the loss of HMS *Sidon* at Portland on 16th June, 1955).

HTP can only be stored in containers or passed through pipes made of 'compatible' materials. These are few – glass, porcelain, PVC, some forms of rubber, certain types of stainless steel and, for a limited exposure time, aluminium. With incompatible materials, such as mild steel, brass, wood, clothing or human tissue, HTP will react vigorously, producing both heat and oxygen – two of the three essentials to establish combustion. It is axiomatic that any HTP leak will start a fire. In contact with oil or grease the decomposition of

HTP is sufficiently rapid and violent to be described as an explosion.

A layman might by now have formed the opinion that HTP was far too anti-social a liquid to be welcome anywhere, least of all in a submarine. But it has one asset, prized above rubies. It can be used as a source of oxygen to support combustion in a submerged submarine.

The HTP plant in *Explorer* was developed jointly by the Admiralty and Vickers from Professor Helmuth Walter's invention, used in later types of German U-boats in World War Two. A Type XVIIB U-boat, U.1407, was captured at Cuxhaven in 1945; she was renamed HMS *Meteorite* and trials were carried out in her after the war. The HTP machinery gave her, and *Explorer*, very high underwater speeds, if only for short periods.

In *Explorer*, the HTP was forced to decompose under controlled conditions by means of a catalyst. The resulting flow of oxygen and superheated steam was passed to a combustion chamber, where kerosene was burnt in the oxygen, causing a rapid rise in temperature and pressure. After some cooling, the hot gases were admitted to turbines which drove the propeller shafts through self-engaging clutches. The turbine exhaust gases were then recompressed and discharged through the hull into the sea. The gases were soluble in sea water and showed no trace on the surface. The whole process of starting and running the HTP machinery was known colloquially on board by the very descriptive term 'fizzing'.

To the unwary bystander *Explorer* 'fizzing' in harbour was like a preview of doomsday. The exhaust gases, emerging at sonic speeds, towered above the submarine in great plumes of pearly-grey smoke, accompanied by an appalling roar which shook windows a hundred yards away, stampeded cattle and caused passing motorists to swerve off the road. When *Explorer* first 'fizzed' after joining the Squadron, *Adamant*'s horrified officer of the watch called out the fire and emergency party and summoned the local brigade, being convinced that *Explorer* had become a fiery holocaust from end to end.

'Fizzing' at full power at sea, *Explorer* fled across the Irish Sea bellowing like some demented sea-monster pursued by twin smoke clouds of apocalyptic shape and colouring. In the early days, when combustion was sometimes faulty, the exhaust clouds would turn from grey to black and then, to the stupefaction of all who saw them, suddenly erupt into cataclysmic fireballs of flame and smoke, as the oxygen in the atmosphere completed the combustion begun inside the submarine. *Explorer* was never an appointment for those of nervous disposition. Her first Engineer Officer was awarded an MBE, an award which, in the circumstances, was not over-generous.

The turbine exhaust gases were composed very largely of carbon dioxide (CO_2), with small amounts of carbon monoxide (CO) and excess oxygen, and traces of other gases such as methane. When the machinery was running the turbine room quickly filled with gas and the plant was therefore started, operated and stopped by remote control from outside the gas- and water-tight forward turbine room bulkhead.

In spite of the bulkhead, small amounts of CO_2 and CO did accumulate at the turbine starting platform and were carefully monitored whilst 'fizzing' dived. If the permitted parameters of gas concentration were ever exceeded, thus risking the health of the ship's company, then the 'fizzing' had to stop for the day. After surfacing, the machinery space was at once ventilated by a fan which exhausted air from the turbine room and discharged it outboard, fresh air being allowed to flow into the turbine room from the rest of the submarine. While 'fizzing' on the surface, the turbine room was ventilated continuously and gas monitoring was not necessary.

Explorer also had a small diesel-generator fitted right forward, where the torpedo tube space would be in an orthodox submarine. It was intended only for internal power supplies and for charging the main battery. Originally, 'E' Class submarines were to be towed to their exercise areas but this arrangement lapsed very early in *Explorer*'s career, if indeed it was ever done, and *Explorer* was left to make her own way. Her single, grossly under-powered diesel-generator gave her a surface speed of about five knots, so that she had to sail at 3.30 a.m. for a serial starting at nine o'clock.

Explorer was first commissioned in 1956, when all major research and development virtually ceased. Her turbines were therefore proto-types, and very temperamental. *Explorer*'s engine-room department was as superstition-ridden as any primitive aboriginal community. If I, as Engineer Officer, failed to do my usual rounds and make my daily obeisances, the turbines would not perform. They would not, in any case, perform on Sundays or holy days; break-downs on these days happened too often to be coincidence. Once, after we had slogged for 36 hours into a raging Atlantic gale, neither turbine would start. Later, I checked and found it was Yom Kippur.

The turbines not only resented rough weather but also strange faces on the control platform and strange hands on the controls. It took weeks to get a new operator accepted. Some members of the ship's company were forbidden by the Chief ERA to come aft of the control room bulkhead while 'fizzing' because of their 'evil eye' effect.

This mental attitude in the turbine operating crew had a bearing on the accident. On that critical afternoon, *Explorer* was 'fizzing' on the surface at about half through-put on both turbines, acting as a target for another, dived, submarine. The sea was flat calm, the day sunny, the wind only occasional light airs. The diesel-generator was running. It was the first 'fizz' of the day, indeed the first for many days, after lengthy and exhausting repairs. There was much jubilation on the turbine platform when both turbines got under way and settled down to the required r.p.m. with only the minimum of bangs and alarms. It seemed that for once we were going to have a good day.

There was no such joy in the control room where, after some fifteen minutes' 'fizzing', the watch-keepers began to be concerned by the great volume of smoke pouring down the conning tower. The First Lieutenant was actually standing at the foot of the tower ladder. His eyes were smarting painfully and he was finding it hard to catch his breath. But he was a newcomer to the ship. This was, in fact, his first 'fizzing' day at sea. He assumed that this smoke was a normal occurrence in *Explorer*. From what he had heard of HTP, anything was possible. Gritting his teeth, he resolved that he would not be the first to complain.

After about twenty minutes, the message was passed aft: 'There's a lot of smoke and gas in the control room'. On the turbine platform this incomprehensible statement seemed highly hilarious, but irrelevant. Watch-keeping on HTP machinery demanded the utmost concentration and the alarm reflexes of a cat. Everything was going well, but we simply dared not take our eyes from the gauges for an instant. If the control room watch wanted to smoke themselves to death, that was their affair entirely. It was nothing to do with us.

However, the word 'gas' touched off a conditioned reflex. Gas content monitoring was started, as a precaution. The Ringrose CO_2 Indicator at the forward end of the motor-room was consulted but was reported to me as *defective because the liquid in the calibrated tube had risen well above the top of the scale*. I accepted the report without query. The Infra Red CO_2 and CO recorders were switched on. Both at once showed unbelievable maximum readings and were consequently reported to me as defective. Again, I did not challenge the reports.

There was one more method of measuring CO content on board. This was the Minchin Tube, which worked in principle rather like a breathalyser. The amount of carbon monoxide present could be determined by measuring the length of discoloured crystals in a tube. A Minchin reading was taken which showed an unprecedented amount of crystal discoloration. The tube was passed from hand to hand, and commented upon with some derision. Clearly, the crystals were defective.

Looking back now, it does seem that I was extraordinarily slow to take the point which was being hammered in on me from all sides. I had been on board for some time, and I knew something of *Explorer* and her funny ways. For us, the monitoring of dangerous gases was almost a daily preoccupation. We, of all people, should have marked the danger signals but with every detection device shrieking warnings we remained oblivious. I myself felt perfectly fit, although one or two men around me were screwing up their eyes in concentration and complaining of slight headaches. But there seemed no reason to stop the turbines. It cost our department so many back-breaking man-hours to maintain them, and we had to overcome so much 'bad joss' to start them, that subconsciously we must all have resisted the idea of stopping the turbines unnecessarily or prematurely.

There was, too, a more insidious factor at work. Carbon dioxide poisoning is a well-known occupational hazard for submariners. A high CO_2 level can reduce a skilled crew to the intellectual status of doped rabbits, befuddling their reasoning, affecting their judgement, and making every breath a burden to them. We must all by now have been thoroughly gassed, and if one symptom of carbon dioxide poisoning is the unbalancing of a man's judgement, then here was a text-book case.

Meanwhile, the Captain had been with the Navigating Officer on the bridge where, of course, where was no sign nor smell of gas. After some twenty-five minutes' 'fizzing' the Captain went down the ladder, to find the control room full of smoke haze. The helmsman was asking to be relieved, because he felt giddy and sick. The Captain ordered the telegraphs to Stop.

Aft, there was an atmosphere of puzzled resentment. Why stop now, when things were going so well? The serial was not due to finish for at least another thirty minutes. Had someone fallen overboard? At this time, the Chief E.R.A. remarked to me quite casually and calmly that if something was not done soon, somebody was going to pass out. At last, all the mental alarm bells began to ring. An Orsat gas analysis apparatus had been set up on the work-bench, to measure the composition of the exhaust gases, indicating plant efficiency. Taking a reading on the turbine platform, I saw that the carbon dioxide content in the air we were breathing was nine per cent. Looking over my shoulder, I noticed the L.E.M. on the main motor switches; his eyes were rolling in his head and his face was, literally, the shade of a rotten plum.

I suppose the order must have been passed to evacuate the submarine, but I have no recollection of it. The same thought seemed to strike everyone on board at once. It was time to go.

The whole ship's company headed for the control room and diesel room ladders, one by one swarmed up them, and tumbled out on to the casing. There, we all with one accord began to experience in varying degree the classic 'off-effect' symptoms of carbon dioxide poisoning: headaches, dizziness, and nausea. Some were very sick. Others lay face down on the casing, their foreheads pressed into their fists, while co-ordinated batteries of bongo drums beat out a tattoo inside their temples. A few just sat, looking bewildered; one moment they had been sitting playing uckers in the mess, the next they were up on the casing feeling like the morning after Hogmanay.

It was a strange sensation, sitting in the hot autumn sunshine, with one's head throbbing and one's stomach turning over and over. Seagulls flew past, looking curiously at us. The sea was so calm I could see a seal swimming off the starboard side. After a short time, those least affected went down in pairs to start the battery fans ventilating outboard, to run the LP blower and restart the diesel-generator. Blankets were brought up. Tea was brewed. All settled down to wait until the submarine was once more fit for human habitation. Hunched in our blankets, we must have been an odd sight. As one wag remarked 'We looked more like a ☀☀☀☀☀☀☀ Arab dhow than a ☀☀☀☀☀☀☀ submarine'.

An hour later, everybody went below and *Explorer* was back to normal. The effects of the poisoning seemed to wear off very quickly, leaving a general feeling that one had just had the worst hangover in the world. Curiously, those who had been ashore drinking the night before seemed the least affected. Later, two ratings were admitted to Campbeltown hospital for observation but returned on board the next day.

There only remained the post-mortem. The turbine exhaust gases were discharged through 'exhaust bends' – short curved lengths of stout pipe, bolted to the pressure hull – which turned the gases through almost ninety degrees to lead them out through the side of the submarine's casing. The port exhaust bend had been worn through by the abrasive effect of the gas so that although the gas clouds still billowed out apparently undiminished a small amount of gas was allowed to escape into the casing. *Explorer* created a relative wind by her speed through the water, but on such a calm day the air inside the casing was comparatively still. The gases therefore filled up the casing, seeking an outlet. Aft there was none, but forward there was the fin and the open conning tower hatch. The gases were sucked down the tower, and thence drawn forward by the diesel-generator, aft by the turbine room ventilation, thus being distributed throughout the submarine.

The 'Great Gassing Day', as it was called, taught us all a sharp lesson, reminding us once again of that old rule: at sea, there really is no substitute for constant vigilance. Circumstances innocent in themselves can suddenly combine to cause a potentially dangerous situation. In this case, a not unusual material failure (exhaust bends had perforated several times before) combined with not unusual weather conditions (it *is* sometimes flat calm in the Irish Sea) had in a few minutes created a serious threat to the ship's company.

I made a note of the readings of gas content in the air at the turbine platform just before it was evacuated. They may have a certain gloomy interest for physiologists.

Ringrose Carbon Dioxide Indicator: off the scale, i.e. more than 5% CO_2.

Orsat Reading: 9% CO_2.

Infra Red Carbon Dioxide Recorder: full scale deflection of needle, i.e. more than 70mm. Hg. partial pressure of CO_2.

Infra Red Carbon Monoxide Recorder: full deflection of needle, i.e. more than 500 parts/million of CO.

Minchin Tube: 0.13% CO.

I am told the lethal level of carbon dioxide content at atmospheric pressure is about 12 to 15 per cent. Those readings therefore prompt the sobering thought that some of us not only had our worst, but very nearly our last, hangover in this world.

JOHN WINTON

Citation for the Albert Medal

The posthumous award of the Albert Medal for gallantry in saving life at sea to Temporary Surgeon Lieutenant Charles Eric Rhodes, M.B., B.S., M.R.C.S., L.R.C.P., of the Royal Naval Volunteer Reserve, who lost his life after the explosion in the submarine *Sidon* in Portland Harbour on 16th June of last year, has been announced in the *London Gazette*. The citation states:

'Surgeon Lieutenant Rhodes was among the first to enter the submarine after the explosion and in spite of darkness and smoke brought out an injured man to safety. He then put on a Davis Submarine Escape Apparatus and re-entered the submarine with morphia to give further help to the injured. In doing so he greatly prejudiced his chance of escape. He was not a submarine officer and was not familiar with the use of the breathing apparatus or the lay-out inside a submarine. In spite of these handicaps and the pitch darkness his only thoughts were for those within the submarine; he had no hesitation in re-entering the *Sidon* and he succeeded in helping two more men to escape before the submarine sank. Surgeon Lieutenant Rhodes's gallant and selfless act in helping to save the lives of others cost him his own life.'

The explosion occurred when the submarine *Sidon* was alongside the depot ship *Maidstone* as she was preparing for sea for practice firing. In addition to Surgeon Lieutenant Rhodes, twelve officers and men were killed.

The accident was caused by a Mark 12 HTP-powered torpedo, codenamed 'Fancy', undergoing trials that summer, which blew up when loaded in one of Sidon's *torpedo tubes. Later another 'Fancy' exploded on the test range at Arrochar in Scotland and the torpedo was withdrawn.*

*

On 12 June 1959, at Vickers, Barrow-in-Furness, HRH The Duke of Edinburgh moved a handle which caused a gamma beam to operate a winch, which in turn drew a 30 feet cylindrical section into position. So was laid the first section of the Royal Navy's first nuclear submarine Dreadnought.

Dreadnought *was a hunter-killer, displacing 3,500 tons on the surface and 4,000 tons dived, armed with six torpedo tubes. Her after body, designed by the General Dynamics Corporation under a contract signed in August 1959, was virtually a copy of the USS* Skipjack *Class, and contained the reactor and the main propulsion and auxiliary machinery. The forward half was entirely British.*

Dreadnought *was launched by Her Majesty the Queen on Trafal-gar Day, 21 October 1960.*

HMS *Dreadnought*

In February 1959, I was a 23-year-old Lieutenant and Navigator of *Sanguine* in Malta. My good friend Jock Campbell was the Torpedo Officer. We were due to sail shortly back to England, having had a happy 18 months in the 1st Submarine Squadron, based in Malta.

At about 1100 one forenoon, a messenger came down to *Sanguine* from the Depot Ship *Forth* and asked for Lieutenant Hale. I said that was me. He informed me that Captain S/M wanted to see me in the Depot Ship right away. Somewhat white-faced, I said I would be straight up.

Jock Campbell looked at me with apprehension. We went through what had happened in the last 48 hours or so, to see what on earth I could have done that was so wrong that Captain S/M wanted to see me. We had not pranged any cars, nor any of the girl-friends, nor got drunk in the wrong places, nor been more than normally rude to anyone important. So I was seriously worried as I hastened to the after end of the dear old Depot Ship.

Lt Cdr Mike Vernon was the Captain's Secretary, and a friend to young submariners. He smiled and took me in to see the Boss. 'Congratulations Tim' said the Boss. 'You've been selected for the first crew of *Dreadnought*.'

My surprise was utter, and it was obvious. It seemed that Captain S/M was also fairly surprised. However, apparently he wasn't aware of anything sufficiently bad about me, that could put a block on this appointment. When I got back down to *Sanguine*, Campbell too was totally surprised. This did not prevent us from having two very large horse's necks.

In due course I learned who the other members of the wardroom were. I was the junior officer of the whole lot. They were all highly talented, and clearly hand-picked. Thus it was clear that I had been selected to provide some light relief – and indeed to take the blame as the most junior officer. The truth of this arose from time to time.

Dreadnought was big and new and fast and very exciting. The Queen did the launch. The builders were Vickers in Barrow, who were even more experienced at building submarines than Electric Boat in Connecticut. The build did take somewhat longer than was originally planned, but we spent the time training and learning about the ship and the systems.

In December 1962, we took her to sea for PSTs – officially 'Preliminary Sea Trials'. We called them 'Political Sea Trials', because the Secretary of State, who I believed was called Orr-Ewing at the time, had said that '*Dreadnought* would go to sea in 1962'. So he got some political *kudos*, and we got further delays in our programme.

The PSTs were interesting. The Walney Channel, which is utterly terrifying at low tide, did fill with water and we did get out and back on one two-day tidal window. We did not dive, but we did get her up on the step at 19 knots on the surface. We also christened Check Point Charlie, the reactor compartment bulkhead of the British to the American Zone – we had an American power plant.

Early 1963 was one of the coldest winters of the century. We did Contractors Sea Trials (CSTs) in February 1963. At my rented farmhouse in north Lancashire, the water was frozen in the ground for nine weeks. However my wife and three year old daughter did survive and are still eminently healthy.

Whilst anchored at one time in Rothesay Bay, the weather blew up severely. The reactor had been shut down, with power on the diesel. We had to get critical quickly, and the pre-critical checks were actually carried out whilst we pulled rods. It all worked. The reasons for the apparent over-abundance of talent in the team were on this occasion clearly justified.

After commissioning on 17 April 1963, we did lots of sea time with lots of trials and lots of VIPs. She did go very fast and at that time there were no restrictions on the use of full power. She was pretty noisy, but we didn't mind. We were very quick.

We also had a lot of fun showing our various friends around from other submarines. Our bar hours were totally normal – for submariners. Faslane had the dear old Depot Ship, which we went alongside. There was none of this over-consciousness of security which seems to prevail these days.

I was Torpedo Officer. It was a great job. I had six torpedo tubes at the front end, with brand new water ram discharge, and 26 reloads. It was a big cavern. We did torpedo discharge trials off Gibraltar in about July 1963. As we worked up in speed, more Mark 8s hit the shutters [streamlining fairings on the hull] on their way out. We lost some. We also fired Mark 20s, which were more difficult for the TRV [Torpedo Recovery Vessel] to find, as they floated horizontally. On one occasion we had to surface to assist the TRV, and had several false calls. At the end, on the roof [surfaced], I had one flooded tube with a Mark 20 in it, and requested permission to fire with latch tripper up – so it would not run, but float up – a lot quicker than unload on board. OK – fire it – we did – it came out, rolled on to its yellow back, and dived straight off to the bottom . . . !

In about August '63 we took 1SL (First Sea Lord) to sea with his NA (Naval Assistant). 1SL was a submariner, David Luce, and the NA was Captain David Williams (later Second Sea Lord). By this time we knew there was a plan for Polaris submarines. I was deputed to suggest some names to 1SL – Sir, what about the George Class? George VI, George Robey, Wee Georgie Wood, George Formby, and the fifth would be The Morning George. Regrettably he was not amused, not at all. I thought it was the end of my glorious career. Many years later, David Williams told me he had to walk away for fear of laughing!

COMMANDER TIM HALE RN

*

Meanwhile, back in the world of orthodox diesel-electric submarines . . .

Diving Debacle

Our new 1st Lieutenant arrived from the nuclear submarine world, one we disparaged and thought too 'big ship' and clever by half. One of his most important jobs was to work out the trim before we sailed so that on first diving we went down quickly, evenly and required only minor adjustments thereafter. It was a matter of pride to get the trim absolutely right and his predecessor had done so on many occasions having taken the advice of our grizzled Chief Stoker who had been in this old class of conventional submarine for over 26 years. But the new man was not receptive to advice. For the whole afternoon before we sailed he covered the Wardroom table with trim statements, tank readings, the trimming 'bible' and slide rule calculations. We were impressed with this new, intellectual approach to the trim. But then he sent for the Chief Stoker and issued his instructions and the Chief left with a shake of his head. During the next six hours the stokers pumped water into and out of just about every internal tank in the ship, and dark were the mutterings.

We sailed next morning and prepared to dive. Jimmy was balanced on the balls of his feet in front of the trimming panel trying to look the part. The Captain ordered dive. The main vents were opened but instead of slipping gracefully beneath the waves we sank about two inches. The Captain was not amused. Jimmy opened every conceivable valve to get water into the tanks but still we stayed on the surface, careering around at 10 knots with planes hard to dive, to the increasing amusement of the destroyers and frigates waiting to exercise with us. After ten minutes the Captain left for a coffee stating that he would return only when the boat was under water. Jimmy was now in charge. Water was still flooding into every tank and our intellectual hero missed the important warning from the chart table team that the R port midships compensating tank gauge was known to under-read by about 200 gallons. He was still doing his ballerina act when the gauge showed nearly full and he ordered the Chief Stoker to keep flooding. Chief did. Immediately the brass dipstick of R port, above which Jimmy was standing and which clearly had not been screwed fully home, erupted with a bang and hit him in a vulnerable place. It was instantly followed by a jet of sea water at 30 psi and painful noises from Jimmy. The submarine took a bow down angle and began to dive. Hearing these kerfuffles, the Captain stepped out of the Wardroom, slipped in the ankle deep water and landed on his backside. Thus we arrived at periscope depth with an injured Captain, a professionally and physically damaged Jimmy and several tens of gallons of sea water sloshing around the control room. We never saw the slide rule again.

CAPTAIN D. G. LITTLEJOHN RN

On Top of the World

HMS *Dreadnought* (Commander A. G. Kennedy RN) surfaced through the ice at the North Pole on March 3rd.

She was under the ice for several days and covered about 1,500 miles while in the area surfacing on six occasions at various points. The aim of the exercise was to study all aspects of operating a Fleet submarine under ice, in high latitudes.

As the submarine broke through the ice to the surface it was described as 'just a shudder like a lift coming to a stop'. The landscape at the Pole was hilly and extremely cold with a temperature of minus 35 degrees Fahr.

Those who went 'ashore' did not go very far afield as they got cold very quickly without realising it – a sharp lookout was kept for polar bears but none were seen. Dr. C. Swithinbank, a glaciologist of the Scott Polar Institute at Cambridge, took passage in the *Dreadnought*, which returned to Faslane on March 11th.

*

The Navy's nickname for RAF personnel is 'Crabs'. Thus

Crabology

We had been at sea dived for two and a half months and were on our way back to Devonport to catch the evening tide on a Friday. Some bright spark at Fleet headquarters had decided that it would be good for inter-service relations if we exercised with an RAF Nimrod aircraft for six hours. This meant that not only would we miss the Friday tide but also, because of dockyard overtime bans, we would not be able to enter harbour until Monday morning. We were not amused.

The Nimrod duly appeared in the south west approaches and we went through the standard routine to effect a rendezvous. He asked us to stick our fin above the surface and we said that we would if he flew with his wheels in the water. After this bit of jollity, I spoke to the Nimrod captain. He was an unhappy bear because he was missing a party in the mess. I told him of our predicament and hinted that if he developed a defect and returned to base he might find, coincidentally, a bottle of whisky in the next post. In less than a minute his radar failed and he developed an engine problem. With great regret we agreed to cancel the exercise. He made the party. We got home for the weekend. It cost us a bottle of Grouse. Good inter-service co-operation.

CAPTAIN D. G. LITTLEJOHN RN

*

On Location

Has anyone not seen the James Bond film 'You Only Live Twice'? The final sequence shows a submarine surfacing under a large, yellow rubber dinghy in which the hero and his Japanese girlfriend had settled for a bit of seclusion after winning another unlikely campaign against the forces of international terrorism, extortion and revenge.

The submarine was *Aeneas*, a streamlined Admiralty A class and the last of its type with a 4 inch gun on the for'ard casing. In the summer of 1967 we had sailed hurriedly from Haifa 24 hours before the start of the Yom Kippur war and were on our way home after an exhilarating three month Mediterranean deployment.

We stopped at Gibraltar to find that we had been leased to a film company for a week and were at that company's disposal (presumably with Her Majesty's approval). The six-strong film team lived first class at the Rock Hotel and had a hired French helicopter at the airport. There were no actors available so our Engineer Officer 'volunteered' to be Sean Connery and each day we took to sea a WRNS officer from HMS *Rooke* to play the girl.

As you cannot surface a submarine under a dinghy without capsizing it, we got the shot they wanted by diving while going slowly astern. What you actually see is the dinghy floating off the casing but with the film run backwards. It is not much fun sitting on the casing of a diving submarine with main vents open and surrounded by the roar of compressed air, but I suspect that our failure to get the same Wren to come out on any two consecutive days owed more to the female producer's methods of squeezing them into a Japanese bikini than to fears of being cast adrift in an open boat with the Engineer.

For less than half a minute's worth of action the cost to the company was the hire of one British submarine and one commercial helicopter for five days, travel from and to London for six with accommodation in Gibraltar, wining and dining some of the ship's company and a substantial contribution to the ship's welfare fund. It was money spent with a profligacy I was not to see again until I became involved with the MOD procurement Executive.

CAPTAIN R. G. SHARPE RN

*

At a meeting at Nassau in the Bahamas in December 1962 between President John F. Kennedy and Prime Minister Harold Macmillan, the President agreed to supply the Royal Navy with Polaris intercon-

tinental ballistic missiles. The warheads would be British. The Polaris programme needed someone to run it.

Chief Polaris Executive

I received the surprise of my life on Friday, 28th December 1962. That morning I had attended a meeting in the Admiralty, not directly concerned with POLARIS; later, returning to Gosport on my way home, I was informed that the First Sea Lord (Admiral Sir Caspar John) wanted to speak to me on the telephone, on the 'scrambler'. I went to my office and was connected, and a conversation on the following lines took place:—

FSL   'You're fully in the picture about POLARIS: well, I want you to head the organization we are setting up in the Admiralty to run the thing through.'

*FOS/M   'Yes, Sir.' (doubtfully)

FSL   'Come and have lunch with me on Monday, at one o'clock at White's in St. James's, and give me your answer then. You can have the weekend to think it over.'

FOS/M   "Yes, thank you, Sir.'

FSL   'I tell you here and now that if you say "no", I'll twist your arm until you bloody well scream.'

FOS/M   (after a pause) 'Right, Sir, I'll see you Monday.'

End of conversation.

Come the Monday (31st December 1962) the answer given was 'Yes', but only after a weekend of much heart-searching. Acceptance would give rise to many personal and family problems and sacrifice, to which was added the disappointment of prematurely relinquishing

* Flag Officer Submarines

258

the enjoyably inspiring and rewarding appointment of FOS/M. But the challenge, however daunting, proved over-riding and the die was cast. Thus came into being my appointment as Chief Polaris Executive (CPE). It was made plain that I could expect to be there until the submarines were operational.

The next day, New Year's Day, 1963, I said goodbye to my staff at Blockhouse and on the following day I found myself in an empty room on the ground floor of North Block of the Admiralty building; empty, that is, except for a chair and a large desk, on which sat a telephone not yet connected and no staff, no paper-work. It was, to say the least, an unusual and perplexing situation. I attended a meeting with the First Lord of the Admiralty (Lord Carrington) that forenoon. At this meeting the First Lord emphasised the importance and urgency of getting POLARIS into service within five years, and the powers that would be given to whoever headed the special organisation to be set up within the Admiralty, an essential factor to achieving the aim.

The provisional terms of the new job indicated that I was responsible to the Controller of the Navy for the POLARIS programme as a whole, but that I had direct and immediate access, at any time, to any member of the Board of Admiralty if I needed assistance in overcoming difficulties or problems arising in that particular member's field. Admiral Le Fanu's three year report, with its proposals and recommendations for the organization required to bring POLARIS swiftly into service in the Royal Navy, was brought out of its pigeon-hole, at his instigation, dusted down, and promptly landed on my desk, to become my bible for the immediate future. It was also fortunate that I, as FOS/M, during a routine visit to Washington the previous summer, had been given a very comprehensive briefing by the Director, Special Projects, (Rear Admiral I. J. Galantin, USN – who had succeeded Admiral Raborn) on all the methods and procedures used in SPO to keep so successfully, the strictest control, on a very tight timescale, of the United States Navy's POLARIS programme. Armed with all this background information, matters quickly clarified and the task began to take on a more definable shape. The Le Fanu report was invaluable as a starting point for a race against all the odds, a race in which it was already clear that many obstacles would arise in the years ahead. Not the least of these could be summed up by the phrase 'We don't know how much we don't know.' In fact, we were at the very bottom of a steep and formidably high learning curve.

VICE ADMIRAL SIR HUGH ('RUFUS') MACKENZIE KCB DSO* DSC

*

In the event, the Polaris programme was completed on time and within budget – an unprecedented and unrepeated feat in British naval history. It had been decided at the start of the programme that the first British Polaris submarine, Resolution, *would fire her first test Polaris missile off Cape Canaveral at 11.15 Eastern Standard Time on 15 February 1968. The test firing duly took place at that time, not without some incident.*

The First Polaris Test Firing

Apart from the many last minute technical blips the initial major problem was the temporary withdrawal of the missile to be fired so as to inscribe 'Royal Navy' rather than the existing 'US Navy' on the part which would be photographed by the attendant chopper when the missile emerged from the ocean.

The firing was to take place on a Monday and the rehearsal and telemetry checks on the preceding Friday. CBNS [Commander

British Navy Staff] arrived on Friday evening from Washington to be met by a posse of slightly distraught officers. During the rehearsal the accompanying US destroyer had reversed course and due to bad communications had failed to inform *Resolution*. This resulted in a collision which bent *Resolution*'s telemetry Mast over and, by a few inches, *Resolution*'s fin had only just failed to rip the bottom out of the destroyer.

The brightest and best of the UK (including Harry Chapman Pincher's team) correspondents and many US reporters were awaiting *Resolution*'s return and the subsequent firing. *Resolution* was told to stay at sea, (the reporters being give some bogus reason). A Top Secret signal to VCNS [Vice Chief of Naval Staff] explained the problem and, *pace* the rules for collisions at sea, added that it was intended to treat this collision as a 'non-event'.

That left the problem of the Reporters and Correspondents. Here the Almighty intervened. As Pincher has described in *Inside Story*, Hubert Humphrey, the Vice-President, was opening a new bridge on Sunday in the nearby Everglades. With their hands on their hearts the RN and USN officers 'in the know' assured the hacks that there would be nothing to see on the Sunday and here was a unique opportunity for them to meet the VEEP. A coach and celebratory lunch would be provided. The latter did the trick.

Hacks out of the way, *Resolution* was then brought in with the mast hanging limp. As quickly as possible (knowing that the supply of liquid at the lunch would eventually run out), the mast was dismantled. Thanks to Admiral Levering Smith USN and Captains Shepherd and Hammer, Royal Navy, a duplicate mast had been flown down overnight by the USN. By the time the cheerful Press contingent returned '*the new mast specially adapted for the actual firing was being fitted*'. The tension of course continued amongst those who knew what had happened . . . 'Was the new mast satisfactory, we asked ourselves?' We put our faith in the fitters. As the final count down before the firing proceeded there was a 'Hold' in the last few seconds. Without hesitation 'Carry on counting' ordered Levering Smith. And so success was achieved.

VICE ADMIRAL SIR LOUIS LE BAILLY KBE CB DL

✳

Polaris crews lived in an enclosed world of their own, in a Submarine Service which was already a world of its own within the Navy. Their daily lives on board were a mystery, which very few outsiders were ever privileged to experience, as in

Have Polaris, Will Travel

For me, it's not just the policemen who are looking younger, it's the submarine captains, too. It comes as a shock to see the young men I used to know now becoming respectable, and highly respected, pillars of the naval establishment. A few days I spent at sea in the British nuclear-powered Polaris submarine HMS *Renown* made me feel about ninety years old, and to be called 'Sir' by the First Lieutenant – a Lieutenant Commander – made me feel not just old but positively antediluvian.

Antediluvian is right. In the decade or so since I left it there has been a flood of changes in the submarine world. It is as though every aspect of the submarine life and technology I used to know has now been raised to a much higher power.

For instance, the Navigating Officer used simply to point at the coffee stain on the chart and tell the Captain, 'We're somewhere about there, sir'. Not so any more: *Renown* has a miraculous table of gyros known as a Ship's Inertial Navigation System (SINS) which can fix her position on the earth's surface to within a few yards. Ship's course, speed, tides, ocean currents, magnetic variations, make no difference to SINS.

The First Lieutenant used to trim the boat by the seat of his pants and a few simple calculations. Every dive was likely to be something of a venture into the unknown. The First Lieutenant in *Renown* still works out the trim, but the depth-keeping, steering and planing can all be done automatically, untouched by human hand.

In the old days the Coxswain was the boat's medicine man, and dispensed from the PO's mess his own empirical brand of diagnosis. Above the waist – aspirin. Below the waist – the Number Nine depth charge, an explosive laxative capable of moving the bowels of the earth. Now, they have a qualified doctor on board, and a properly-equipped sickbay.

Submarine food always used to have a certain spectacular unpredictability; quality and quantity depended upon the progress of the Chef's sex-life and the accuracy of the Coxswain's arithmetic. We seemed to subsist on a staple diet of 'bangers, beans and babies' heads' (babies heads: an especially glutinous variety of steak and kidney pudding) often with a rib-sticking Cabinet pudding, known as 'figgy duff' or 'zizz pud', for afters. And there was always that favourite brand of tinned, skinned tomatoes known as 'train smash'.

Actually they still do have 'train smash' in *Renown*, but it looked much less macerated than of old, and it was just one item from a very good menu. The food in *Renown* was excellent, with a choice of main courses and frequent salads, served cafeteria-style, in a dining-hall – a vast compartment by old submarine standards. Polaris submarines carry Supply Officers, the first time officers of this branch have gone to sea in submarines – yet another innovation.

That *smell* has gone, that characteristically pervasive submarine attar of diesel oil, rubber boots and boiled veg, underlaid with something more sinister, as though there had been a recent human sacrifice somewhere down in the bilges. Compared with that, *Renown* smells like a rather superior clinic.

They don't even wear the same clothes at sea any more. Where are all those exotic 'steaming rigs', striped football shirts, leather jackets, Davy Crockett hats and woolly caps? All gone, apparently for ever. They wear uniform now, blue shirts and trousers, with smart gilt lapel badges.

No more 'hot bunking' – where a man climbed into the bunk vacated by his relief. Every man has his own bunk, with ventilation louvre and reading light. Never more the great glad cry of 'One all round!'; smoking is virtually unrestricted. They've never heard of the old ritual of Ditching Gash, when bins of rubbish were hauled up the conning tower and ditched over the side from the bridge. *Renown*'s garbage is chopped up, packed in special weighted containers and fired overboard through a garbage ejector – a fitting like a miniature torpedo tube.

No need to do your dhobeying in a bucket. They have a laundry. No more rationing of fresh water on a long patrol. They have hot showers and distilling capacity to spare. Above all, no more jealous hoarding of every amp in the main battery. The reactor has enough power to supply a small town.

But *surely*, I thought, looking around me, it can't *all* be changed? What about the blokes? Well, at first sight, they are a typical submarine company: typically cheerful, and cynical, and competent – *Renown* still has an unmistakable small ship atmosphere. There are still some tattooed forearms to be seen. Wilsons are still called 'Tug'. They can still coin apt nicknames and phrases, and they still have that special submarine brand of black humour.

They have changed, though. For one thing, there are very few ordinary bods about – the plain hewers of wood and drawers of water. One of the most common remarks heard in *Renown* was 'too many Chiefs and not enough Injuns'. Of a total ship's complement of about 150, more than half are chief petty officers or petty officers. The Chiefs' mess in *Renown* – though, again, a huge compartment by old submarine standards – is seriously overcrowded. A Polaris submarine crew requires a quite unusually high proportion of men with sophisticated skills – nuclear engineering, computers, electronics, fire control systems – who are normally senior ratings.

The Polaris programme has made extraordinary demands on the Navy's manpower. Each submarine has two complete crews, designated Port and Starboard, who relieve each other on a three-monthly cycle. The 'On' crew carries out maintenance, pre-patrol training, and the deterrent patrol of sixty days. Meanwhile, the 'Off' crew go on leave, attend courses, and generally support the boat from shore.

Besides the crews, there are many men coming up in the training 'pipe-line'. Many of *Renown*'s ship's company have come straight from general service, some even from the Fleet Air Arm, with no intervening apprenticeship period in orthodox submarines. By no means all were volunteers for submarines. The wonder is that they take to the life so quickly; though some of them are serving in their first submarine (some of the junior rates in their first *ship*) they all look as though they have been doing it for years.

The wardroom has the same mixture of old-and-new-type submariners. *Renown* has thirteen officers, half of them with University degrees, and normally another three or four additional officers borne for training or understudying the men they are going to relieve – some duties take a whole patrol to turn over.

The Captain, who is a full Commander, has been through the traditional mill of the submarine service, starting years ago as a junior 'fourth hand' and working his way up through third hand, first lieutenant and finally to command. He might also have had experience in a fleet nuclear submarine or as first lieutenant of a Polaris. With the comparatively junior rank of Commander, he has awesome responsibilities which hardly bear thinking about. At the same time he must lead his crew through the long tedium of their patrol – yet keep them on their toes. In this sense, he is like a coach training a team to run a steady successful marathon and yet be ready to sprint a hundred yards in even time at any moment in the race.

His First Lieutenant, a Lieutenant-Commander, is also a submarine captain in his own right, having passed the Periscope Course (the 'Perisher', as it is popularly called) and commanded his own submarine. The other executive officers, the Torpedo and Sonar, Navigating and Communications Officers, and the Senior Technical Officer and his assistants, will also probably, but not necessarily, be submariners of long standing; such is the Polaris programmes' rapacious appetite for men that some of the junior engineer and electrical officers may well be new to submarines. The Supply Officer and the Medical Officer are also likely to be newcomers. In *Renown*'s Polaris Department – popularly supposed to be nicknamed 'the Polaroids', although I never actually heard anyone in *Renown* use the word – the Polaris Systems Officer and his assistant were electrical officers, both new to submarines, and neither was a volunteer. However, now that they were there, they felt they 'would rather like to stay'.

At sea, *Renown* is a totally enclosed and private world, hot and rather noisy, and abounding in buzzers and bells, dials and gauges and indicators. Submarines always were happy hunting grounds for the instrument-makers, but the instrumentation in *Renown* is like wallpaper in a house. There are instruments everywhere, some mounted in neat display consoles, worthy of an executive suite, but others gathered in great amusement arcades of colours and glass and levers, looking as though they were just waiting for some mad twenty-first century theatre organist to sit down and play them.

Polaris sailors work an average 70-hour week and many of them spend most of their working lives just looking at instruments. Design attention has been paid to ergonomics, but watchkeepers still complain that they find some of the displays tiring.

Renown is a creature of the deep and with a length of 425 feet and an underwater displacement of nearly 8,000 tons – the size of a pre-war cruiser – she is clearly not built for periscope depth acrobatics. A submarine's role, traditionally, was to detect and identify a target, and then close and attack it. In Polaris, this concept is completely reversed. If a target is detected, no matter how tempting, *Renown*'s duty is to evade. Only when the missiles have been successfully launched can *Renown* take up the 'hunter-killer' role for which she is fitted with long-range sonar equipment and six torpedo tubes.

The popular press and public's notion of the Polaris captain running amok – 'the madman with his finger on the button' – is simply not possible. No one man can launch a missile on his own. The active co-operation, and the physical presence, of several others are needed. The firing system is so encompassed about with precautions, key combinations, cross-checks, inter-locks and verifications that the order to fire must be proved to be authentic beyond any possible doubt. Furthermore, every senior member of the firing team must be convinced of its authenticity. Officers and senior ratings have discretion to refuse to play their necessary parts if they are not so convinced. However, a man cannot refuse unreasonably or whimsically; every member, even the Captain himself, can be over-ridden.

In other words, the system ensures that the missiles cannot be fired unless the country really means it, and if the country really means it then the missiles will be fired.

Renown carries sixteen A3 Polaris missiles with an operational range of nearly 3,000 miles. The 'sharp end' – the re-entry body, nuclear warhead, fusing and arming devices – is British-designed and built, but the rest of the missile, and the stowage, launching and fire control equipment are all American, supplied under the

'Nassau Agreement' between Harold Macmillan and John F. Kennedy.

The missiles are stowed in colossal vertical tubes, 33 feet long and seven feet in diameter, which reach down through the three deck levels of the Missile Compartment like great white columns. The compartment is supposed to be called 'Sherwood Forest' but, again, I never heard anyone in *Renown* call it that; usually, it was just the Missile Compartment, or perhaps the 'rocket shop'.

To be effective, a deterrent must be reliable and credible. Polaris is fantastically reliable and is kept so by constant practice drills and by treating each missile as though it were an 'Old Master' painting, cosseting it, keeping it warm and dry and comfortable, at a steady desirable temperature, pressure and humidity.

The ship can be ready to fire in a few minutes – as, of course, she must be. Information on the ship's position is fed to the missiles from SINS until the last moment before firing. The targets' positions are pre-programmed and fed into the fire control system on prepared tape; many tapes are carried on board, each relating to different targets. The fire control system incorporates eleven separate computers, and there is another in each missile. Once away, the missile's own guidance package governs the flight path.

The missiles can be fired from the surface but are normally fired when submerged. A gas/steam generator launches the missile and boosts it to the surface where the rocket first stage ignites automatically. On board, a launch is entirely unspectacular: a hissing noise, a very slight trembling of the deck underfoot. And that is all.

What do the ship's company think about the weapon on board? The question has hoary whiskers on it, having been asked ten thousand times before. A patient, long-suffering look comes over a Polaris sailor's face when it is asked yet again. Actually, there is no clear-cut answer. Broad generalisations about a Polaris crew's feelings can be dangerously misleading.

'Drop-outs' on moral grounds are very rare, but that does not mean that the great majority are insensitive.

There are, of course, some doubters who suppress their misgivings and say 'Anyway, it'll never happen'. There are those who are 'all for it'. And there are some who clearly have never thought about it at all: to them it is, in a quite literal sense, unthinkable.

But most have given the subject a great deal of thought and now console themselves with the absolute certainty that under no conceivable circumstances would Britain ever start a nuclear war. Polaris is therefore a 'second strike' weapon, used as morally justified retaliation. With that certainty to support them, the ship's company are free to get on with the job they are paid to do, to address themselves to its undoubted professional challenges, and to achieve a high degree of personal involvement. The Polaris Systems Officer says, 'During a practice missile firing I get so absolutely absorbed in what I'm doing. I'm so pleased to see all those green lights coming up just as they should, quite honestly I don't think any further than that.'

When *Renown*'s two crews each fired a practise missile on the Cape Kennedy range in July 1969, the predominant emotions on board were exultation and triumph, tempered with a certain relief. When, after a lengthy count-down, the missile went off successfully it was a deeply satisfying moment for all on board: 'Everybody was grinning, and talking too much; it was just like being intoxicated.'

But practise launch drills, which can be and are ordered at any time, are only brief flurries of excitement in a patrol, when the ship's pulse seems to slow right down, and the hours pass in a suspended state rather like a controlled hibernation. All the normal parameters of submarine existence – speed, depth, course, even time itself – no longer have the same meaning or relevance. The routine eats time and a patrol passes strangely quickly, in a way which the crew almost resent: 'It's two months out of your life, cut out just like that. It's gone. When you get back and meet somebody, you forget it's weeks since you last saw them. It hasn't been weeks to you.' Although time of day means nothing, the watches change, meals are served, the lights are dimmed and raised again, as though obeying some atavistic memory of a solar day. As one wag said, 'We're like battery hens.'

The Navy has paid much attention to the physical and mental well-being of Polaris crews on patrol. It was thought that men would have time and inclination for study, but in practice this has not happened. A few ambitious men study for GCE 'O' levels or take correspondence courses, but most spend their leisure time reading, sleeping, playing cards, crib or uckers (coarse submarine ludo). Some do embroidery, rug-making, marquetry or tapestry work, or model making. For the energetic there is weight-lifting, rowing and cycling machines, and table tennis. Ship's contests, quizzes, bridge tournaments, darts competitions, are all organised. There is a film-show every night. Each man gets a daily issue of canned beer. The Chiefs also have keg beer on tap in their mess. *Renown* has a ship's newspaper, the *Hi-Ho Journal*, with all the news that's fit to print, contributions from all departments, and Andy Capp cartoons, supplied *before* national publication, by courtesy of the *Daily Mirror*.

Personality clashes on board are inevitable, but rare, – 'the ship's big enough to get out of each other's way'. Towards the end of a patrol, according to the Doctor, a few may get symptoms of a mild form of 'twitch' – 'they may go off their food a bit, and get vague feelings that they're not doing their jobs as well'. But in general, British Polaris experience confirms the American – 'You only get psychological problems on board when you get a psychologist on board'.

Although they do have a tendency to be overweight, Polaris crews are generally healthy and the Doctor expects to treat only minor ailments: cuts, abrasions, stomach upsets, headaches, constipation, rashes. If needed, a portable operating table can be set up in the Chief's Mess. This would be clean but not sterile and the policy for Polaris submarines is to avoid surgery if at all possible; a rumbling appendix, for example, would be treated with antibiotics for as long as possible. In the event of a death on board, the body would be brought back; the authorities would certainly require a full postmortem. (If the doctor wants another symptom to mull over, I can tell them that my eyesight, not very good anyway, deteriorated rapidly and noticeably while I was on board, to the point where I was worried about it. It took a couple of days to recover.)

The Doctor's main concern is the monitoring and control of air pollution. A Polaris submarine is a unique environment: totally sealed off, for very long periods, with an artificially controlled atmosphere. Oxygen is made from water by electrolysis. Impurities such as carbon monoxide, carbon dioxide and hydrogen, are burned or chemically 'scrubbed out'.

Oddly, the most obstinate pollutant is the coolant gas used in the ship's refrigerators. There is no way of removing it except by ventilating and although it is basically non-toxic itself, it gives off the lethal gas phosgene when at high temperature (for example in contact with a lighted cigarette). Although the quantities are minute, they are very carefully watched.

Radiation is *not* a health hazard, although the levels are constantly monitored. When they are developed, the sensitive film badges everyone on board wears only show how little radiation there is rather than how much; in fact, a man would get more radiation from cosmic rays standing on the submarine's casing in the open air than he would down below in the submarine.

Samples from the reactor coolant liquid are tested daily, in a delicate process known colloquially as 'Drinka Pinta Gamma'. Alarm clocks and wristwatches with luminous hands, or indeed any fitting with luminous paint, are firmly banned on board. Their emissions are tiny but they do accumulate over a long period until they trigger the boat's hypersensitive radiation alarms. This is irritating and distracting, and could be dangerous.

The principal power source (there is, of course, a battery for emergency use) is the British-built pressurised water reactor which drives the single shaft through steam turbines. To fit a reactor and propulsion machinery inside a submarine at all is a marvellous technical achievement, but it is still disappointing to find in *Renown*'s machinery spaces habitability conditions no better than those of small surface warships of twenty years ago.

Renown's machinery compartments are very hot, very humid, very difficult to keep clean, and large portions of them are virtually inaccessible for repairs or maintenance. There must be some residual Puritanism in the British national character, which believes that to be comfortable is also to be sinful; or perhaps we all secretly believe that air conditioning is somehow cissy and unnecessary. Whereas American nuclear submarines have ample air conditioning capacity, the British system is barely adequate, particularly in the after spaces.

Renown's Starboard Crew are lucky to have an artificer who has a way with air conditioning machinery and can 'tweak' it to optimum performance. But even when he has done his best, most of the machinery spaces aft are, as the watchkeepers down there describe them, 'do-it-yourself sauna baths'.

It is disappointing, too, to see by the apparently random routing of pipe systems that British ship-builders have seemingly not forsaken the competitive, 'Olympic' method of ship-building – 'the fastest dockyard matie won, you see. If he was quick, he got there first and got a clear run with his bit of pipe. All the slower dockyard maties then had to bend their pipes around his. And it didn't matter what size the pipes were'.

On patrol, a Polaris submarine can receive messages but cannot transmit. Therefore, before sailing, every man decides what action he wants taken in the event of family emergency, such as his wife or child's illness or a parent's death. Many opt not to be told. There is nothing they can do, and the knowledge might distress them. (The recall of a Polaris submarine from patrol is a decision for the Defence Secretary.)

However, they are not entirely cut off. There are the 'Family-grams' – twenty-word messages from families, transmitted periodically to the submarine when signal traffic permits. They are discreetly handled, by as few people as possible. The need for brevity sometimes lends wives an almost epigrammatic wit; nearing the end of one patrol one *Renown* wife signalled: 'Put away your toys boys nearly time to go to bed.'

Polaris crews will never get a traditional 'run ashore' in a foreign port, but the three-month changeover cycle between the crews is inviolate and the sailors can therefore plan their private lives – dates of holidays, weddings, house removals, and so on – with a degree of confidence unusual in the submarine service. Nevertheless submarines, and particularly Polaris submarines, have notorious reputations as marriage breakers. The figures are, of course, impossible to check reliably but the proportion of men in the Polaris programme with broken or troubled marriages was put as high as one in five.

Certainly the establishment of a huge Polaris base has created social problems ashore – and not just from the nuclear disarmament demonstrators who still make their migratory appearances at certain times of the year. The Clyde Submarine Base is on the Gareloch, at Faslane in Dunbartonshire. The nearest town of any size is Helensburgh. The population of the whole area has nearly doubled in ten years. Whole hillsides, fields when I was last there, are now married quarter estates. (For one of them the sailors have coined the perfect name – Moon City.) The neighbourhood's educational and medical facilities are under strain. Despite good intentions on both sides, there has so far been little social mixing between the sailors and their families and the solid Scottish bourgeoisie of Helensburgh.

Originally, there were to have been five Polaris submarines which, allowing for maintenance periods and refits, would have guaranteed at least two submarines on patrol continuously. The fifth boat was cancelled when the Socialist Government took office in 1964, leaving a maximum potential of 1.7 boats on patrol (whatever '1.7 boats' may mean in strategic terms).

The names of the four in commission – *Resolution*, *Repulse*, *Renown* and *Revenge* – reflect the Polaris submarine's present capital ship status. *Renown* is the tenth ship of her name in the Royal Navy, and her battle honours stretch from the Battle of the Gabbard in 1653 to the bombardment of Sabang in 1944. Most of the honours – Norway, Atlantic, Cape Spartivento, Mediterranean, Bismark, Malta Convoys, Arctic, North Africa and Sabang – were won by the ninth *Renown*, the battle-cruiser.

Nobody wants any battle honours for the tenth *Renown*. If the missiles are ever used, then the deterrent will have failed to deter and the £350,000,000 so far spent on the Polaris programme might just as well have been torn up note by note and scattered on the sea.

However, it could still be said that the Polaris submarines and the men who serve in them will have bought us all a little time – time indeed for the occasional lucky Ancient Submariner like me to have had a fascinating and humbling experience. There were moments in *Renown* when I felt like Orville Wright having a ride in Concorde. When I got home my wife was spring cleaning and had one of my old uniform jackets out of the wardrobe. 'Funny', she said, 'I can't smell the moth-balls.'

But I could.

JOHN WINTON

Polaris submarines had, of course, every facility for the recreation of the crew, including a

Submarine Library

It was only my second day in command of the Port Crew of the nuclear submarine *Repulse* when I was told that the following day I should be visited by the Supreme Allied Commander of all the NATO ground forces in Europe, the US Army's General Goodpaster. He was scheduled to visit the submarine base at Faslane and as we were the only Polaris submarine alongside, it was to be our lot to impress on him that the British nuclear deterrent was in capable hands. The rest of the day was spent in much spitting and polishing, whilst I struggled to find my way around in my new 8,400 ton command – larger by far than the 36 ton midget submarine I had first commanded in the mid-50's! As a newcomer to the boat's layout, it wouldn't do for me to take a wrong turning during his tour.

At 1030 sharp on the following day, I greeted our visitor as he mounted the gangway and came aboard. A quick handshake and then introductions to my First Lieutenant before leading off to the hatch which took us down into the interior of the submarine.

The missile compartment with its 16 launch tubes, each loaded with a 2,500 mile range Polaris missile, was fairly old hat to him as he had seen similar in American submarines. Further aft, the reactor compartment and engine rooms left him somewhat bemused I thought, and by the time we had returned to the Control Room, he was beginning to exhibit something of a glazed expression as more and more technicalities were explained to him.

Proceeding forward, I felt that some alleviation from all this technical jargon was needed so told him that we would shortly arrive at the library – something which no other class of British submarine had ever previously had space for. His eyes lit up; here obviously was a straw he could clutch at; something with which his military mind could grapple. As we reached the door I made to slide it open but it would not budge. It was firmly locked. With a glower at the First Lieutenant I apologised and assured him we would get it unlocked in time for him to visit it before his departure.

After visiting the torpedo tube space (with more technical descriptions), our route took us back past the library door – still firmly locked. I glibly lied to him that the rating with the key was presently ashore but had been sent for and if he arrived back before the end of the visit, we would certainly come back to see it.

To my acute embarrassment, the visit came to an end still with no sign of the library key and as the General crossed the gangway to the shore, I turned angrily to my First Lieutenant for an explanation as to the cause of this dreadful gaffe. Without saying a word, he reached into his jacket pocket and pulled out a key. Beckoning me to follow, he led off down below to the library whose door he proceeded to unlock. As he slid it back, my anger turned to gratitude; I clapped him on the back and congratulated him on his initiative. It was stacked to the deckhead with cartons of beer.

COMMANDER DAVID LUND RN

*

1983 nuclear submariner's typical menus

	Breakfast	**Lunch**	**Dinner**
Monday	Standard Choice	Steak & veg. pie	Roast Lamb & mint
	Eggs to order	Omelettes to order	sauce
	Bacon, sausage, baked	Salad selection	Liver & bacon
	beans, tomatoes		Cottage pie
	plus extra	Chipped & boiled	
		potatoes	Fondant & creamed
	Black pudding	Choice of veg.	potatoes
		Fruit flan & custard	Cabbage, butter beans
			& peas
			Cheese & biscuits
Tuesday	Standard choice	Cheesy Hammy Eggy	Boiled silverside &
	plus extra	Omelette to order	dumplings
		Salad selection	Sweet & sour pork
	Fish cakes		Rabbit pie
		Chipped & boiled	
		potatoes	Boiled & creamed
		Choice of vegetables	potatoes
			Turnips, green beans,
		Sultana roll & custard	broccoli
			Cheese & biscuits
			Fresh fruit
Wednesday	Standard choice	Choice of fish dishes	Roast chicken &
	plus extra	Omelettes to order	stuffing
		Salad selection	Shepherds pie
	Sauté kidney		Pork chops & apple
		Chipped & boiled	sauce
		potatoes	
		Choice of vegetables	Roast & marquis
			potatoes
		Chocolate pudding &	Cabbage, carrots &
		custard	brussels
			Cheese & biscuits

Thursday	Standard choice *plus extra*	Pizza pie Omelettes to order Salad selection	Baked gammon & peach sauce Braised liver & onions
	Kippers		Lamb chop & veg
		Chipped & boiled potatoes Choice of vegetables	Lyonnaise & baked potatoes BITS, peas & carrrots
		Apple crumble & custard	Cheese & biscuits Fresh fruit
Friday	Standard choice *plus extra*	Brown stew & dumplings Omelettes to order	Grilled & fried steak Cod portions Spaghetti Bolognaise
	Pork luncheon meat fritters	Salad selection	Chipped & creamed potatoes
		Chipped & boiled potatoes Choice of vegetables	Fried onions, sweetcorn & peas
		Fruit & ice cream	Cheese & biscuits
Saturday	Standard choice *plus extra*	Cottage pie Omelettes to order Salad selection	Chicken pie Savoury mince Gammon steak & pineapple
	Smoked haddock	Sauté & boiled potatoes Choice of vegetables	Scallop & creamed potatoes
		Rice pudding & jam sauce	Swede tomatoes & green beans
			Cheese & biscuits Fresh fruit
Sunday	Standard choice *plus extra*	Roast beef & Yorkshire pudding Roast turkey & stuffing	100% salad
	Grapefruit segments Mushrooms	Roast pork & apple sauce	
		Roast & braised potatoes Cabbage, carrots & cauliflower	Baked potatoes
			Cheese & biscuits
		Jelly, fruits & cream	

Despite the RAF Vulcan bombing of Port Stanley runway on 1 May and the air attacks on Glamorgan *and* Arrow *the same day, there was still a general feeling that this affair in the Falklands would not come to anything really serious. However, the very next day, 2 May, an event occurred which convinced everybody once and for all that the Falklands conflict was now 'for real' – the first torpedo attack on a surface target carried out in earnest by a submerged submarine since the Second World War. It happened during*

Conqueror's War Patrol

Before I tell you about my experiences in Operation 'Corporate', let me give you a brief description of HMS *Conqueror*, the submarine I commanded.

She is a 4½ thousand ton, 280 feet long, nuclear-powered submarine with a primary operational role of anti-submarine warfare, but she is equally capable of attacking surface ships.

Her acoustic sensors included active and passive sonars, one of which was a long range passive towed array. Her communications fit included a recently installed satellite system which rapidly became our primary means of sending and receiving signals. She was fitted with electronic surveillance equipment for detecting radar transmissions and finally, perhaps of most importance in Operation 'Corporate', two periscopes, the smaller for use in close proximity to ships and the larger for surface search.

Almost all of my ship's company of 110 kept watches. To operate a modern SSN effectively, watchkeepers forward of the reactor compartment keep one watch in two; for an indefinite period while at sea, they spend six hours on watch and six hours off, changing over around 7 and 1 o'clock, day and night.

Those on watch are responsible for manning all the sensors and other watchkeeping positions, as well as defect repair, maintenance that has to be done at sea and domestic routines, such as keeping the submarine clean, operating the laundry and the periodic ditching of gash.

This was a well established routine, which they liked, because it gave them time off watch when, apart from sleeping, they were able to watch films, play cards and other games, work for professional and academic exams and generally relax in their mess.

Because of space limitations on board, even with a severely reduced ship's company, it was necessary for several watchkeepers to share bunks with their opposite numbers – this is known as 'hot-bunking', when the bunks of those going on watch are taken by those they have just relieved.

The propulsion watch, those watch-keeping back aft and responsible for the safe operation of the nuclear reactor, main engines and auxiliary machinery, keep watches in a one-in-three routine, four hours on and eight hours off, under the direction of an Engineer Officer of the watch, stationed in the manoeuvring room.

Food plays an important part in a submariner's life when away for a long period. After about three weeks, the fresh food runs out, so the chefs rely on tinned or frozen. Variety is important, and so is freshly baked bread. We embarked enough food for at least 75 days at sea. We had to lay a 'false deck' of boxes of tinned food laid all along Two Deck accommodation space passage, in exactly the same way as they did in the submarines of World War Two.

I actually took command of HMS *Conqueror* some three weeks before we sailed for Operation Corporate. During that time we spent one week at sea before starting a routine maintenance period at Faslane, our base on the Clyde in Scotland. As events round the Falkland Islands developed, like most of the Royal Navy we were very interested as to whether we would be involved.

I was told on 31 March to prepare the submarine for sea and to sail as quickly as possible. Preparation included recalling some of the ship's company from leave, and embarking a full war outfit of torpedoes, comprising a mixture of the old Mark 8 straight running diesel torpedo, used for anti-shipping attacks, and the Mark 24 Tigerfish electric torpedo, for both anti-submarine and anti-ship attacks, which was wire-guided on its run out to the target.

Meanwhile, the operations team and I were busy planning our passage south, obtaining information, charts and intelligence, while my engineers were involved in the essential task of finishing the fore-shortened maintenance period as rapidly as possible and making the submarine in all respects ready for sea.

As a further complication, just before we sailed we were told to embark nine Royal Marine members of 6 Special Boat Squadron and all their equipment, which came to some thirteen tons in weight and had to be stored in the torpedo compartment.

We eventually sailed on Sunday 4 April, with instructions to proceed south as fast as possible. We were the third of our nuclear submarines to deploy and, after diving in the Irish Sea, we proceeded at full power for the best part of two weeks, only slowing down once or twice a day to receive signal traffic, and to conduct various necessary domestic routines such as ditching gash, pumping bilges and getting rid of sewage.

On sailing it was still unclear exactly what we would be doing when we arrived in the Falklands area. In my own heart I hoped that our Task Force would be sufficient deterrence to persuade the Argentines to withdraw from the Falklands without a fight, but it soon became clear that we would be involved in some form of conflict.

We were a fully worked-up, operational submarine and an experienced crew, but nevertheless during the passage south I took every opportunity to harden my men's minds to the prospect of fighting and to prepare for any eventuality. For example, we ensured that we instinctively knew our drills for evading torpedo attack or containing damage caused by a fire or a flood.

Another important aspect was to restow correctly all the equipment that we had embarked so hastily, to make sure it would not move about when the submarine manoeuvred at speed. It was also necessary to consider which type of torpedo to load in the six torpedo tubes and to ensure that the correct reloads were available. As we moved south, we received in our signal traffic a vast quantity of data that required analysis: the rules of engagement under which we would operate, intelligence assessment of the Argentine Navy, updates on the oceanographical environment in which we were going to operate, and an assessment of where we might find icebergs.

The last was of great interest to me, as shortly after crossing the Equator we were told that our first area of operation would be off the islands of South Georgia. A look at the Admiralty Pilot for that area suggested that we could find ourselves amongst icebergs at that time of the year.

We arrived off South Georgia in the early hours of the morning of 19 April, after a cautious over-night transit. We had been told that South Georgia was occupied by Argentine forces and I had been ordered to establish an anti-shipping patrol to intercept any units that might be attempting to resupply the garrison.

Prior to starting this patrol, to the north-west of the island across the direct route from the Argentine mainland, I decided to conduct a periscope reconnaissance of the coastline to confirm the absence of Argentine shipping. The morning was foggy with poor visibility and as we made a slow approach at periscope depth the only acoustic contact we held was the Fortuna Glacier making a tremendous groaning and creaking noise that was clearly audible on our sonars.

When we were about two miles off the island, the fog cleared and we had our first view of land after our two week and 6,000 mile passage. I carried out a reconnaissance search as closely as I thought prudent, bearing in mind the charts on board had been compiled from surveys conducted during the last century and were designed for mariners who sailed on the surface rather than those who spent their time underneath.

We found nothing, so withdrew to the north-west and settled down over the next few days on an anti-shipping patrol. The weather varied but on occasions it was very rough and severely degraded our search. It was during one of these rough periods that the wireless mast that we had to raise while at periscope depth to receive our satellite communications traffic was damaged.

The mast was actually bent forward by heavy waves and for the remainder of the patrol we were only able to receive incoming traffic with great difficulty, with a resultant impact on how I conducted operations. Although I could still send signals, receiving them was very much a hit and miss affair and very time consuming, requiring protracted periods at periscope depth trying to access the satellite.

On at least two nights we spent several hours on the surface in very rough weather, with the submarine rolling violently, while my technical staff tried in vain to repair the mast. For the remainder of the patrol we streamed a long floating wire aerial which to a certain extent assisted the receipt of signals.

South Georgia was recaptured on Sunday 25 April. The next morning we were instructed by CinC Fleet headquarters, North-wood, to transfer our Royal Marines to HMS *Plymouth*. We surfaced in choppy seas and began a fairly lengthy helicopter transfer of the men and stores we had embarked nearly a month earlier. During this operation two of my ship's company and one of the Royal Marines went overboard, requiring prompt action to rescue them before hypothermia set in.

We were sorry to see the Royal Marines depart, because although they were not conditioned to living in the cramped quarters of the submarine, they had fitted into our routine very well. I will have an ever-lasting memory of their officer's amazing ability to eat food any time it was put in front of him. Furthermore, despite the limited choice, he was always appearing in the wardroom in the wrong uniform which normally resulted in the mess president fining him a bottle of port.

Once we had disembarked the Royal Marines, we dived again and set off for the Falkland Islands, to take up an initial patrol area to the south of the islands to counter the possibility of surface ship attacks on our Task Force.

Towards the end of April, the United Kingdom established a 200nm Maritime Exclusion Zone around the Falklands and had further declared and I quote 'that any *approaching* Argentine military vessels which could amount to a threat would encounter the appropriate response'.

By the time our surface forces under the command of Admiral Woodward in HMS *Hermes* arrived in the area, we had three nuclear submarines on patrol to the west of the Falklands but outside this Exclusion Zone. We were operating in separate but dedicated areas and under very clear rules of engagement which explained in precise detail the circumstances under which we could engage Argentine units.

I entered my patrol area, between the relatively shallow waters of Burdwood Bank to the south of the Falklands and Los Estados Island to the south-west of the Argentine mainland, on 30 April. One of the first tasks for a submarine entering a new patrol area is to establish the environmental conditions and assess the likely detection range of the passive sonars.

In the South Atlantic the oceanographical conditions were such that we usually made very long-range passive detections on surface ships. However, we were unclear about the movements of the two remaining Argentine diesel submarines, and as they were very quiet we were conscious that we might find ourselves within their torpedo range without being able to detect them. To counter this threat, on the infrequent occasions we conducted some noisy onboard evolution, I subsequently used high speed to displace ourselves from that position and deny the opportunity of an attack.

Shortly after establishing my patrol, we made sonar contact on what I classified as a group of ships to the west. I was confident that they were at long range and as there was very little other shipping in the area I decided to close them, to establish visual contact. The sonar contact was steady, about fifty miles east of Los Estados Island, as though whoever it was was waiting for something.

I spent the night proceeding down the sonar bearing and at dawn the next day returned to periscope depth to have a look round. It was a lovely day, flat calm sea and perfect visibility, but there was nothing to be seen. The contact had been growing steadily noisier, which suggested that we were getting closer, so I went deep again and increased speed.

Late in the forenoon of 1 May I again returned to periscope depth and sighted four ships which I classified as the cruiser *Belgrano* with her two escorts [the ex-US Navy Exocet-armed *Sumner* Class destroyers *Hipolito Bouchard* and *Piedra Bueno*] in the process of refuelling from a tanker.

At that time my rules of engagement were specific, in that I could only attack warships if they actually entered the Maritime Exclusion Zone which was some way to the east. So I worked my way around the group to take up a trailing position some three nm on their port quarter.

When the ships had finished refuelling, the tanker moved off to the west and the three warships formed up in a loose formation and, increasing speed to about 13 knots, set off to the south-east. I sent my first locating report via satellite – only a short transmission of a few seconds – to Northwood and went deep to follow them.

We settled down into an uneventful trail. We remained several miles astern and deep below them. Trailing a surface ship from deep in a submarine is not difficult. The contact is tracked on sonar and the range periodically established by an alteration of one's own course or speed.

We followed for over 30 hours, all that day and through the night, continuing to send regular position reports back to Northwood, while they steamed steadily south-eastwards and then east, avoiding the TEZ by about 25 miles and conducting a fairly simple zigzag, but heading towards the shallow Burdwood Bank.

During quiet moments, as I lay on my bunk in my cabin, I considered the next moves. We were the first submarine to maintain contact with enemy units and although the rules of engagement in force did not allow me to attack, I was in no doubt that those back in the UK would realise the tactical implications of what we were doing and form the conclusion that it would be militarily sensible to engage these enemy units before they threatened our Task Force.

I also considered how I would go about my attack when the time came, if it came, so that I had everything clear in my mind, knowing exactly what I was going to do. I decided I would attack the cruiser, aim to get within 2000 yards range of her, on her beam, and I would fire a salvo of the older Mark 8 torpedoes because they had bigger warheads and therefore a better chance of penetrating the warship's armour plating and anti-torpedo bulges – good World War Two stuff; ships aren't designed like that these days. If I could still use my second option of the wire-guided Tigerfish, I planned to attack as soon as they entered the exclusion zone and before I had to slow down for the shallow water.

However, that was not to be, for at eight o'clock on the morning of 2 May the situation changed. They suddenly altered course to the west and began to carry out another kind of zigzag, in an apparently aimless sort of way. I think the ship's company in *Conqueror* felt we were waiting for things to develop. I felt it was bound to escalate.

It must have been about this time that they realised at home that if the *Belgrano* group chose to make a dash across the shallows, we might not be able to keep track of all of them and they might get within Exocet range of *Hermes* and *Invincible* before anybody could take action to stop them. In the early afternoon I eventually received a signal from CinC Fleet changing my rules of engagement, permitting me to attack any Argentine warships outside Argentine territorial waters – in other words, the group I was trailing.

Maintaining radio contact with the UK required a mast to be raised with the submarine travelling at slow speed at periscope depth and was therefore incompatible with maintaining a relative position on the units we were trailing. By the time I had confirmed this vital signal we were some seven miles astern of the group.

I spent more than two hours working my way into an attacking position on the port beam of the cruiser, the opposite side from the two escorts. It was still daylight. The visibility was variable. It came down to less than 2,000 yards at one time. I kept coming up for a look – but when at periscope depth I had to slow down so we were losing ground on them. I had to go deep and run fast to catch up. I did this five or six times. They were not using sonar – just gently zigzagging at about 13 knots. Twice I was in reasonable firing positions but found they had moved off a few degrees.

Listening later to the tape of the attack, it was remarkable how like an ordinary drill it was. It sounded like a good attack in the Attack Teacher at Faslane, everything tidy, no excitement. I'm not an emotional chap and I had been concentrating the whole time on getting into a good position. It was tedious rather than operationally difficult.

We eventually got there – ourselves on the cruiser's port beam, with the two destroyers on her starboard bow and beam. I think the escorts were mainly thinking of a threat from the north, while we were to the south. I was at periscope depth, doing a visual attack. We fired three Mark 8s at 18.57 Zulu, at a range of 1,400 yards. They were fired at short intervals. The object was never to hit with all three but to fire a spread, to cover any inaccuracies in the fire-control solution.

We knew the range and had timed how long it would take the torpedoes to run. We heard the weapons run on the underwater telephone and then heard two torpedo hits; we'd got two out of three. We were still at periscope depth. I looked through the periscope and saw two of the torpedoes hit. I distinctly recall seeing an orange fireball in line with the main mast – just aft of the centre of the target – and shortly after the second explosion I thought I saw a spout of water, smoke and debris from forward.

A big cheer went up from the Control Room and only then did I realise how many extra people were crowded into the corners listening. My immediate thoughts then were to evade; in the Attack Teacher at Faslane we would have stopped to have a cup of coffee at that stage. But my immediate reaction was to clear my position from where I had fired, and judging by the looks on the faces in the Control Room, this met with everyone's approval. We went deep and used our speed to move away to the east. I was then concentrating on avoiding what I presumed would be a counter-attack by her escorts which carried some form of depth charges.

We heard their sonar about six minutes later, when they started their counter-attack, and then distant depth charges. They did come a bit closer but then we moved off to the east.

Returning to periscope depth at dusk, I sent my attack report to Northwood by satellite and started to work my way out of the area. I was conscious that the Argentines were operating Neptune maritime patrol aircraft and I was concerned that they might be instructed to conduct a search of the area. In fact, the aircraft were only ever used on surface search, appeared to have no anti-submarine capability, and were not tasked to look for us.

I remained in the general area for the next two days and on 4 May, while at periscope depth, I watched for some time the two destroyers, a merchant ship and several helicopters and aircraft searching for survivors. I let them go without attacking.

After the attack, I was both relieved and exhilarated that it had been successful. I had had no doubt about our capabilities and we had spent countless times practising; nevertheless, there was a certain sense of relief that the team had got it right.

Afterwards I had a certain amount of regret about the loss of life. I did not know the numbers involved, but one presumed it was considerable. But I feel we did just what we were invited to do and I would have no hesitation in doing it again. It is a fact of life that if you want to go to war, you must expect losses.

Judging by the way the Argentine ships were operating, I think that they had not anticipated coming under attack. However, the Argentine Government had been clearly warned by our Government on the establishment of the Maritime Exclusion Zone that any approach on the part of any Argentine warships would be considered a threat to the British forces, and would encounter an appropriate response. To me that is a very clear indication that they could expect trouble if they approached the Exclusion Zone.

The Argentines had been told this on 23 April and indeed the full text was released to the world's press the following day. However, it was obvious from the reaction to what we had done that some areas of the media had failed to pay any attention to this statement and as a result there was some ill-considered comment in our national press that many of our relatives found disturbing.

We remained on patrol until the middle of June. Our patrol area was periodically changed as further submarines were deployed into the area and as a result we spent the best part of the next month operating to the west and north of the Falklands Islands, tasked mainly to an anti-submarine patrol, with orders to prevent the Argentine diesel submarines attacking our surface forces.

So far as detecting other submarines was concerned, the period was uneventful. One of the resultant problems was maintaining the ship's company's alertness while we spent long hours at periscope depth. We were often surrounded by wild life, in particular whales and penguins, and as a result the periscope watchkeepers often found it difficult to concentrate on searching for aircraft and ships when observing the antics of all this wild life was more interesting.

The whales also affected our sonar and on several occasions we were quite excited about a sonar contact before we were able to classify it as 'non-submarine'.

It was during this period we managed to wrap around the propeller some of the floating wire aerial we had streamed earlier to receive our signal traffic. This meant that whenever we went above a fairly low speed the propeller started to cavitate, which could have been heard at long range by another submarine. Maintaining a low speed for the rest of the patrol was too restrictive on my operations, so I decided to surface at night and put a diver in the water to cut the wire away from the propeller.

I had no lack of volunteers from the small diving team on board. The man whom I selected, Petty Officer (Sonar) (SM) Graham Libby, was in the water in total darkness for about twenty minutes, holding on to the propeller with one hand and working by feel to cut the wire away with a knife in the other.

I knew that the Argentines were flying surface search patrols at this stage and I was conscious that I might have to dive the submarine in a hurry while there were still members of my ship's company on the upper deck. Before Libby went out, I had to warn him that, if there was an air attack, I would have to dive and this would have given him very little time to get back on board. I think he was outstandingly brave. It is just the sort of thing I would expect from him.

To add to the interest of the night while he was underwater, the officer taking charge on the submarine's upper deck was washed over the side, but fortunately was pulled back on board by the other members of his team.

COMMANDER CHRISTOPHER WREFORD-BROWN RN
CONQUEROR'S CO

Commander Wreford-Brown was awarded the DSO, and Petty Officer Libby the DSM.

✻

Very little has been revealed about the work of the submarines during the Falklands Conflict. Much of their doing is still classified secret. Five nuclear fleet submarines took part: Conqueror, Courageous *(Cdr. R. T. N. Best),* Valiant *(Cdr. T. M. le Marchand),* Spartan *(Cdr. B. Taylor), and* Splendid *(Cdr. R. C. Lane-Nott).*

There was one diesel-electric patrol submarine, HMS Onyx. *Ideal for inserting parties of SAS and SBS on clandestine missions all over the Falklands,* Onyx *is the least known but was in fact the most closely involved in the campaign of all the submarines. Her CO, Lt.-Cdr. A. P. Johnson, describes:*

The 116-Day War Patrol

I remember listening to the Saturday morning House of Commons debate on the radio with my wife, thinking it was the most extraordinary situation to be getting into a confrontation over and wondering how it might be resolved, not even considering that I might eventually end up in the South Atlantic. Even when troops and ships were preparing to depart, was there any real likelihood of a diesel submarine, with a surface speed slightly less than that of the modern ocean racing yacht, being sent 8,000 miles to take part in what seemed just a show of force?

Obviously, the use of conventional submarines would be considered, although, lacking the speed of their nuclear-powered cousins, a diesel submarine can be used close inshore for reconnaissance and special operations. Bearing in mind the paucity of accurate hydrographic information for the area around the Falklands Islands, they also represented a much less costly asset to put at risk amongst the rocky islets.

When it became clear that a diesel submarine might be deployed, a short list was drawn up. I seem to remember that HMS *Onyx* was fourth or fifth on the list. Others took priority because of their general state of repair, recent experience or future programme. However, one by one, they were discounted for a variety of reasons and, finally, *Onyx* came to the top of the list.

We arrived in Plymouth one Friday evening – a treat for me since my family was only twenty minutes from the dockyard. Over half the ship's company went off back to Portsmouth for the weekend, but I had only a short drive to my house. I had hardly greeted my family before the telephone began to ring. The 'phone call was fairly cryptic, and included allusions to various events which I could not quite understand, and an enquiry into the state of my (*Onyx*'s) hydraulic system.

The telephone rang with increasing frequency over the weekend and by Sunday morning I was preparing to say goodbye to my family, ready to sail with a skeleton crew back to Portsmouth as quickly as possible. What a strange cocktail of emotions! Firstly, sadness at having to leave home so abruptly, then the surge of adrenaline at the prospect of testing the skills I and my crew had spent years acquiring and honing, thinking furiously of the multitude of preparations which would need to be made in the few days before we left to head south, then trying to reconcile the possibility of going into action, with all that might entail, against the probability that we should not be required to proceed further than Ascension Island before a settlement was reached.

The week at Portsmouth passed in a flash. While most of the crew were involved in the more physical preparations: storing, loading weapons, carrying out every conceivable piece of maintenance and testing of our equipment, there was also a need for briefing, planning and the assimilation of large quantities of data concerning both our own and Argentine units, not least of which was a geography lesson. Few of us had any idea of the size or exact location of the islands we were off to recover!

As the sole unit deploying from the submarine base at Gosport, we received the best possible attention from all within the shore-based support facilities and other submarines in our squadron. There was genuine goodwill for both our personal safety and the success of our mission, although there was also an undercurrent of envy – that we should be the ones to share in what could be a momentous event.

We sailed early one morning, with the whole of the base (or at least it seemed like it) there to see us off. Our formal departure, with traditional salutes and pipes on the bosun's call, was put in perspective by my two-year-old daughter. Although my wife and son were prepared to watch from a discreet distance, Helen pushed between the legs of the Captain of the submarine squadron and some of his staff to give me a final wave from the edge of the jetty. Although I'm sure she was totally unaware that anything special was happening, she very clearly reminded all of us by that simple act just what we were leaving behind.

Having left harbour and whilst making preparations for our test dive, it became clear that all of the ship's company were very tired. The efforts of the previous week and the relief of finally sailing were marked by many uncharacteristic mistakes made in those first few hours. It was all rather an anticlimax, since we had to return to Gosport for some final repairs late that day, and then once again just before midnight to land one of the crew who was taken ill with an unidentified breathing problem, requiring him to be resuscitated by the Engineer Officer before medical help arrived from ashore. When we finally cleared the Solent at about 0200, we were certainly relieved to be on our way – anywhere – and spent the next couple of days catching up with our rest, re-stowing the plethora of stores and equipment which had literally been thrown onboard and starting to think about the task which faced us.

It is about 8,000 miles from Portsmouth to the Falkland Islands, therefore getting there in good condition was a feat in itself, and would take a month. We began a concentrated period of training, diving every other day to carry out a variety of drills, travelling surfaced in between to cover the ground as quickly as possible. There was plenty of motivation to achieve the highest possible readiness for any eventuality, but we were all still convinced that a diplomatic solution would be found and we would be turned back.

Our refuelling stop at Ascension Island is a good example of the isolation we felt and the technical problems with which we had to contend. As we approached the island, an engine overspeed started a small fire and damaged much of the valve gear on one of our two main engines. We had no method of landing on the island, and were at the mercy of other ships and the logistics team ashore, who were occupied with the many other ships for most of that day and were unable to assist.

The following morning we carried out what was probably the first submarine refuelling at sea from a tanker in forty years, but in the process punctured one of the submarine's external fuel oil tanks.

We had sailed from the island before the leak was noticed, but then had to return in order to find sheltered water for our ship's divers to attempt a repair. Even close to the island, the divers were repeatedly thrown against the hull by the heavy swell, in a race to stop up the leak as the escaping diesel fuel dissolved the rubber wrist and neck seals of their diving suits, causing them to flood with water.

Our one social event of the outward passage occurred shortly after leaving Ascension. Even in these circumstances, crossing the Equator could not be allowed to go unacknowledged. In true submarine tradition, we crossed the line surfaced, then returned 'under' it submerged. We then surfaced for the traditional celebrations – the initiation of those as yet unknown to 'King Neptune' and the punishment of many of the ship's characters for a variety of transgressions, trumped up by the members of Neptune's court.

As we proceeded south, we spent more time dived and therefore travelled more slowly. Despite the odd aircraft sighting, we were still very much alone, kept in touch with the rest of the world by our daily signals from the headquarters at Northwood and what we could hear of the news on the World Service.

Even though events such as the attack on HMS *Sheffield* caused significant shock onboard, morale remained high and we had to continually remind ourselves that this was 'for real'. Operating a submerged submarine is a demanding task which takes the utmost concentration and professionalism, even in peacetime. It was therefore hard to notice any difference between this and many other patrols we had undertaken previously. There was one subtle difference, however; we knew that we would be given tasks to plan and execute and that we would be very much on our own, trusted to do the job to the best of our ability without reference to higher authority, only required to report on completion. This would be a little different from the fairly proscriptive control of peacetime.

As hostilities commenced, we realised that we would at least be sent all the way South. Whilst at Ascension, a fellow officer had remarked that 'all those who are going to the Falklands can't wait to get there, but all those who are there can't wait to leave'. I thought of this as a variety of surface ships, reinforcements and supply vessels overtook us on our slow journey.

We all found the passage a trial, particularly after we left the tropics and entered the South Atlantic winter. Surfaced at night to travel faster was wet, cold and uncomfortable, dived in the day was quieter, but it seemed we would be travelling for ever. Unlike a normal peacetime exercise or patrol, we were deployed indefinitely at that stage. Various contingency plans had been made to refuel and store, but there was no planned date to return home. As a result, we all tended to live very much from day to day, rather than having a long-term perspective.

Once in the theatre of operations, we embarked a number of additional personnel. When we stored prior to our departure, we had laid a complete 'false deck' of canned food and stores throughout the submarine, reducing headroom from six to four feet in some places. Even the showers were full of stores. I can remember the three occasions in the entire 116 day patrol on which I was able to have a proper wash, rather than just a dip in a bucket! Living with eighty-four people in a space designed for sixty-eight, as well as all the extra equipment, was the epitome of 'cheek by jowl'. Remarkably, however, there was no friction, and our 'visitors' soon became fully integrated into the crew, taking a full part in the day-to-day operation of the boat.

When we were eventually released to return home, we made the best of a surface passage through the tropics to enjoy a late summer, stopping occasionally for 'hands to bathe' and spending a little of each day sunbathing on the casing when the sea was calm.

Unfortunately, one of our main generators developed a fault when we were still five thousand miles from home. Not only did our already extremely low speed decrease with only one engine, but we became extremely assiduous in our care and maintenance of that survivor. Being stopped in mid-Atlantic with no propulsion and a dwindling battery would have been an interesting but singularly unpleasant experience. Whilst we faced this setback fairly philosophically – there was little choice – we felt particularly sorry for the support ship which was detailed to escort us at half her normal surface speed. This delayed her return to home and families by some two weeks.

The opportunity to swim also allowed us all to examine the submarine's bow, damaged in a collision with an uncharted rock. We knew that the bow doors of two torpedo tubes were slightly damaged, but in the pale blue waters of the tropics, it did not appear too serious. It was only after our return, when *Onyx* was put in a floating dry dock, that we discovered that one torpedo was actually jammed in its tube, leading to the partial closure of Portsmouth Harbour while the torpedo was cut apart and dragged out in small pieces.

Before that drama unfolded, we had actually to return to our base at Gosport. We arrived in the Solent in time to catch the tide and enter harbour at about 2300. However, we were instructed that we must anchor and make a formal entrance the following morning. Our preference would have been to get alongside as quickly as possible and all go home. But we had no idea of the preparations which had been made to welcome us back.

Unfortunately, in the morning we were delayed for an hour when the anchor winch failed. Having carried an anchor for 20,000 miles without needing to use it, we were forced to break the cable and leave it buoyed, two miles from home. Added to this, we had planned to allow as many of the ship's company as possible on the casing for our entrance, firstly because by now we had some idea of the reception we might be getting and also to allow the earliest possible glimpse of loved ones.

Unfortunately, we were greeted by a typical mid-August day –

pouring rain and a force eight gale! Undeterred, we still got everyone up on deck as we entered the shelter of the harbour. A further instruction required us to proceed right up the harbour and turn, rather than 'making a quick right' into the submarine base. As we did so, the noise from the other ships in harbour sounding their sirens and the cheers of their crews who turned out to welcome us back was so great that the coxswain could hardly hear my conning orders over the microphone. It was certainly a moment to savour before we all returned to the real world and stopped breathing the heady mixture of wartime patrol.

LT.-CDR. ANDREW JOHNSON RN

Commander Johnson was appointed MBE. Commanders Le Marchand, Taylor and Lane-Nott were all mentioned in dispatches.

*

Absent Friends

By the time this appears I shall be preparing myself mentally, physically and alcoholically for the biggest party of the year. It so happens that I spent about seven years of my life in the Submarine Service, and am thus entitled, indeed summoned, to attend the annual Submariners' Reunion. For some reason it is always held on a Friday evening early in October, often on the day before the Cesarewitch is run.

The Reunion is held (down in Gosport) at Fort Blockhouse (the Alma Mater of submariners) and is very nearly a religious festival, attended faithfully by many who served in submarines. The first of the faithful generally begin to assemble some days beforehand; the last of them is not normally carried away until some days afterwards.

It is a pretty distinguished gathering, in its own way; at least a couple of V.C.s, with shoals of D.S.O.s, and D.S.C.s two a penny. Everybody turns up, from slightly shy and abashed young sub-lieutenants fresh and green from their training class to grizzled old submariners who went to sea in primitive boats when every dive was like a new (and possibly irreversible) venture into the unknown.

Luckily our Reunion is not a dinner, but what is known as a 'stand-up charge and cheer' following a traditional pattern: drinks, buffet supper, more drinks, the odd speech or two, very many more drinks. Thus we have no knife-and-fork military strategists, slugging out old campaigns amongst the cutlery – 'that fork there is Rommel's H.Q. and we're here, by this fish-knife', and no ex-aircrew waving their arms, making internal combustion engine noises through their teeth and boring our ears off with 'There I was, upside down, nothing on the clock, and *still* laughing' non-anecdotes. Much of the Reunion talk seems to be about gardens, and daughters' marriages and, in these days when every other person is writing a book, publishers' advances.

It is not until much later, in the small hours when the whisky has expanded the soul and activated the memory, that the stories begin— stories witty and fabulous and bibulous and libellous and nostalgic and downright impossible. I remember one aged submariner once pinning me in a corner and telling me about the day just after the First World War when his captain was trying to find the entrance to Dartmouth harbour, on a high spring tide and in thick fog. To cut a long story short (as he said, quite untruthfully) the submarine eventually ran aground on Slapton sands so hard and fast that the bow projected over the beach road where the local postman, pedal-ling on his early morning round, crashed into it and fell off his bicycle. Picking himself up, the postman saw the figures in oil-skins on the submarine's bridge anxiously peering down at him through the murk. Roundly and at some length he told them his opinion of submarines which obstructed the King's highway, to the detriment of His Majesty's servants. The captain heard him out, then said 'But my dear fellow, why didn't you ring your little bell?' A soft answer turneth away wrath.

It seems to me reunions are essentially a modern innovation. There is no record, as far as I know, of the armies of Xenophon or Hannibal or Charlemagne or Marlborough or even Napoleon, foregathering to have a chat about the good old days when they were up to their necks in muck and arrows/axes/musket balls. Did Nelson's gunner's mates revisit *Victory*? Not likely, mate, not with the Press Gang around, eager to make the reunion permanent. Nor was a pikeman who had taken six weeks to get home from the Wars of the Roses likely to make the pious pilgrimage to Bosworth Field, just to swap reminiscences. Improved inland communications and regular terms and conditions of service are clearly prerequisites for reunions.

Shakespeare had the essence of reunions. He hit it exactly with his soldier of Henry V's army who will yearly on the vigil feast his neighbours and remember with advantages what feats he did that day. As the years go by the enemy grows stronger, our own opposing forces weaker, the hardships greater, even the bombs get bigger. Twenty-five years after, the solitary incendiary at the bottom of the garden has become a 2,000-pounder on the fire-place – 'right where you're sitting'. At the time, we were in no danger really; a quarter of a century later, we were lucky to escape with our lives.

It is fashionable these days to sneer at reunions, along with all things military. The mental image of the 'regimental dinner' is always good for a chuckle. But people who criticise reunions on the grounds that they glamorise war, or in some way foster wars, are missing the point completely. Reunions are the very opposite of wars; they are all that war is not. (Wasn't it H. L. Mencken who said that there would be no wars and the world would be a much better place if everybody in it was always just a little tight?)

Surely the point of reunions is that they are just one rather special-
ised example of belonging to a group – and particularly a group
who have collectively something they are proud of. It doesn't matter
much what the group is. Why shouldn't the 365th Anti-Aircraft
Battery (Ilfracombe Volunteers) Royal Artillery have their annual
reunion and tiddy oggy hot supper? So what if their entire wartime
record was one near-miss on an astonished Dornier and several direct
hits with a boot on the vicar's cat? They can still gather once a year to
watch each other growing fatter and balder and slower, and remember
the high point of their lives, when they were all really alive.

There are some very unexpected reunions. The Victoria Cross
and George Cross winners had theirs at Buckingham Palace in July
1968. One wondered what on earth they talked about. They must
have been the most oddly-assorted bunch of men and women imaginable. Very few can have served with each other; some of the submariners and the bomb disposal experts might, just possibly some
of the aircrew, and one or two men from the same regiment. But
most of them must have been complete strangers to each other.
What, apart from their awards, can an R.N. destroyer captain or a
colonel in the Saskatchewan Regiment or a woman who was para-
chuted into occupied France have in common with, say, a havildar
in the Gurkha Rifles, or a sergeant in the Royal Dublin Fusiliers or
an ex-school-teacher who could charm the fuse out of the most
recalcitrant bomb?

Yet, curiously enough, I happen to know that they *did* find their
reunion most valuable and rewarding. My mother is just completing
a vast tome, a sort of definitive encyclopaedia of V.C. winners, and
five Commonwealth V.C.s called on her while they were in England.
They demolished her bottle of whisky and told her that their reunion
had been a wonderful experience, well worth coming halfway across
the world to share in the spirit of comradeship.

Certainly this is the time of year for reunions and everybody is doing it. You've only got to look at the right columns of *The Times* or the *Telegraph* to see that everybody who can possibly reunite is busy reuniting: not only submariners but girls' schools and Eton Houses and ex-prisoners of war in the Far East and individual regiments and corps and squadrons and ships. The Tank Corps meet to relive the days when they fought through mud and blood to reach the green fields beyond, and the Desert Rats of the Eighth Army dine Monty out and remember the last gentleman's war there will ever be in history. The Old Contemptibles meet to march through the streets of London to the Cenotaph – although I understand they are giving it up. They are all getting on a bit now.

That, of course, is the trouble with reunions based on a particular event or drawing their members from a particular body of men at a particular time. In what seems no time at all, there are far fewer faces. As the years go by and the numbers dwindle there must eventually be a last survivor of such reunions. What are his feelings as the table is set for fewer and fewer places? Does he, the last trustee of their fellowship, continue until he dines alone with his memories? Does he go on, looking down an empty table, in a room peopled with ghosts and ringing to the laughter of absent friends? It doesn't bear thinking about.

There is no danger of that at the submariners' reunion. It is true that there are very few left of the generation who fought submarines through the Dardanelles in the Kaiser's war and even those who served in submarines from the Arctic to the South China Sea in the last war are beginning to drop out. But there is always a new generation coming up. One day, maybe it will be *my* turn to button-hole some likely young lad, draw him aside and say: 'Did I ever tell you about the day I sold the forward periscope to an Arab Sheikh?' He will say 'No, sir, you haven't.' And I will say: 'Well, to cut a long story short . . .'

JOHN WINTON

Submarine Old Comrades

Although Faslane, as the base for the nuclear Fleet and Polaris Submarines, was growing in importance, *Dolphin* continued as an Alma Mater for many old Submariners. Apart from those who came on duty or casual visits there was, every Autumn, a Submarine Officers' Reunion taking the form of a prolonged evening reception cum buffet. This was followed on the next day by the Reunion of the Submarine Old Comrades Association.

The Old Comrades have active branches all over the British Isles and some overseas. It is an all ranks organisation and, apart from social functions, help is given to those who find life hard through health or other reasons. The Dolphin Reunion is a nostalgic affair; some of those attending are well up in the 80s and were in submarines pre 1914. There is a service in the Church of St. Ambrose (converted by Dolphin's Shipwrights and others in the 1930's from an old wet canteen) and they visit modern submarines, also the Memorial Chapel and Museum. At a brief ceremony an Old Comrades' Efficiency Shield is presented to a selected submarine's crew. About dinner the bars are thronged, the smoke thickens and tall stories and reminiscences abound. After one such Saturday evening an elderly Old Comrade is reputed to have stayed in *Dolphin* till the following Wednesday.

CAPTAIN J. S. STEVENS DSO DSC RN

Index